THE POLITICS OF PENSION REFORM IN CENTRAL AND EASTERN EUROPE

To Carol and Mark,

For their unending guidance
and support, for being both
a source of inspiration and
a helping hand in time of
need, and for taking it all
with a grain of humor.

Oana

THE POLITICS OF PENSION REFORM IN CENTRAL AND EASTERN EUROPE

Political Parties, Coalitions, and Policies

Oana I. Armeanu

First published in 2010 by
PALGRAVE MACMILLAN®
in the United States—a division of St. Martin's Press LLC,
175 Fifth Avenue, New York, NY 10010.

Where this book is distributed in the UK, Europe and the rest of the world,
this is by Palgrave Macmillan, a division of Macmillan Publishers Limited,
registered in England, company number 785998, of Houndmills,
Basingstoke, Hampshire RG21 6XS.

Palgrave Macmillan is the global academic imprint of the above companies
and has companies and representatives throughout the world.

Palgrave® and Macmillan® are registered trademarks in the United States,
the United Kingdom, Europe and other countries.

ISBN: 978-0-230-62028-5

Library of Congress Cataloging-in-Publication Data

Armeanu, Oana I.
    The politics of pension reform in Central and Eastern Europe : political
parties, coalitions, and policies / Oana I. Armeanu.
        p. cm.
    ISBN 978-0-230-62028-5
        1. Pensions—Government policy—Europe, Eastern. 2. Pensions—
Government policy—Central, Eastern. I. Title.

HD7164.7.A85 2010
331.25′220943—dc22   2010017102

A catalogue record of the book is available from the British Library.

Design by Newgen Imaging Systems (P) Ltd., Chennai, India.

First edition: December 2010

10 9 8 7 6 5 4 3 2 1

Printed in the United States of America.

For my parents

CONTENTS

Figures and Tables

Figures

Tables

Acknowledgments

This book benefited from the support of many people, to whom I owe a debt of gratitude. Much of the initial research for this book received the support of the faculty and graduate students in the Department of Political Science at the University of Illinois at Urbana–Champaign, and I thank them all. I am particularly grateful to Carol Leff, who provided me with invaluable input and unending guidance throughout my entire career. Many thanks also to Brian Gaines, Bill Bernhard, and Mark Leff for their insightful criticism, sharing of their knowledge, guidance, and support. I owe a special debt to James Kuklinski and Paul Diehl for their always informative advice, for teaching me that good research requires hard work and endurance, and for their mentorship. My appreciation also goes to the colleagues and friends who encouraged and supported me during this long process, in particular to Seden Akcinaroglu and Elizabeth Radziszewski, who gave me helpful criticism, and, most of all, to Florin Feşnic, for his friendship, sense of humor, and intellectual motivation.

I am most thankful to Ken Benoit, who generously shared his knowledge and data, and to Hanna Popowska, Andrea Varga, Monika Kubisiak, and Peter Pénzeš for helping with my access and translation, and making sense of the data. Dan Perjovschi, who would always brighten my day back at "22" magazine in Bucharest, has graciously accepted my request to design the art for the cover, for which I am grateful.

My colleagues in the Political Science Department and the College of Liberal Arts at the University of Southern Indiana provided me encouragement and support during the entire process of completing this book. Special thanks to Karyn Sproles for her comments and advice. I appreciate the two Liberal Arts Research Awards that allowed me to focus on writing. I am also thankful to the University of Southern Indiana and the Lilly Endowment for their financial support of my research.

Thanks also to *Europe Asia Studies*, for allowing me to reprint my article, "The Battle over Privileges," which now appears as chapter 3 and the Polish case study in chapters 4, 5, and 6 (*Europe-Asia Studies* 62 (4), 2010 © Taylor & Francis).

Last but not least, my deepest gratitude goes to my family. Most of all, I wish to thank my husband, for always being there for me, for sharing with me all the good and bad of life, and for helping me believe in this project. I also wish to thank my parents and my mother-in-law for their love, patience, and unconditional support, and my children, who had to put up with my long working hours, and to honor the memory of my father-in-law, who has always been a source of help and encouragement.

Abbreviations and Political Party Acronyms

ANO (Aliancia Nového Občana): Slovakia	Alliance of a New Citizen
AWS (Akcja Wyborcza Solidarność): Poland	Solidarity Electoral Action
CDR (Convenţia Democrată Română): Romania	Democratic Convention of Romania
CEE	Central and Eastern Europe
CNPAS (Casa Naţională de Pensii şi Alte Drepturi de Asigurări Sociale): Romania	National House for Pensions and Other Social Security Rights
CSSD (Česká strana sociálně demokratická): Czech Republic	Czech Social Democratic Party
DeSUS (Demokratična stranka upokojencev Slovenije): Slovenia	Democratic Party of Pensioners of Slovenia
DPS (Demokrātiskā Partija "Saimnieks"): Latvia	Democratic Party "*Saimnieks*"
DS (Demokratická strana): Slovakia	Democratic Party
DU (Demokratická únia): Slovakia	Democratic Union
FDSN (Frontul Democrat al Salvării Naţionale): Romania	Democratic National Salvation Front
Fidesz (Fiatal Demokraták Szövetsége): Hungary	Alliance of Young Democrats
Fidesz-MPP (Fiatal Demokraták Szövetsége–Magyar Polgári Párt): Hungary	Alliance of Young Democrats–Hungarian Civic Party
FKgP (Független Kisgazdapárt): Hungary	Independent Smallholders Party

FSN (Frontul Salvării Naţionale): Romania	National Salvation Front
HDZ (Hrvatska demokratska zajednica): Croatia	Croatian Democratic Union
HZDS (Hnutie za demokratické Slovensko): Slovakia	Movement for a Democratic Slovakia
IMF	International Monetary Fund
JP (Jaunā Partija): Latvia	New Party
KDH (Kresťanskodemokratické hnutie): Slovakia	Christian Democratic Movement
KdNP (Kereszténydemokrata Néppárt): Hungary	Christian Democratic People's Party
KDU-ČSL (Křest'anská a demokratická unie–Československá strana lidová): Czech Republic	Christian and Democratic Union–Czechoslovak People's Party
KNP (Klub nezávislých poslancov):	Slovakia Independents' faction
KOZ SR (Konfederácia odborových zväzov Slovenskej republiky): Slovakia	Trade Unions Confederation of the Slovak Republic
KRUS (Kasa Rolniczego Ubezpieczenia Społecznego): Poland	Farmers' Social Insurance Fund
KSS (Komunistická strana Slovenska): Slovakia	Communist Party of Slovakia
LC (Latvijas Ceļš): Latvia	Latvia's Way
LDS (Liberalna demokracija Slovenije): Slovenia	Liberal Democracy of Slovenia
LNNK (Latvijas Nacionālās Neatkarības Kustība): Latvia	Latvian National Independence Movement
LS-HZDS (Ľudová Strana–Hnutie za demokratické Slovensko): Slovakia	People's Party–Movement for a Democratic Slovakia
LVP (Latvijas Vienības Partija): Latvia	Latvian Unity Party
LZS (Latvijas Zemnieku savienība): Latvia	Latvian Farmers' Union

MDF (Magyar Demokrata Fórum): Hungary	Hungarian Democratic Forum
MDNP (Magyar Demokrata Néppárt): Hungary	Hungarian Democratic People's Party
MIÉP (Magyar Igazság és Élet Pártja): Hungary	Hungarian Justice and Life Party
MSzMP (Magyar Szocialista Munkáspárt): Hungary	Hungarian Socialist Workers' Party
MSzOSz (Magyar Szakszervezetek Országos Szövetsége): Hungary	National Confederation of Hungarian Trade Unions
MSzP (Magyar Szocialista Párt): Hungary	Hungarian Socialist Party
MUNKÁS (Munkáspárt): Hungary	Workers' Party
NSi (Nova Slovenija—Krščanska ljudska stranka): Slovenia	New Slovenia–Christian People's Party
ODA (Občanská demokratická aliance): Czech Republic	Civic Democratic Alliance
ODS (Obedineni Demokratichni Sili): Bulgaria	Alliance of Democratic Forces
ODS/KDS (Občanská demokratická strana/ Křest'anskodemokratická strana): Czech Republic	Civic Democratic Party/ Christian Democratic Party
OPZZ (Ogólnopolskie Porozumienie Związków Zawodowych): Poland	All-Poland Alliance of Trade Unions
PAC (Partidul Alianţa Civică): Romania	Civic Alliance Party
PAR (Partidul Alternativa României): Romania	Alternative for Romania Party
PAYG	Pay-as-you-go pension system
PC (Partidul Conservator): Romania	Conservative Party
PCR (Partidul Comunist Român): Romania	Romanian Communist Party

PD (Partidul Democrat): Romania — Democratic Party

PD-L (Partidul Democrat Liberal): Romania — Democratic Liberal Party

PER (Partidul Ecologist Român): Romania — Ecologist Party of Romania

PDSR (Partidul Democraţiei Sociale din România): Romania — Party of Social Democracy in Romania

PNL (Partidul Naţional Liberal): Romania — National Liberal Party

PO (Platforma Obywatelska): Poland — Civic Platform

PNŢCD (Partidul Naţional Ţărănesc Creştin Democrat): Romania — National Peasant Christian Democratic Party

PRM (Partidul România Mare): Romania — Great Romania Party

PSD (Partidul Social Democrat): Romania — Social Democratic Party

PSDR (Partidul Social-Democrat Român): Romania — Romanian Social Democratic Party

PSL (Polskie Stronnictwo Ludowe): Poland — Polish People's Party

PSM (Partidul Socialist al Muncii): Romania — Socialist Labor Party

PUNR (Partidul Unităţii Naţionale a Românilor): Romania — Romanian National Unity Party

PUR (Partidul Umanist Român): Romania — Humanist Party of Romania

PZPR (Polska Zjednoczona Partia Robotnicza): Poland — Polish United Workers' Party

ROP (Ruch Odbudowy Polski): Poland — Movement for the Reconstruction of Poland

SDK (Slovenská demokratická koalícia): Slovakia — Slovak Democratic Coalition

SDKU (Slovenská demokratická a kresťanská únia): Slovakia — Slovak Democratic and Christian Union

SDL (Strana demokratickej ľavice): Slovakia — Party of the Democratic Left

SdRP (Socjaldemokracja Rzeczypospolitej Polskiej): Poland — Social Democracy of the Republic of Poland

SDSS (Sociálnodemokratická strana Slovenska): Slovakia — Slovak Social-Democratic Party

SKD (Krščansko-demokratska stranka): Slovenia — Christian Democratic Party

SLD (Sojusz Lewicy Demokratycznej): Poland — Democratic Left Alliance

SLS (Slovenska ljudska stranka): Slovenia — Slovenian People's Party

Smer (Smer–sociálna demokracia): Slovakia — Direction–Social Democracy

SMK (Strana maďarskej koalície–Magyar Koalíció Pártja): Slovakia — Party of the Hungarian Coalition

SNS (Slovenská národná strana): Slovakia — Slovak National Party

Sociálna poisťovňa: Slovakia — Social Insurance Agency

SOP (Strana občianskeho porozumenia): Slovakia — Party of Civic Understanding

SzDSz (Szabad Demokraták Szövetsége): Hungary — Alliance of Free Democrats

SZS (Strana zelených na Slovensku): Slovakia — Green Party of Slovakia

TB (Tēvzemei un Brīvībai): Latvia — Fatherland and Freedom

TP (Tautas partija): Latvia — People's Party

UDMR (Uniunea Democrată a Maghiarilor din România): Romania — Democratic Alliance of Hungarians in Romania

UP (Unia Pracy): Poland — Labor Union

US-DEU (Unie Svobody–Demokratická unie): Czech Republic — Union of Freedom–Democratic Union

UW (Unia Wolności): Poland — Freedom Union

WB — World Bank

ZChN (Zjednoczenie Chrześcijańsko-Narodowe): Poland	Christian National Union
ZKPP (Związek Komunistów Polskich "Proletariat"): Poland	Union of Polish Communists "Proletariat"
ZLSD (Združena lista socialnih demokratov): Slovenia	United List of Social Democrats
ZRS (Združenie robotníkov Slovenska): Slovakia	Association of Workers of Slovakia
ZUS (Zakład Ubezpieczeń Społecznych): Poland	Social Insurance Institution

CHAPTER 1

Introduction: Dilemmas of Pension Reform in Central and Eastern Europe

Since the beginning of the 1990s, pension reform has reached the top of the political agenda in numerous countries worldwide because of severe pressures on the pension systems caused by adverse demographic trends. After a first wave of reforms in Latin America in the 1980s and early 1990s, countries in Europe, East and Southeast Asia, and Africa have embarked on restructuring their pension systems, with varying degrees of success. Early experiences made apparent the unpopularity of pension reform with the public and the divisiveness of the issue among the political elites, who were caught between economic and international pressures for reform on the one hand and massive domestic opposition on the other. In Central and Eastern Europe, as elsewhere, pension reform has encountered enormous difficulties with adoption, implementation, and sustainability, and generated bitter debates. According to a World Bank analysis that evaluated pension reform progress in Europe, pension reform attracts "more attention in countries throughout Western, Central and Eastern Europe than any other topic on the economic reform agenda, but in no area of European policy has progress been more uneven" (Holzmann et al. 2003: 1).

The Pension Problem in Central and Eastern European Countries

The collapse of communism in Central and Eastern Europe and the former Soviet Union and the sweeping political and economic transformations that followed left a deep mark on the systems of social protection across the postcommunist region. In some countries, particularly in the former Soviet republics, the welfare institutions collapsed in the face of unprecedented demands for social protection generated by the economic transition. Most of the other countries experienced at least some degree of financial deterioration of their public pension systems. A number of factors contributed to the imbalances of their pension funds, the most prominent being population aging due to increased life expectancy and a decline in fertility rates. In addition to the demographic factor, the pension systems inherited from the communist era were granted very generous benefits and had lax eligibility requirements. The so-called "cradle to grave" protection that the communist systems provided to their citizens included the pension systems. Given the fact that there was no separate pension budget—pension benefits were paid from the general revenues—there was no need to tie contributions to benefits.

The postcommunist era brought further deterioration of the pension systems through economic developments and policies that altered even more the already fragile balance between revenues and expenditures. Economic restructuring led to growing unemployment, which reduced the number of contributors. To counter unemployment, during the first years of transition many governments offered the option of early retirement from the age of 50, thus simultaneously tremendously increasing the number of beneficiaries and reducing that of contributors. Moreover, an increasing informal sector and diminished tax compliance substantially reduced the revenues. System dependency ratios[1] dramatically increased by the mid-1990s, reaching values ranging from 60 pensioners for every 100 workers in Poland, Romania, and Slovakia to over 80 pensioners for every 100 workers in Albania and Bulgaria (Palacios and Pallarès-Miralles 2000). In other words, for every pensioner there are fewer than two workers to support him or her,[2] placing a tremendous burden on current working generations. Pension fund deficits ran as high as 4 percent of the gross domestic product (GDP; Müller 1999), thus requiring transfers from the state budget and causing pension arrears in Russia and other former Soviet republics. In addition, projections for the medium and long term showed unfavorable trends with many countries being expected to build up enduring pension fund deficits in the coming decades in the absence of major reforms. Therefore, the question of pension system reform had appeared on the political agenda of many governments across the postcommunist region.

Competing Perspectives on Reform

The mainstream view on reforming pension systems nowadays is represented by the so-called "new pension orthodoxy" (Müller 1999), which is largely shared by economists and is vigorously advocated by international financial institutions, in particular the World Bank and the International Monetary Fund (Andrews and Rashid 1996; De Castello Branco 1998; Holzmann 1993; Holzmann and Palacios 2001; Holzmann and Stiglitz 2001; Lindeman, Rutkowski, and Sluchynskyy 2000; World Bank 1994). International financial institutions saw pension crises as a major source of budget deficits and made their loans conditional on governments taking action to place their pension systems on sustainable bases. In this perspective, the solution to the existing problems of the pay-as-you-go (PAYG) public systems is their partial replacement with privately funded systems. In PAYG systems, workers finance from their contributions the retirement benefits of the current pensioners through an intergenerational transfer. In contrast, in privately funded systems, each worker's contribution is deposited into an individual account, invested, and returned to the worker as an annuity or a lump sum at retirement.

According to international financial institutions, privatization of the public pension schemes is expected to counteract the problem of population aging and place pension systems on sound financial footing. By providing a close link between contributions and benefits, privatization is said to discourage moral hazard and free-rider behavior and reduce the labor market distortions associated with them. The problem of the moral hazard is related to a defined-benefit pension system, which does not condition benefits upon the payment of a corresponding contribution, and creates the perverse incentive to limit one's contribution in the absence of a penalty. Related to the moral hazard is the free-rider behavior of individuals who do not contribute their share of the costs but can still receive benefits from the public pension system. As a result of these perverse incentives, some individuals choose to remain inactive and the opportunities created by the job market are not fully exploited.

Privatization is also expected to bring a higher return on savings, because contributions are long-term invested rather than being spent on the spot to cover current pensions, as in the public system. In addition to addressing the imbalances in the pension system, privatization is said to have beneficial consequences for the economy as a whole by promoting savings and capital accumulation and encouraging the development of financial markets (De Castello Branco 1998).

The critics of the "new pension orthodoxy" argue against privatization and propose instead a thorough reform of the public system (Beattie and McGillivray 1995; Fultz 2002; Fultz and Ruck 2001a, 2001b). In principle, the controversy is about the desirable level of state involvement in the provision of retirement benefits. The critics raise four main objections to pension privatization: (1) it is expensive, (2) it does not guarantee higher benefits compared to the public system, (3) it is politically difficult to ensure its long-term sustainability, and (4) it does not necessarily overcome the resistance to change of entrenched interests (Fultz and Ruck 2001a). While the first two concerns are economic, the other two relate to the political process of pension reform. I will discuss them in turn.

First, privatization assumes that the contributions of current workers are diverted from the public system to private funds, therefore leaving a gap in the public system that requires additional revenues. Contribution rates are high in the region, in the range of 35 to 45 percent of the gross wage in many countries, and raising them further is not an option. The governments thus need to mobilize resources from outside the pension system to cover the gap, and the amounts needed may prove to be quite substantial, as the experiences of Hungary, Poland, and Slovakia show. In Slovakia, for instance, which implemented the largest pension privatization in Europe, directing half of the total old-age contribution to the private pillar, the short-term gap in the public system was covered from the privatization of state gas and electricity companies (ILO 2007). Second, because the financial markets are underdeveloped in the region, they cannot absorb the savings deposited in the private funds. As a result, many private funds invest in public securities, which inevitably bring a lower rate of return than private securities. Coupled with higher administrative costs to run the private funds—mainly due to high marketing costs generated by the competition among private funds—compared to administering the public scheme, the insufficient return on savings may lead to lower than expected benefits in the public scheme.

Third, given the frequent changes in government that are characteristic of the postcommunist region and the controversial nature of pension reform, many countries experience mid-course changes in policy, making reform sustainability problematic. A more moderate, politically sustainable approach to reform is, according to this view, preferable. Finally, privatization did not prove to be more efficient than public system reform in overcoming the resistance of groups with entrenched privileges in the old pension system. In Poland and Romania, privatization did not shatter previous pension privileges, while in the Czech Republic, Lithuania, and Slovenia privileges were cut back in the absence of privatization (Fultz and Ruck 2001a).

Critics of the "new pension orthodoxy" instead propose a thorough reform of the public system, with the goal of tightening the link between contributions and benefits. This could be achieved through four main measures. First is to increase the retirement age in an attempt to counteract population aging. A second measure involves changing the pension formula used for the calculation of benefits in order to make it less redistributive and using a uniform formula for all occupational categories. Third, to keep up with inflation, benefits should be indexed using a price-based rather than a wage-based indexation, because the former does not take into account increases in wages due to economic growth, which usually exceed increases in prices. Finally, incorporating the separate pension schemes into the general one will curtail occupational privileges. The above measures produce a shift from a defined-benefit to a defined-contribution system, and therefore they are expected to reduce labor market distortions produced by the moral hazard and free-riding behavior through a mechanism similar to that of privatization. In addition, it is argued, public system reform without privatization has two main advantages. On the one hand, it escapes the transition costs incurred by privatization, which diverts part of the contributions toward the private pension funds, and instead keeps the resources designed to finance the benefits of current pensioners within the public system. On the other hand, managing the public system requires lower administrative costs compared to the private pension funds because it avoids the marketing costs.

The promoters of the "new pension orthodoxy" have had, through international financial institutions, more leverage over the postcommunist region than their opponents. Not only did the "new pension orthodoxy" constitute the dominant discourse across the region, but international financial institutions also exerted direct pressures by conditioning their loans on the accomplishment of comprehensive pension reform that includes pension privatization. In a number of Central and Eastern European countries, the World Bank set up task forces that worked closely with the governments to elaborate all-encompassing pension reform proposals.

THE RESEARCH QUESTION

As a consequence of the economic and international pressures for reform, a majority of the countries in the postcommunist region have embarked on pension reform. The result, however, has been in most cases very different from the blueprint provided by the World Bank. On the whole, Central and Eastern European countries made more progress than their Western counterparts. The frontrunners of the region have been Bulgaria, Croatia, Hungary, Latvia, and Poland, which have adopted during the 1990s mandatory funded schemes and at the same time have tightened the link between contributions and benefits within their PAYG systems. Some Central and Eastern European countries, such as Romania and Slovakia, have been marked by deep divisions and a prolonged process of reform adoption, which in Romania was still ongoing in 2010. Other Central and Eastern European countries, such as the Czech Republic and Slovenia, have not pursued major reforms. How can one explain such a diversity of outcomes given the relative similarity of starting points? What is the role of political factors in explaining the success or failure of pension reform? How could governments that implemented major reforms overcome the economic and political obstacles to reform? What is the interplay between economic and international pressures on the one hand and political factors on the other in shaping the outcome of reform? These are the general questions that this study addresses.

More specifically, the study pays particular attention to politics: what is the role of political parties and processes of coalition formation in the outcome of pension reform? Although some Central and Eastern European countries achieved remarkable results in overcoming opposition to reform and forging a consensus, in many others reform is still a matter of debate. Contrary to the conventional wisdom, the strongest opposition does not come from the social democrats, but from a variety of political parties on both sides of the political spectrum, including Christian democrats and nationalists. Analysts of pension reform in Central and Eastern Europe are therefore faced with a puzzle. Whereas in numerous cases center-right governments radically restructured the previous pension system despite opposition from the left, in others center-left coalitions were the engine of reform and were challenged by the conservative right. What accounts for the cross-country variation in the type of pro-reform coalitions? How is the outcome of reform related to the characteristics of the coalition that adopts it? What are the implications for the long-term sustainability of reform? These are the more specific questions that this study addresses. Although these questions are asked in the context of pension reform, they pertain to a whole range of unpopular policies, of which pension reform is an exemplar case.

The dominant trend in the literature on pension reform has been a concern with the economic and international pressures for reform and their impact on the outcome. Implicit in this approach, which is based on macroeconomic theory, is the assumption that countries whose pension systems do worse are more likely to attempt reform than countries where the problems of the pension system are moderate or limited. In contrast with this view, which attempts to explain political outcomes through economic factors, this book argues that political factors ultimately shape the outcome of pension reform. The need for reform does not automatically carry the political solution to that need; only the domestic political institutions and actors can provide this.

The main argument of this book is that political parties and coalitional politics largely account for the cross-national variation in the outcome and long-term sustainability of pension reform. The characteristics of the parties and the configuration of the party system define the available options for coalition formation. The outcome of reform ultimately depends on the relative strength of pro-reform and anti-reform coalitions. Unlike the accounts that focus exclusively on the role of ideology in attempting to explain political parties' positions on pension reform, I argue that, in addition to their ideological orientation, political parties are subject to a whole array of additional constraints, such as maintaining internal cohesion, satisfying the demands of their constituents, and forming alliances with other parties. The strategies that parties adopt in order to maximize competing goals represent the main determinant of policy output. Among the various constraints on party behavior, I argue that parties' ideologies and their connections with privileged groups that have entrenched interests in the old pension system are consequential for the outcome of pension reform.

For Central and Eastern Europe, several authors have pointed to the hostility toward pension reform of political parties that are strongly tied with privileged occupational groups (Müller 1999; Orenstein 2000). However, the strong empirical evidence supporting the impact of special interests on the outcome of pension reform has yet to be incorporated into a more general framework of pension politics. This is the task this book undertakes. Using a two-dimensional spatial model of pension reform as a heuristic device, it attempts to relate various configurations of the party system to pension reform outcomes and predict the chances for reform sustainability. Although this theoretical argument was designed with Central and Eastern European experiences in mind, it is useful for understanding pension reform beyond the postcommunist setting.

Within the paradigm of the new institutionalism to which the present study belongs, I combine a structuralist-institutionalist approach characteristic of historical institutionalism with an actor-centered approach belonging to the rational choice institutionalism. In line with the structuralist-institutionalism is a preoccupation with the redistributive effects of institutions and a view of the political process as a struggle for scarce resources among actors differently endowed with power. The path-dependent view, in which past choices constrain present options, also fits in this tradition. From rational choice institutionalism, this study borrows the assumptions that actors are rational and that they try to maximize the fulfillment of their objectives within the constraints imposed by institutions. Also essential to the actor-centered perspective is a focus on the immediate causes of institutional choice, which are attributed to the strategic interaction among actors, and a view of institutions as solutions to collective action problems.

IMPORTANCE OF THE QUESTION AND CONTRIBUTIONS OF THIS STUDY

Why is it important to study pension reform? Political scientists are interested in pension reform and, more generally, welfare state reform for a number of reasons. First, the welfare state is by nature concerned with redistribution, and thus it is meant to be at the heart of the divisions that characterize a given society. The welfare state not only reflects existing tensions, but reforming it also proves extremely difficult, as those who stand to lose have an incentive to oppose. Welfare state reform has proven to be one of the most unpopular reforms, which makes it the most interesting to study. Second, special concerns of intragenerational and intergenerational solidarity are raised by pension reform in particular. It is a very sensitive issue, which few democratic governments would approach without securing some degree of consensus. Third, pensions represent the largest item of social spending, accounting for up to 40 percent of total social expenditures and up to 16 percent of the GDP in both Western Europe and postcommunist countries (Palacios and Pallarès-Mirales 2000; Pierson 2001). The structure and operation of the pension system are thus consequential for the economy as a whole, to which it is tightly connected. Any imbalances in the pension fund are likely to affect the functioning of the entire economy.

This book strives to make several contributions to the study of welfare reform and more generally to the field of comparative politics. (1) It brings to attention an important type of reform that has deep implications for the system of social and economic relations, and which has received only partial and unsystematic scholarly treatment. (2) It sheds more light on the politics of welfare reform by bringing a new perspective that reconciles some of the previous disputes in the literature. (3) It uses cases from an under-explored region of the world (Central and Eastern European countries) that pose new questions and force the reconsideration of previous theories. (4) It deepens our understanding of how unpopular policies are adopted. (5) It has important policy implications that go beyond the social sphere. (6) Methodologically, it combines comparative cross-national research with roll call analyses of voting in Central and Eastern European legislatures, thus bringing together diverse research traditions to approach the study question from various angles.

Outline of Subsequent Chapters

Chapter 2 proposes a general framework for analyzing pension reform in Central and Eastern Europe that centers on the role of domestic political factors. The framework is structured by the distinction between the demand and supply for reform and argues that both types of factors are necessary for reform to occur. The chapter discusses the welfare state literature in light of the recent reform experience of the postcommunist region.

In chapter 3, I develop the theoretical argument of this study. I present a theoretical framework of the role of political parties and coalitional politics in pension reform adoption and sustainability. I discuss the relative role that parties' ideologies, their connections with privileged occupational groups, and their interactions with other parties play in defining the available options for reform. The last section of the chapter uses a two-dimensional spatial model as a heuristic device that relates various configurations of the party system with different reform outcomes to generate the research hypotheses.

Chapters 4, 5, and 6 provide empirical tests of the argument. In chapter 4, I present the results of a cross-national comparative analysis of pension reform that covers four Central and Eastern European countries: Hungary, Poland, Romania, and Slovakia. The four cases vary in the timing and extent of the reforms accomplished, and they also differ in the configuration of their party systems, which is depicted using public opinion surveys that spatially position parties' constituencies. The chapter analyzes how the past development of the main political parties led to the current configuration of the party system in each country and how it constrains available options for coalition formation. The four-case comparison allows for the empirical testing of the hypothesized relationships between certain configurations of the party system and specific reform results. The chapter ends with an evaluation of emerging patterns of pension reform in Central and Eastern Europe.

In chapter 5, the focus shifts from the historical development of the party system to the interaction of political parties in the legislature, and from the macro-level of analysis to a lower level of aggregation, represented by political institutions and actors. Using roll call analyses of voting in four Central and Eastern European legislatures—Poland, Hungary, Romania, and Slovakia—I estimate the configurations of the party systems at the time when pension reform was adopted. I then analyze how these configurations influence the formation of pro-reform and anti-reform coalitions and shape the end result of pension reform. Roll call analyses provide a more refined picture of party spatial positions: they highlight the divisions between and within parties, estimate legislators' ideal points, and show the formation of coalitions on particular votes. In addition to the roll call analyses, I use the results of an expert survey to provide an alternative way of mapping party positions.

In chapter 6, I offer a direct empirical test of the hypothesized mechanism underlying the observed relationships at the aggregate level between the configuration of the party system, the coalition formation process, and pension reform outcome. Using the case of Poland, I analyze in detail the legislative process surrounding the passage of the public pension system reform bill. I utilize a roll call analysis of voting, but this time I focus on voting on the amendments to the public pension system bill rather than on all final bills, as in the previous chapter. This analysis identifies the main lines of conflict among parties and legislators regarding the specifics of the public system reform and shows the formation of pro-reform and anti-reform coalitions on individual items within the pension bill. It thus provides direct evidence that ideological differences and connections with privileged groups are the two major divisions regarding pension reform.

Chapter 7 concludes the analysis with a summary of the main results and a discussion of the theoretical and policy implications. The last section of the chapter outlines several directions for future research.

CHAPTER 2

Assessing the Impact of Domestic Political Institutions

Why do countries faced with severe economic crises and international pressures for pension reform achieve such a diversity of outcomes? How do domestic political institutions and actors interact with economic and external forces in shaping the outcome of reform? To explain why we see variation in the outcome of reform despite the relative similarity of starting points, this chapter outlines a theoretical framework for the analysis of pension reform in Central and Eastern Europe (CEE) that is centered on the role of domestic political factors.

Pension reform in postcommunist countries represents a far more complex case than the cutback of existing social programs encountered in Western European countries because of the unprecedented scope and scale of reforms. The rationalization of the pay-as-you-go (PAYG) public systems in the sense of tightening the link between contributions and benefits is indeed similar to Western retrenchment. However, the partial or total replacement of the PAYG systems (first pillar) with mandatory privately funded systems (second pillar) is more radical than most Western pension reforms. This type of reform constitutes a fundamental departure from the existing PAYG systems, whose payoffs are not well known to those involved (including policy makers) because relatively few countries have experimented with it, most of which are new democracies in Latin America and some postcommunist states. The high degree of incertitude surrounding the outcome adds to the complexity of reform and the difficulty of studying it. At the same time, incertitude makes pension reform particularly unpopular because it is difficult to convince individuals to give up benefits that are certain under the current PAYG system for future uncertain benefits in a funded system.

As many scholars have argued in regard to economic reforms (Haggard and Kaufman 1992; Haggard and Webb 1996; Nelson

1992, 1993; Williamson 1994), pension reform produces short-term, concentrated, and highly visible costs, while its potential benefits are long-term and diffuse (Müller 1999; Pierson 1994). Moreover, because pensions involve an intergenerational transfer, current generations have an incentive to shift the costs onto future generations and hence postpone reform. Given these individual and group incentives that act against reform, the main issue becomes not why governments do not adopt pension reform in the face of mounting budget deficits and threatening demographic forecasts, but under what circumstances do governments confronted with a pension crisis attempt reform, and what factors make reform possible in some countries when failure seems so likely?

The surprising outcome throughout the postcommunist region has been the broad scope of reforms accomplished compared to the much more limited revisions of pension systems in industrialized countries. Central and Eastern European countries started from large welfare states that provided universal coverage and generous benefits. Esping-Andersen (1990) classifies welfare states into three types: social democratic, Christian democratic, and liberal. In social-democratic regimes, the strength of the working class and of social-democratic parties led to a welfare state characterized by universalism and high equality. The generous welfare state contributed to the development of a middle class that relies heavily on public services and is devoted to social democracy. In Christian-democratic regimes, the working class was comparatively weak and the left was unable to fundamentally alter the inherited corporatist and etatist structures. The middle class remained committed to the occupationally segregated social insurance, which produced a welfare state that has a limited redistributive function and preserves the class differentials. In liberal welfare states, the commitment of middle classes to market social insurance isolated and stigmatized the poor as the only recipients of state-provided welfare, contributing to the creation of a residualist welfare state. Of the three types of welfare states, communist welfare states conform best to the social-democratic model, based on universalism and high redistribution. Their postcommunist reforms attempt to transform the large welfare state in a liberal direction, in which the role of the state in the provision of social benefits will be partially replaced by the market. In pension provision, the previously large and universal public system is partially or totally replaced by a privately funded system.

The literature on pension reform generally focuses on three categories of factors: (1) demographic and economic factors, (2) domestic factors, and (3) international factors. This study belongs to the literature concerned with the role of domestic political institutions and actors. The focus on domestic factors is not an attempt to disregard or minimize the contribution of the other two bodies of theory in the explanation of pension reform. As I will discuss further in this chapter, economic and demographic factors are essential to placing pension reform on the political agenda, but they cannot account for the timing, direction, and success of reforms. Likewise, international factors are useful in understanding the diffusion of ideas and the evolution of the prevalent models of pension systems over time. They cannot explain, however, the pattern of cross-country variation in adoption, implementation, and sustainability of reforms. For example, neither economic and demographic factors nor international factors can account for the virtual absence of reforms in Romania and Slovakia during the 1990s, despite a deepening fiscal crisis for their pension systems, while Hungary and Poland, also facing a pension crisis, achieved early reforms. Other authors discovered a similar pattern across the postcommunist region, with reforms being blocked in the Russian Federation in the 1990s despite the presence of an economic crisis (Cook 2007).

The explanations centered on political institutions and actors account better for the large cross-country variation in pension reform. They are essential to accounting for the timing of reform. As this study argues, it is necessary that a pro-reform coalition of parties accedes to power for reforms to be launched. If anti-reform parties dominate the party system, neither a deep recession nor strong pressures from international financial institutions will make reform happen. Domestic political factors are also important in determining the magnitude of the reform as well as the specific mix of state and private provision of retirement benefits to be chosen. Although the prevalent pension reform model since early 1990s has been the World Bank's three-pillar system, there has been substantial variation in how each country has adopted this model. Kazakhstan, for instance, has achieved one of the most radical reforms in the postcommunist region, and in the world, by phasing out its public pension system over a period of 40 years and replacing it with a minimum pension guarantee (Hinz, Zviniene, and Vilamovska 2005). Other postcommunist countries have partly privatized their public system, ranging from a 9 percent mandatory private pillar (as a percent of the gross wage) in Slovakia to only 2 percent in Romania. There has also been substantial variation in the extent to which postcommunist states have sheltered elements of the old pension system from reform. Poland and Romania, for example, have left previous occupational privileges largely untouched, and so has Kazakhstan, despite its otherwise radical reform. The tendency of the previous pension system to leave behind institutional remnants that are very resilient to change can be understood only in the context of domestic political factors.

DEMAND FOR AND SUPPLY OF REFORM

Building on the existing literature on pension reform in both indus-trialized and postcommunist countries, and on the distinction drawn by Kitschelt (2001) between demand and supply factors, this study proposes a broad framework for thinking about pension reform in postcommunist countries (Table 2.1). The main theoretical explana-tions of pension reform mentioned above can be grouped together as factors that create a demand for reform, such as demographic and economic factors that create a fiscal deficit in the pension system. International factors could also be subsumed under this category, as international financial institutions have conditioned their loans on the reform of the pension system, and new policies spread across countries through policy diffusion. On the supply side are domestic factors, such as domestic political institutions and actors. They are the ones who ultimately adopt or prevent the adoption of reform. Although this framework is not all-inclusive, it highlights the theo-retical trends in the literature that have proven to be the most pro-ductive and to hold the most promise for future research. It is not necessary to have all factors at work simultaneously, and different fac-tors may carry different weight cross-nationally. Although it is not a theoretical requirement to have some demand for reform in order to place reform on the political agenda, empirically it is difficult to find

Table 2.1   Demand for and supply of pension reform

Demand for reform	*Supply of reform*
Pension crisis due to: • Demographic factors • Economic factors	Political institutions: • Power concentration • Level of democracy • Partisan differences ("power resources theory")
International factors: • International financial institutions • Policy diffusion	Interest groups: • Trade unions • Pensioners associations • Privileged occupational groups

governments that are willing to embark on unpopular reforms such as pension reform motivated solely by ideological considerations.

Conversely, it is necessary to have at work some of the political factors that ensure the supply of reform, because the demand for reform alone cannot provide the reform. Fiscal crises do not automatically carry their own solutions, and international financial institutions are not the decision makers: they have to act through domestic structures. I argue, therefore, that it is necessary to have both some demand factors and some supply factors present in order for reform to occur. Neither of them alone is sufficient for a policy change.

Without attempting to downplay the importance of demand factors, the pervasiveness of fiscal crises across the world, often accompanied by international pressures, suggests that demand factors account for the large cross-national variation in pension reform outcomes only to a limited extent. In contrast, provided that the demand for reform is present, the focus on the supply side offers promising avenues to explore. Important questions can be addressed by paying attention to the domestic political institutions and actors. Why, in the face of a crisis, do some governments choose to reform their pension systems while others do not? Why in some countries does the political right promote pension reform while in others support comes from the left? How are the outcome and long-term sustainability of pension reform related to the characteristics of the governing coalition that passes the reform? In the following sections, I will discuss how the main theories outlined in Table 2.1 contribute to a better understanding of pension reform in Central and Eastern Europe and beyond, and how the evidence based on the experience of the postcommunist countries supports or undermines those theories.

The Role of Crises in Pension Reform

Fiscal constraints are often considered the main factor driving welfare cuts because of the pressure they put on governments irrespective of their political coloring (Clayton and Pontusson 1998; Garrett 1995, 1998; Huber and Stephens 2001; Müller 1999; Pierson 1994; Rodrik 1998). There are several sources of fiscal constraints. First, demographic factors place a heavy burden on the welfare state, especially on pension systems, due to the pronounced aging of the population in advanced industrial states as well as the postcommunist states, and the concomitant increase in the system dependency ratio (ratio of pensioners to contributors). Second, globalization exerts downward pressure on wages and social benefits because high wages and benefits lead to a lack of competitiveness in the international markets. At the same time, globalization strengthens the position of capital vis-à-vis labor because of the threat of capital being located elsewhere. In addition, globalization constrains government capacity to regulate domestic markets, because governments cannot simultaneously control the interest rate and the exchange rate (Huber and Stephens 2001). Finally, the shift from manufacturing to services has also been seen as a source of fiscal constraints, because productivity growth in the service sector lags behind that in manufacturing, leading to pressures on the welfare state (the postindustrialism thesis).

There are various types of fiscal constraints, but the most important one to pension reform is a pension crisis, which is evident through reoccurring pension fund deficits that need to be covered by transfers from the state budget. A pension crisis may not be manifest, but may be expected in the near future, as indicated by an aging population and a projected decline in the ratio of contributors to beneficiaries in the pension fund. World Bank and International Monetary Fund (IMF) data show that countries that reformed their pension systems (measured by the size of the mandatory private pillar and the scope of the public pillar reforms) experienced worse crises on average, as manifested in much higher system dependency ratios, as well as higher rates of unemployment compared to countries that did not reform their pension systems (World Bank n.d.; World Economic Outlook 1999). There are, however, exceptions to this pattern; for example, in the mid-1990s both Albania and Hungary had very high system dependency ratios, but only Hungary had a major pension reform, while Albania at the end of 2009 still had no mandatory private pillar.

Fiscal constraints continue to provide a powerful explanation for welfare state retrenchment because they drive most instances of cutbacks. Few governments would engage in unpopular reforms were they not forced by some kind of crisis. There have been, however, some cases of so-called "ideological retrenchment," in which a conservative party attempted to reduce social provision, despite the absence of an imminent crisis (e.g., Thatcher in Great Britain). The main criticism raised against this line of argument is that it is to some extent tautological. As Kitschelt has noted, fiscal constraints represent only the demand side of reform, and they provide an insufficient explanation for the observed variation between the outcomes (Kitschelt 2001). The need for some policy does not automatically provide the supply of that policy. One should look also at the supply-side factors—political institutions and actors. This is exactly the approach that this study takes.

The Role of International Factors

International factors are believed to influence the pension reform process through various mechanisms, but mostly through the diffusion of ideas and the pressures of international organizations (IOs). Policy diffusion and the role of international organizations in the spread of policy ideas have received recently growing attention because of the highly visible role that international financial institutions have played in pension reform in Latin America and Central and Eastern Europe. The policy diffusion approach is based on the premise that policy solutions are not necessarily readily available to the governments facing a crisis, and that a crisis is not a sufficient condition for policy innovation. This strand of literature attempts to identify the ways in which policy innovation is transmitted to other countries and regions of the world and the countries that are more likely to adopt innovation early versus late (Brooks 2001, 2005; James and Brooks 2001; Orenstein 2003, 2008). This approach contributes to our understanding of the interdependence among countries in terms of the timing of policy change and the particular type of policy design chosen, which is influenced by similar developments in peer nations and by regional leaders. Although policy diffusion theories explain why major reforms occur in waves as well as the regional clustering of reforms, they cannot account for the variation within each wave and region in terms of the timing and content of reforms. For this reason, these theories are often accompanied by domestic-level explanations, which they complement to give a fuller and more nuanced account of the reform process.

Although the existence of some degree of policy diffusion's influence on pension reform is accepted without much debate, the role that international organizations play in the diffusion and adoption of policy innovations is much more controversial (Brooks 2004). There is controversy about whether the IOs play a direct or indirect role in pension reform. Those who argue that the IOs directly influence the adoption of new policies also tend to attribute to the IOs hidden agendas and evil motivations. Huber and Stephens, for instance, contend that "[e]xecutives were pushed and supported in the drive for privatization of pension systems by large and internationally well connected business interests, particularly from the financial sectors, and by international financial institutions" (2000b: 19). In contrast, other scholars have found that the direct influence of the IOs is limited and argue instead for an indirect influence through the diffusion of reform ideas (Brooks 2004). While the international financial institutions propagate neoliberal ideas that emphasize the need to privatize, the International Labor Organization and the International Social Security Association support more cautious reforms limited to the public pension system. The European Union does not uphold a particular type of pension reform, but requires new members to limit their budget deficits, which implicitly reduces their ability to finance the transition from a public to a private pension system.

Supporters of the second view also believe that fiscal crises increase the influence of the international financial institutions over domestic governments. Müller (1999), for example, argues that the financial deterioration of the pension fund and the presence of external debt give the international financial institutions leverage over the reform process through the means of loan conditionality. According to this argument, countries whose pension funds are in crisis and have external debt are more susceptible to the international financial institutions' influence than countries with balanced pension funds and no debt. This line of reasoning is difficult to disentangle from the fiscal crisis argument discussed above, because in many cases a pension crisis is accompanied by international pressures and some degree of reform. However, the IMF and World Bank data suggest that the level of the IMF loans and a country's overall level of external debt do not adequately explain the variation in pension reform outcomes in Central and Eastern Europe. There are indeed countries with high levels of external debt that have accomplished radical reforms, such as Hungary and Bulgaria, in which external debt surpassed on average 50 percent of their gross national product in the period 1990–1999. Others, for example, Georgia and Tajikistan, had equally high levels of external debt during the same time frame, but lagged either in the adoption or in the implementation of pension reform, suggesting a need to consider domestic factors (World Bank n.d.; World Economic Outlook 1999). While international factors are no doubt useful, they illuminate only part of a complex picture in which domestic-level factors need to be brought in. To these factors I will turn in the following pages.

The Role of Domestic Factors

While fiscal constraints and international factors explain the demand side, domestic factors explain the supply of reform. The main domestic explanations for welfare state retrenchment in both industrialized and postcommunist countries can be roughly divided as follows: (1) political institutions, such as power concentration, partisan

IMPACT OF DOMESTIC POLITICAL INSTITUTIONS ✦ 19

differences ("power resources theory"), and the level of democracy; and (2) interest groups, such as trade unions, pensioners associations, and occupational groups that held pension privileges under the old system (Table 2.1).

Power concentration
The theories of power concentration emphasize the importance of government capacities, such as bureaucratic and financial capacities, as well as previous experience with specific programs in the adoption of pension reform. Most of the studies argue that greater centralization of power tends to increase the ability of governments to accomplish reform because there are fewer veto points to prevent the adoption of social policies (Brooks 2002; Cook 2007; Hicks and Swank 1992; Huber, Ragin, and Stephens 1993; Orenstein 2000). In this view, multiple veto points such as federalism, presidentialism, strong bicameralism, single-member districts, and provisions for referenda are obstacles to welfare reform. Orenstein (2000), for instance, in analyzing Central and Eastern European cases, found that countries with more veto actors accomplish less radical reform than countries with fewer veto actors. Similarly, also based on the Central and Eastern European region, Brooks (2002) argued that fragmentation of legislative power in multiparty systems poses an obstacle to pension reform.

Some scholars, among them Arend Lijphart (1984), argue the opposite that more dispersed power increases the representativeness and capacity of governments to respond to diffuse societal interests. Others emphasize the complex and often indeterminate effects of centralization on welfare state reform. On the one hand, concentrated authority does not necessarily provide an advantage to the incumbent government because it also concentrates accountability (Pierson 1994). On the other hand, some authors have noted that veto points are not all alike. Some veto points constrain welfare reform, while others have enabling effects (Crepaz 1998). The constraining veto points create competitive incentives for actors operating through distinct institutions with mutual veto powers, such as federalism, strong bicameralism, and presidentialism, and lead to "lowest common denominator politics." In contrast, the enabling veto points create incentives for collective decision making when actors operate in the same body and interact on a face-to-face basis, such as in proportional representation electoral systems, multiparty legislatures, and multiparty governments, and they favor the "highest common denominator politics" (Crepaz 1998). Therefore, the sheer number of veto points tells little about the probability of welfare reform.

The role of institutions in pension reform is complex. As Pierson (1994) has noted, particular institutional arrangements represent mixed blessings for policy makers. Federalism, for instance, constrains welfare state growth but has both positive and negative influences on retrenchment (Pierson 1994). Similarly, parliamentary systems concentrate both authority and accountability, and therefore are not necessarily more conducive to retrenchment than presidential systems (Pierson 1994). Government capacities also seem to matter less for retrenchment than for expansion. Several authors have noted that bureaucracies can explain neither long-term change within a country nor variation across countries (Huber and Stephens 2001; Pierson 1994). They argue that neither government capacities nor autonomous bureaucratic activity shape ultimate outcomes in fundamental ways because politicians, not bureaucrats, are the crucial actors (Pierson 1994).

In the same vein, a number of scholars contend that there are fewer obstacles to reform in presidential systems, in which reform is largely insulated from electoral protest (Cook, Orenstein, and Rueschemeyer 1999). In contrast, other authors note that the distinction between parliamentary and presidential systems offers little leverage in explaining the outcome of pension reform (Brooks 2002). Although presidential systems have accomplished a greater number of radical reforms than parliamentary systems, variation in the outcome of reform within the presidential group is also much wider, and therefore the distinction has little predictive value (Brooks 2002). The evidence of this study, based on the experience of the postcommunist region, does not offer support for the role of presidentialism in reform either. With the exception of Armenia, all presidential regimes across the area occur in semiauthoritarian and authoritarian political systems, such as Azerbaijan, Belarus, Georgia, Kazakhstan, the Russian Federation, Tajikistan, and Uzbekistan, whose patterns of policy making are different from those of democracies and thus the two should not be analyzed together. Moreover, authoritarian regimes have accomplished less reform on average compared to democracies in the region (see the discussion about the level of democracy below). In addition, looking only within the democratic and semidemocratic categories, the institutional diversity is rather limited. Most of the democracies and semidemocracies are unitary states, have unicameral or bicameral asymmetrical legislatures, and are parliamentary systems, with the exception of Lithuania, Poland, and Romania, which are semipresidential.

The Level of Democracy

The level of democracy argument has been developed to specifically address the diversity of democratic institutions and practices across the postcommunist region, and it is relevant to all new democracies and countries struggling to democratize. It is based on logic similar to the veto actors approach discussed above and focuses on the insulation of government power from societal pressures. The more democratic and inclusive the political process is the more potential obstacles there are to pension reform, because the government is more concerned with the distributional needs of the society (Brooks 2002; Cook 2007; Orenstein 2000). Conversely, authoritarian regimes that are insulated from society are seen as being better able to pursue radical reforms than democratic regimes, as reforms in Kazahkstan and Croatia under Tudjman show.

The evidence based on the entire postcommunist region does not support this argument. On the contrary, it supports the opposite view, according to which the more inclusive the political process is the more likely it is to accomplish reform. The democratic regimes[1] tend to cluster together and accomplish a high degree of pension reform, with the notable exceptions of the Czech Republic and Slovenia (see Table 4.1). Of the eight consolidated democracies (according to the Freedom House ratings) in the region, six have accomplished radical reform, including both reform of the public system and the introduction of a mandatory funded system. In contrast, most authoritarian regimes, with the exception of Kazakhstan, have not attempted reforms or have abandoned them. Among the middle categories there is also a high rate of pension reform completion: four of the five semiconsolidated democracies, with the exception of Albania, have adopted radical reforms, and one of the two hybrid regimes (Ukraine) has adopted limited reform. The overall pattern suggests that consolidated and semiconsolidated democracies have accomplished radical reforms, with few exceptions (3 out of 13 countries), while the semiconsolidated and consolidated authoritarian regimes have not made reforms or have not implemented them, with the exception of Kazakhstan.

The Power Resources Theory

The "power resources theory," relating the expansion of social provision in Western Europe to the political and organizational resources of labor movements and social democratic parties (Esping-Andersen 1985, 1990; Korpi 1983; Stephens 1979), was a powerful theory in the welfare state literature in the 1980s but has declined in importance with the mounting pressures for cutbacks on the European welfare states (Pierson 1994, 2000). As numerous scholars have noted, partisan differences over retrenchment declined in importance due to severe constraints faced by both left and right governments (Bonoli 2000; Huber and Stephens 2001; P. Pierson 1998; Schludi 2003). The right was often not able to implement major cuts because the welfare state was very popular. The left, on the other hand, was forced to curtail some of the benefits when faced with mounting unemployment and low levels of economic growth. The new literature on pension reform in Central and Eastern Europe has revived the debate around the role of partisan differences (Cook, Orenstein, and Rueschemeyer 1999; Lipsmeyer 2000). These works treat political parties as central actors in the decision-making process and analyze how their ideological orientation interacts with various constraints that parties face in order to produce a given outcome. In line with the power resources theory, some scholars have attributed a significant role to ideology, contending that the right favors radical reform while the left defends existing pension arrangements (Lipsmeyer 2000; Scarbrough 2000).

In contrast, other works follow the retrenchment argument according to which ideology's role in pension reform has declined; such scholars adopt a more cautious view of ideology, stressing the constraints that parties in power face (Cook, Orenstein, and Rueschemeyer 1999). These authors, while acknowledging that the left has a distinct pro-welfare agenda, highlight important differences within the left camp due to the variation in the environments that left parties face. Coalitional politics, for instance, was an important obstacle to maintaining a generous welfare state, because most of the left parties in postcommunist Europe governed in coalition with parties that had a different social agenda (Cook, Orenstein, and Rueschemeyer 1999). Likewise, the avoidance of difficult reforms by the right put the left under pressure to pursue liberal economic policies in order to stay on the road to Europe (Cook, Orenstein, and Rueschemeyer 1999). This argument, which provides a powerful explanation for cross-national variation in pension reform, is at the core of the approach of this study and will be explored in detail in chapter 3. The criticisms to this perspective come mostly from the promoters of international and fiscal crises approaches, who consider parties and coalitions in power to be severely restrained in their policy decisions by international and economic forces beyond their control.

The Role of Interest Groups

Interest group theory attributes various groups with entrenched interests in the old pension system the power to derail the reform process in order to preserve previous pension privileges (Cook, Orenstein, and Rueschemeyer 1999; Kapstein and Mandelbaum 1997; Müller 2002). Commonly invoked are the trade unions, pensioners' associations, and the groups with pension privileges, such as members of the military, civil servants, and workers in heavy industry. Müller (2002), for instance, claims that in Slovenia reform-minded politicians could not privatize the pension system because of strong opposition from powerful interest groups. Likewise, Kapstein and Mandelbaum (1997) argue that massive rent-seeking opportunities made it difficult to reform postcommunist welfare systems. The role of trade unions is more controversial because unions in some countries became entrepreneurs in the new private industry and supported privatization, while in other countries they took an oppositionist stance. The main criticism against theories based on interest group politics is that interest groups are not the decision makers and therefore such theories need to incorporate the mechanisms through which interest groups affect the decision-making process. There have also been more and more instances of retrenchment despite the existence of strong constituencies that opposed reform, particularly in Latin America and Central and Eastern Europe, thus contradicting the theory of interest group power. In contrast with the later findings, this study provides evidence that interest groups play a powerful role in pension politics and combines an interest group approach with a theory of political parties and coalitional politics.

Conclusion

The distinction between supply and demand factors in pension reform provides a useful framework for analyzing the political economy of pension reform and helps explain the need of many researchers to combine economic and international explanations with explanations centered on domestic factors. Both demand and supply factors need to be present for pension reform to occur, but not all factors are equally important. On the demand side, pension reform correlates positively with the presence of a pension crisis, bringing support to the prevalent idea in the welfare state literature that reform for purely ideological reasons is rare. In contrast, economic crises do not show a positive correlation with pension reform, suggesting a more complex role for economic factors. Similarly, the role of international factors is complex. International organizations play an important role in policy diffusion and provide an incentive structure for completing pension reform. How governments respond to these incentives ultimately depends on the domestic institutions and actors.

On the supply side, the level of democracy, the partisan differences, and the interest groups emerge as promising explanations for pension reform across the postcommunist region, sometimes in unexpected ways. There is a clear pattern across the postcommunist area showing a positive correlation between the level of democracy and the degree of reform, which goes against the common argument made in the literature that relates reform to the insulation of executive power from public pressure. The explanations focusing on the role of party systems and interest groups will be explored in depth in the following chapters.

CHAPTER 3

Parties, Coalitions, and Policies: A Theoretical Framework

The focus of this book is on the political determinants of pension reform in Central and Eastern Europe. The analytical framework that I develop draws on theories of political parties and coalitional politics. Theories of political parties stress the central role of parties in policy making, whereas coalition theories focus on the dynamics of inter-party competition and their impact on the policy output. While treating political parties as essential political actors, this study highlights the environments in which they operate, which raises a multitude of constraints on their behavior. The strategies parties adopt in order to maximize competing programmatic, organizational, electoral, and governing goals are consequential for the outcome of pension reform. Among the various constraints on party behavior, this book pays special attention to the role of ideologies, the influence of key constituencies with entrenched interests in existing welfare arrangements, and coalitional politics.

Within the new institutionalist paradigm, this work combines structuralist-institutionalist and actor-centered approaches (Immergut 1998; Thelen 1999). It shares with the structuralist-institutionalist perspective a concern with long-term processes of development and a path-dependent view, in which past choices constrain present options. Also along the structuralist-institutionalist line is a preoccupation with the redistributive effects of institutions and a view of the political process as a struggle for scarce resources among actors differently endowed with power and resources. The complexity of actors' goals and the trade-offs between short-term maximization and long-term benefits, such as trading off one's favorite policy for future electoral gains, are also structuralist-institutionalist concerns.

From the actor-centered approach, this study borrows the assumptions that actors are rational, that they try to maximize fulfillment of their objectives within the constraints imposed by institutions, and that they have complete information about other actors' preferences and the rules of the game. Essential to the actor-centered perspective are (1) a focus on the short-term causes of institutional change, such as external shocks, which break down the equilibrium that institutions provide and create opportunities for actors to establish new institutions, and (2) a view of institutions as solutions to collective action problems—in this case a Prisoner's Dilemma situation in which rational individual choices produce irrational collective outcomes. For example, individual incentive regarding the welfare state is to contribute as little as possible and receive as much as possible in benefits, irrespective of what the other participating individuals do. However, if all individuals contribute less than their own share, the system is not financially sustainable over the long-term and everybody ends up worse off.

I bring together the structuralist-institutionalist and actor-centered traditions on two levels. First, I treat institutions as serving a two-fold purpose: they solve collective action problems, such as the moral hazard and free-rider behavior associated with a defined-benefit pension system (for an explanation of the perverse incentives created by a defined-benefit system, see section Competing Perspectives on Reform, chapter 1); at the same time they have a redistributive function within the economic system through the allocation of resources between generations, income groups, and occupational categories. Second, institutional change is the result of two distinct and complementary processes. On the one hand, a path-dependent process constrains available options for reform through the inherited pension system, the political choices made during the early transition, and the historical development of political parties. On the other hand, the strategic interaction among political parties during the coalition formation process ultimately shapes the pension reform outcome.

I begin this chapter by developing a theoretical argument in which political parties, the party system, and the process of coalition formation play a central role in explaining pension reform outcomes. I discuss the role of ideology, the impact of special interests, and the consequences of the coalition formation process. In the second part of the chapter, I use a two-dimensional spatial model as a heuristic device that attempts to relate various configurations of the party system to pension reform outcomes and sustainability. Although this theoretical framework has been built with Central and Eastern European experiences in mind, it is also useful for understanding pension reform beyond the postcommunist context.

ROLE OF POLITICAL PARTIES, PARTY SYSTEM, AND COALITIONAL POLITICS IN PENSION REFORM

In this section, I lay out the logic of a pension reform theory based on political parties and coalitional politics. The main argument of this book is that the supply-side variables, particularly political parties, the party system, and the coalition formation process, largely account for the variation in pension reform outcomes and their sustainability (Figure 3.1). The available options for coalition formation are defined by parties' ideological orientations, their connections with interest groups, and their relative strength and strategic interactions with other parties. These, in turn, influence the characteristics of the pro-reform coalition and the relative strength of pro- and anti-reform coalitions, which determine the political feasibility of a reform proposal and shape the end result. This approach can be used to explain not only cross-national variations in pension reform outcomes, but also the variation in outcomes over time within a country. Cross-nationally, countries differ in the configuration of their party systems and in the types of governing coalitions formed, and this study will provide evidence that this variation accounts for the variation

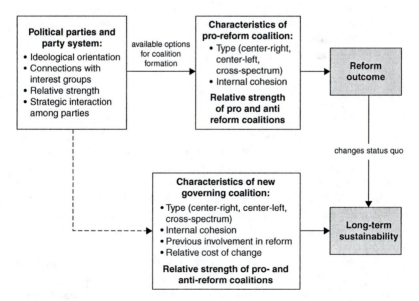

Figure 3.1 Role of political parties, party system, and coalitional politics in the outcome and long-term sustainability of pension reform

in pension reform outcomes. Similarly, in a given party system the changing of governing coalitions over time explains why reform fails at one time but passes at another time under a different coalition.

Not all reforms adopted have proven to be durable. Parties dissatisfied with the outcome may attempt to alter the outcome of reform. I argue that the long-term sustainability of reform depends on the characteristics of subsequent governing coalitions and the results of reform, which changes the status quo against which political parties weigh new proposals (Figure 3.1).

In the next subsection, I focus on the characteristics of political parties and party systems that influence the process of pension reform. I then turn to the impact of the coalition formation process on the outcome. In the last subsection, I discuss the role of political parties and coalitional politics in the long-term sustainability of reform.

Role of Political Parties and Party Systems in Pension Reform

The dominant approach to pension politics in both the Western and the Central and Eastern European literatures has been to explain it in terms of ideological differences between parties. Some scholars have contended that the right favors reform while the left defends existing pension arrangements (Lipsmeyer 2000; Scarbrough 2000). Meanwhile, others have pinpointed an increasing number of cases that do not fit the typical pro-reform-right versus anti-reform-left pattern and have claimed that ideology's role in pension reform declines because of mounting demographic, economic, and international pressures for reform that left and right governments equally face (Bonoli 2000; P. Pierson 1998; Schludi 2003).

This book advances a different explanation, arguing that the role of ideology in pension reform is complex and its influence is circumscribed by interest group politics. Pension reform has far-reaching costs and benefits, only some of which reflect the left-right distinction; others represent concentrated interests. Parties, irrespective of their political color, could be connected with groups that have an entrenched interest in the old pension system and/or with new managerial groups that benefit from reform. In reality, the alleged convergence between the left and the right with respect to pension policy masks a divergence of views not only between the left and the right about the diffuse costs and benefits of reform, which are spread across large segments of the population, but also within each camp regarding the allocation of concentrated costs and benefits. Based on the strategic interaction among parties, these divisions may translate into a variety of pro-reform and anti-reform coalitions that overlap and sometimes obscure ideological differences. The specific shape of reform and its long-term sustainability ultimately depend on the type, internal cohesion, and relative strength of these alignments, which explains the puzzling diversity among cases despite the relative similarity of starting points.

Role of Ideology in Pension Reform

The literature on pension reform has focused almost exclusively on the role of left and right ideologies in the reform outcomes and neglected the important impact of the nationalists. Given that no theory directly relates nationalist parties with specific pension reform outcomes, I will discuss more extensively the nationalist influence on pension reform.

The role of the left in pension reform is controversial. The common assumption is that the left opposes pension reform, which involves a reduction in the role of the state in pension provision and favors the free market and the individual. The left does not want the redistribution embedded in the previous pension system to be eliminated, nor does it seek pension privatization. Empirical evidence shows that some left parties conform to the expected pattern while others do not. I argue that in the postcommunist context the modernization of the former communist party, or lack thereof, not only determines the attitude of the left toward pension reform, but is also likely to have a major impact on reform outcome and sustainability because it conditions the policy preferences of the communist successor party and the likely alliances it will form. A reformed ex-communist party that has embraced a social democratic outlook is more likely to support pension reform and enter into coalitions with liberal parties that promote reform than an unreformed communist party. Conversely, an unreformed ex-communist party is more likely to oppose reform and form coalitions with other left parties and the nationalists. As the evidence based on the cases of Poland, Hungary, Romania, and Slovakia will show, the timing of transformation is also important: pension reform is likely to occur early in countries in which the former communist party had modernized early and late if the former communist party suffered a late modernization.

Although the right pole is generally expected to promote reform, the extent to which it does so and its effectiveness depend on its ideological and organizational coherence, as well as its connections with interest groups. A strong, liberal right is more likely to accomplish pension reform than a fragmented right or a right divided between a liberal camp and a nationalist camp. For instance, a number of right parties have embraced a nationalist rhetoric in order to attract support from those dissatisfied with the results of market-oriented reforms, such as Klaus' Civic Democratic Party in the Czech Republic and the Fidesz in Hungary. The right may also be connected with privileged occupational groups, such as the Polish AWS (Solidarity Electoral Action, Akcja Wyborcza Solidarność), and thus will oppose those aspects of pension reform that adversely affect their constituents. In other countries, such as Romania and Slovakia, divisions within the right have contributed to delays in the adoption of reforms. Overall, in all four cases examined in the book, the right has been responsible for delays, partial reforms, or partial reversals of reforms.

As the empirical evidence that I present in the following chapters will show, nationalist parties tend to be more strongly opposed to pension reform than many left parties. The role of nationalists in pension reform has not been systematically analyzed because the literature has focused almost exclusively on the left and the right. This is partially a result of the assimilation of the nationalists into the left-right continuum. In contrast with this tendency, I argue that nationalists constitute a pole of the party system distinct from both the left and the right, and moreover that nationalist parties can have either a left or a right orientation. The unusual combination of left and nationalist ideologies is characteristic of the postcommunist context in which nationalist parties blend nationalist appeals with nostalgia for the communist paternalist system of economic relations.

There are a number of theoretical reasons to assume that nationalists would oppose pension reform, such as the involvement of international financial institutions in pension reform, the opportunity to capitalize on the unpopularity of pension reform, and the connections of nationalist parties that originated in the former communist regime with occupational groups that had privileges under the old pension system. Nationalist parties oppose the involvement of international financial institutions in the pension reform process. Western institutions (such as the IMF and the World Bank) and the policies associated with them are common targets of nationalist attacks. International financial institutions condition their loans on the adoption of a radical version of pension reform. Their intervention in the postcommunist reforms fuelled the nationalist discourse which portrays international financial institutions as hostile external forces that use their ideas, values, and institutions to subdue nations.

Nationalist parties also tend to capitalize on the unpopularity of proposed reforms. The introduction of market forces in previously heavily regulated economies has generated a form of economic nationalism. As Jack Snyder noted (1993), "[P]articularly intense nationalism results from a gap between a group's inadequate capacity for collective action and acute threats to the group's military or economic security." Those who lose as a result of an economic transition expect more, not less, social protection and regard the retreat of the state from the provision of social services as a failure to deliver the social protection that communism had promised. Many of them turn toward nationalist parties, which promise to continue paying subsidies to state-owned enterprises, ensure job security in the state sector, keep inflation under control, and restore the state's capacity to protect individuals from the vagaries of the market (Snyder 1993).

Key constituencies of nationalist parties who held pension privileges under the previous system, such as workers in uncompetitive industries and members of the military, often lose these privileges after the reforms. Feeling frustrated about the relative loss they have incurred compared to their pretransition socioeconomic status, they may attempt to use their connections with nationalist parties to further their parochial interests. While protecting such privileged groups, nationalist parties often use propaganda to present themselves as the champions of the general national interest, which is being threatened by Western forces through neoliberal policies.

Nationalist parties and the groups that support them are the most virulent critics of market-oriented reforms because they possess elements of both nationalism and left protectionism, such as Mečiar's HZDS (Movement for a Democratic Slovakia, Hnutie za demokratické Slovensko) in Slovakia and the Greater Romania Party in Romania. However, some right parties have also embraced nationalism, as the above-mentioned examples of Klaus' Civic Democratic Party in the Czech Republic and the Fidesz in Hungary show. Therefore, the distinction between left and right is not sufficient to position such parties ideologically. A second, nationalist-cosmopolitan dimension is necessary.

Role of Special Interests in Pension Reform

Several authors have pointed out the hostility toward pension reform demonstrated by political parties strongly tied with occupational groups that held privileges under the old pension system (Aleksandrowicz 2007; Müller 1999; Orenstein 2000; Wenzel 1998). However, the strong case study evidence supporting the impact of special interests on pension reform has yet to be incorporated into a more general framework of pension politics. The present study undertakes this task. This section discusses the constraints that interest groups pose on political parties and how they impact the reform process.

The theoretical framework of this work is based on the distinction between the diffuse and concentrated costs and benefits of pension reform, which is essential for understanding political parties' positions toward reform. Rationalization of the public system and creation of private pension funds have, for the most part, diffuse effects that are spread over large categories of the population. Private pension funds favor higher income workers at the expense of lower income workers and therefore reduce the redistribution that is embedded in the old pension system, but the benefits are not aimed at a well-defined occupational category or interest group in particular. In addition, privatization also reduces intergenerational redistribution by favoring younger workers, who will save for their own retirement instead of paying the pensions of current pensioners, at the expense of pensioners and older workers, whose benefits will inevitably erode.

In contrast, eradication of pension privileges inflicts concentrated costs on both the beneficiaries and the providers of pensions in the old system. In postcommunist countries, occupational privileges could come in two different forms. Some consist of a more favorable calculation of benefits and early retirement provisions for certain categories of workers within the public system, such as miners and workers in heavy industry, implying redistribution from less privileged workers to more privileged workers according to their political clout. A far-reaching reform of the public system would entail a uniform formula for the calculation of benefits.

Other privileges are in the form of separate pension systems, for instance, those for uniformed groups in the Czech Republic and Romania and for uniformed groups and farmers in Poland, which are highly subsidized by the state. The separate pension schemes could have considerable scope. In Poland, for instance, these schemes provide approximately one-third of the total old-age benefits (Müller 1999). Elimination of occupational privileges assumes incorporation of the separate pension schemes into the general public system.

Workers in the occupational categories that benefited under the previous system share four main features: (1) they occupied privileged positions under the communist regime and some, though not all, have managed to preserve these positions during the postcommunist period; (2) they have a strong sense of their social importance as a direct result of the way they were portrayed by the communist discourse; (3) they tend to be well organized and articulate their interests through powerful trade unions and political parties originating in the communist regime; and (4) those who have not succeeded in transforming their previous political power into economic power under the new system do not expect the free market to compensate for the loss of their privileges. The combined effect of these characteristics is that workers in these occupational categories are likely to fiercely oppose any attack on their previous entitlements. Likewise, trade unions and other administrators of public pension funds that were the pension providers under the old system are also negatively affected by reform, which deprives them of control over the pension funds and erodes the economic bases of their power.

Typically one can find among the privileged groups workers in mining and heavy industry, the police, and the armed forces, as well as civil servants. They have strong ties with the unreformed communist parties or with the hard-line factions of the former communist parties, as well as with other parties that originated in the communist regime. They are also likely to articulate their demands through nationalist-populist parties, which are willing to capitalize on their discontent. They could also find more limited support in the right parties that advocate a traditionalist view of society, such as Christian democrats, which are likely to see a special role for some of the privileged groups (mainly the armed forces) as defenders of the nation and, at the same time, might fear the consequences of upsetting the already fragile balance of social relations.

The restructuring of the pension system generates not only concentrated costs, but also concentrated benefits, most of which come in the form of administrative positions in the restructured pension system. Pension reform mobilizes vast amounts of capital, only part of which returns to the contributors in the form of retirement income. A large portion of the expected return on this money[1] is spent on administering pension funds and providing spoils to a new range of interest groups, such as banks, insurance companies, pension fund managers, and supervisory agencies. The new special interests compete, sometimes within the same party, against the old privileged groups for the division of profits, leading to splits within the parties and the formation of pension coalitions cross-cutting party lines.

James Q. Wilson's (1980) framework for analyzing policies based on their perceived costs and benefits provides useful insights into the politics of pension reform. According to Wilson's theory, pension reform most closely reflects *entrepreneurial politics*, which "will confer general (though perhaps small) benefits at a cost to be borne chiefly by a small segment of society" (Wilson 1980: 370), similar to auto-safety bills or antipollution acts. The incentive for the opponents to organize is strong, but for the beneficiaries it is weak since in the case of pension reform the potential benefits are long-term and diffuse (Müller 1999; Pierson 1994); therefore, we are witnessing a collective action problem. The efforts of an entrepreneur are needed to organize support for the proposed policy and to overcome organized opposition. The attempts by international financial institutions to play such a role have in large part been unsuccessful because they were regarded with hostility throughout Central and Eastern Europe due to the austerity programs that they had imposed in the region. Among the domestic actors, the most likely entrepreneurs were the pro-market political parties that were not connected with groups that have entrenched interests in the old pension system, such as the liberal parties. Most liberal parties were relatively small; in order to succeed, they needed to build coalitions with other parties. The structure of these coalitions depends on the configuration of the party system, which in turn determines the reform outcomes.

Ideology and Interest Groups: Convergent or Competing Incentives?
This book argues that parties in favor of both an increased role for the free market in the provision of retirement benefits and the elimination of previous pension privileges, such as the liberals, are the most likely pension reformers. Their right ideology and lack of connections with privileged occupational groups converge toward strong support for reform. Conversely, parties that oppose a free market and elimination of pension privileges, such as unreformed communists and nationalists, are the least likely to support reform, and in this case their left orientation and strong connections with privileged occupational groups are also in agreement.

This is no longer the case for the other two types of parties. Parties that favor a major role for the state in pension provision but have no connections with privileged groups, such as some social democrats, have mixed feelings about reform and support it selectively. For instance, a social democratic party may support elimination of pension privileges but oppose the elimination of redistribution embedded in the public pension system. Likewise, pro-market parties connected with privileged groups, such as some Christian democrats and nationalists of the right, may favor public system reform and privatization but oppose the eradication of occupational privileges. For these types of parties, their ideology and connections with privileged occupational groups create competing incentives. The position that these parties adopt toward pension reform depends on their internal cohesion and the likely alliances they can form.

Parties that are internally divided over reform can easily swing one way or the other, depending on the internal balance of power and their coalition partners. For instance, the Democratic Left Alliance (SLD, Sojusz Lewicy Demokratycznej) in Poland was split between a liberal faction inclined toward radical reform and a unionist wing that opposed elimination of privileges (Müller 1999; Orenstein 2000). When the liberals in the party held the leadership, the party launched an ambitious reform project. When the leadership went to the conservatives, the party opposed continuation of reform. The case of the SLD is also illustrative of the role of the coalition formation process in shifting the position of those parties that are torn between competing incentives. The SLD's first choice for a coalition partner was the liberal Freedom Union (UW, Unia Wolności), but the latter did not want to compromise itself by entering into an alliance with the former communists. The SLD had no choice but to turn toward its former communist era ally, the Polish People's Party (PSL, Polskie Stronnictwo Ludowe), which was a natural enemy of reform. As a result, the SLD kept away from the difficult reform of occupational privileges, which the unionist faction of the SLD and the PSL opposed. One can speculate that if an alliance between the SLD and the UW were possible, the SLD would have been a strong promoter of reform, following the Hungarian path.

As this example suggests, parties facing competing incentives for reform raise important theoretical difficulties because their behavior is not amenable to simple explanations. For such cases it is necessary to know, on the one hand, the party's position within the party system, which defines its available options for coalition formation. On the other hand, it is also necessary to know the party's specific position toward pension reform, which constrains the range of policy options available to the respective coalition.

Role of Coalitional Politics in Pension Reform

As the above discussion stressed, the configuration of a party system defines the available options for coalition formation, which in practice are relatively limited in number (Figure 3.1). When a pro-reform coalition comes into power, its chances for accomplishing reform depend on its relative strength versus the anti-reform coalition and its internal characteristics. Minority governments are unlikely to approach pension reform because it is highly controversial and unpopular. For example, of the 15 governments that embarked on pension reform in Central and Eastern Europe during the period 1994–2010, only two were minority governments: the LC (Latvia's Way, Latvijas Ceļš) government in Latvia, which in 1994–1995 did not finalize the reform, and the Social Democratic Party (PSD, Partidul Social Democrat) government in Romania, which passed the second pillar reform with broad support from all major parties (see Table 4.1). Similarly, a coalition that has a small majority may avoid the issue, as did Klaus' coalition in the Czech Republic (1993–1997), which held 52 percent of the seats (see Table 4.1). In contrast, 5 of the 15 pro-reform coalitions were surplus coalitions, containing at least one party that was not necessary to form a majority (see Table 4.1), and 9 of the 15 coalitions commanded large majorities, suggesting that the strength of the coalition might be a factor in its decision to launch a major pension reform.

Of the internal characteristics of the governing coalition, I argue that the type of coalition—center-right, center-left, or cross-spectrum— and its internal cohesion influence reform outcomes. Given the constraints examined above, there are a limited number of pro-reform coalitions possible:

- **Center-right**: a coalition of center-right and right parties, excluding parties connected with privileged groups and nationalists of the right. Such a coalition could include the liberals and Christian democrats.
- **Center-left**: a coalition of center-left parties that are not connected with privileged occupational groups. This coalition is built around the social democrats.
- **Cross-spectrum**: a cross-spectrum coalition of center-left and center-right parties that are not connected with privileged groups. This could be a coalition of social democrats with the liberals.

The types of coalitions that are more likely to form in a given country depend on the characteristics of the party system. In the postcommunist context, the fate of the successor communist party is of great importance to reform outcomes. If the former communist party has been marginalized (as in the Czech Republic) or has disappeared altogether (as in Latvia) and a modern social democratic party occupies the center-left, a pro-reform coalition can include the social democrats, which are likely to support at least some degree of reform. In such countries all three types of coalitions are possible and the chances of reform success are high. Likewise, if the successor communist party has become a modern social democratic party that accepts a free-market economy, it can become part of a pro-reform coalition (as in Hungary and Poland). In contrast, in countries where the successor communist party has modernized late (e.g., Bulgaria and Romania), the unreformed party is likely to block the reform process, and pro-reform coalitions can form only on the right side of the political spectrum, which diminishes the chances for reform. The strength of the nationalists is also relevant for the end result of reform. In Slovakia, for instance, pension reform did not stand a chance as long as Mečiar's HZDS, which was both left and nationalist, dominated the political scene.

Role of Political Parties, Party Systems, and Coalitional Politics in the Long-Term Sustainability of Reform

The configuration of the party system and the process of coalition formation also influence the long-term sustainability of reform through a similar mechanism to that of reform adoption, which is by limiting the available options for coalition formation and the governing coalition's strength and position toward reform outcomes (Figure 3.1). The characteristics of the new governing coalition define its position toward the outcome. The closer in type and composition the new and previous coalitions are, the more likely it is that the new coalition will accept the outcome of reform, and thus the chances that the reform will endure are higher.

However, two main factors break this symmetry, both of which are intrinsic to the reform process that had taken place. On the one hand, the adopted reform changes the status quo (SQ) against which parties weigh new proposals. Even if the new status quo is far from ideal for many parties, it is not necessarily worse than alternative proposals. A shift in the status quo influences parties' relative costs and benefits of altering the outcome. It is often costly to change a policy once it is in place because of a path-dependency phenomenon, which leads to the creation of new constituencies supporting the new policy and an increase in the public acceptance of that policy. On the other hand, parties' experiences with the reform process may modify their initial positions. For instance, parties' exposure to new information and opinions, along with their direct and indirect contributions to the elaboration of the reform proposal, parliamentary debates, and voting, may transform their attitudes regarding the outcome and also their incentives to amend it.

For these reasons, many policies prove to be "sticky" and tend to endure even if a majority dislikes them. It takes greater effort to reverse a policy once it is in place than to prevent its adoption in the first place.

A Two-Dimensional Spatial Model of Pension Politics

The distinction between the diffuse and concentrated costs and benefits of pension reform suggests that the logic of my argument in this book should be amenable to portrayal in a two-dimensional spatial model of pension politics. At one pole of the diffuse dimension (corresponding to the classic left-right distinction and depicted horizontally in Figure 3.2A) are situated those who favor a low redistributive function of the pension system. Such groups support a tight link between contributions and benefits as well as a substantially diminished role for the public system and an increased role for the market in the provision of retirement benefits, which advantages the better-off segments of the population. The opposite pole is occupied by those who support maintaining the income redistribution embedded in the old system and a dominant role for the state in pension provision.

The concentrated dimension lies between a trade unionist pole that defends existing occupational privileges and a liberal pole that wishes to eliminate them (the second dimension is depicted vertically in Figure 3.2A). The analysis of party positions and potential pro-reform and anti-reform coalitions in this space provides answers to the following questions: first, what are the most likely pro-reform and anti-reform coalitions; second, how does the coalition formation process under various configurations of the party system relate to different pension reform outcomes; and third, what are the conditions for reform sustainability?

The argument is based on the following assumptions: that there is a party system with four parties, each of which is located in one of the four quadrants defined by the two axes of pension system, as depicted in Figure 3.2A; that each party is a unitary actor represented as a single ideal point; and that each party's preferences are single peaked and symmetric.[2] For ease of presentation, the two dimensions are assumed to be equally salient to each party. Following P. Pierson (1998) and Schludi (2003), I place the status quo (SQ), which represents the pension system inherited from communism, in an extreme position in the lower left quadrant. In substantive terms, such a position reflects the large redistribution inherited from the communist system, in which old-age pension was a social right granted by the state to every citizen (diffuse dimension), coupled with the award

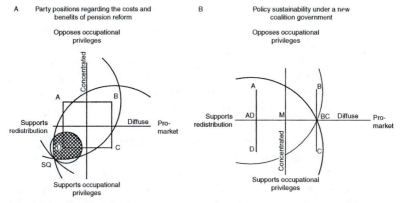

A   Party positions regarding the costs and benefits of pension reform

Parties A, B, C, and D differ in their relative positions regarding the diffuse and concentrated redistributive functions of the pension system. Status quo (SQ) is characterized by high redistribution and high pension privileges. The darkened area represents the zone of agreement among all four parties.

B   Policy sustainability under a new coalition government

When the outcome of reform is BC and parties A and D form the new government, they are likely to shift policy from BC to AD. When the outcome is M, the benefits of shifting policy from M to AD are comparatively lower; therefore policy M is more sustainable than policy BC, all else being equal.

Figure 3.2 Comparison of party positions regarding the costs and benefits of pension reform and policy sustainability under a new coalition government

Source: Reproduced with permission from Europe-Asia Studies. © 2010 Taylor & Francis.

of substantial privileges to particular categories of workers well positioned within the party-state hierarchy (concentrated dimension).

Parties' indifference curves drawn through the status quo show that departures from the status quo with which all four parties would agree are limited (darkened area in Figure 3.2A), and that these departures represent marginal changes to the existing pension system. The existence of two major groups of parties is apparent in Figure 3.2A: on the one hand, party D, whose ideal point is close to the status quo, does not want a large policy change; on the other, parties A, B, and C favor radical reforms, albeit of different varieties. Therefore, the first implications of the model are:

> **Proposition 1**. Coalitions dominated by parties who oppose both diffuse and concentrated costs of reform make only marginal changes to the existing pension system.

> **Proposition 2**. Parties that accept both types of costs support all pro-reform coalitions because any move away from the status quo brings the outcome closer to their ideal.

> **Proposition 3**. Parties that accept one type of cost but not the other do not always benefit significantly from a move away from the status quo. They support a reform proposal provided that it is closer to their ideal point than the status quo.

The politics of radical reform is therefore about finding an equilibrium among parties A, B, and C. We know from social choice theory that majority rule decisions tend to produce unstable outcomes. Shepsle and others have addressed this by adding structure to the decision process in the form of institutions (Shepsle 1979; Shepsle and Weingast 1981). Taking into account institutional constraints, such as being in the governing coalition or in the opposition, being the senior or the junior coalitional partner, and the history of participation in previous coalitions (Pridham 1986), and assuming that no single party has a majority on its own, there are two main theoretical possibilities that predict different policy outcomes. In the first case, two of the three parties (for instance, B and C) form a majority government and party A is in opposition. The policy proposal lies on the contract curve uniting parties B and C's ideal points, labeled BC (Figure 3.3A). The stronger party of the two pulls policy BC closer to its ideal point. BC is invulnerable to any alternative because any point off the BC line is dominated by BC. Policy BC is close to the median voter[3] on the vertical dimension, but far away from it on the horizontal dimension. Similarly, policy AB represents the equilibrium outcome of a coalition government formed by parties A and B.

The second case is when all three parties—A, B, and C—form a government (Figure 3.3B). Assuming that each party in the coalition has veto power over a proposal, the outcome is either M, which represents the ideal of the median voter on both dimensions, or it is located in M's win set (Figure 3.3B). The analysis of the two possibilities of coalition formation leads to the following:

> **Proposition 4**. The equilibrium outcome of a coalition government formed by two parties lies on the contract curve connecting their ideal points and is close to the median voter on a single dimension. When multiple parties participate in the coalition, the outcome is either the median voter on both dimensions or is located in its win set.

This proposition implies in substantive terms that whether the reform coalition includes only two parties or reaches toward other parties is consequential for reform outcomes. Two-party coalitions tend to adopt a more radical version of reform, while broader coalitions are more likely to achieve a more moderate solution, closer to the median voter M. Proposition 4 has important consequences for reform sustainability, which depends on the incentives and capabilities of future coalitions to change the outcome. Here I examine medium-term sustainability, which I define as the outcome of reform

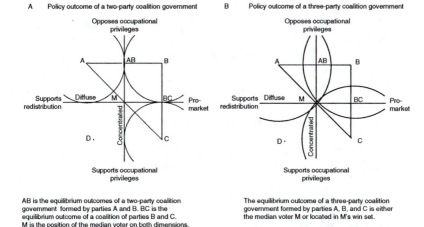

AB is the equilibrium outcomes of a two-party coalition government formed by parties A and B. BC is the equilibrium outcome of a coalition of parties B and C. M is the position of the median voter on both dimensions.

The equilibrium outcome of a three-party coalition government formed by parties A, B, and C is either the median voter M or located in M's win set.

Figure 3.3 Comparison of policy outcome of a two-party coalition government and a three-party coalition government

Source: Reproduced with permission from Europe-Asia Studies. © 2010 Taylor & Francis.

that remains unchanged under a coalition government that resulted from new elections and whose composition is different from that of the coalition that adopted reform. There are three main scenarios possible that are contingent on the reform outcomes and the type of coalition that forms the new government.

Scenario 1: The outcome of reform is BC and a coalition of parties A and B forms the new government.

Policy AB is situated in BC's win set (Figure 3.3A). Party A clearly prefers policy AB to BC, while party B prefers AB only if it is closer to B's ideal point than BC. It is thus possible that parties A and B agree to shift policy from BC to AB. If policy AB is chosen, it is invulnerable to any other policy because it can beat any alternative situated off the AB line. However, changing policy is costly, which explains the stickiness of certain policies even if a majority does not like them. Because party B contributed to the adoption of policy BC, changing it leads to a credibility loss for party B, both with the public and party C, and affects its future ability to win votes and participate in coalitions. Party B thus faces a trade-off between its policy ideal and credibility. In addition, if reform is unpopular, parties A and B might be better off leaving it to BC rather than provoke a popular backlash, and thus they trade off their policy ideal for future votes. On the whole, a coalition government of parties A and B can shift policy from BC to AB, but this decision is subject to strategic calculations. A scenario of this type occurred in Poland in which a reform designed by an informal coalition of social democrats and liberals was subsequently altered by a Christian democratic-liberal coalition. The liberals maintained their support for the initial reform design, but their senior Christian democratic coalition partner overpowered them.

Scenario 2: The outcome of reform is BC and a coalition of parties A and D forms the new government.

Policy AD is the preferred outcome of a government formed by parties A and D (Figure 3.2B). Because neither party A nor party D participated in the government that adopted policy BC, they are not bound by previous commitments. Moreover, if policy BC is unpopular, shifting it to AD, which is closer to the status quo, may also be well regarded by the public and thus may bring future votes to parties A and D. In this scenario, the policy and vote-seeking goals of parties A and D concur to shift policy from BC to AD, and hence policy BC is not sustainable. This was the case in Romania in which a center-right coalition of Christian democrats, liberals, and the party of the Hungarian minority adopted a radical type of reform that the subsequent social democratic government partly reversed.

Scenario 3: The outcome of reform is M^4 and a coalition of parties A and D forms the new government.

Indifference curves through M reveal that policy AD is in M's win set (Figure 3.2B). Party D unquestionably wants to move the policy from M to AD. Party A, which participated in the adoption of policy M, faces a loss of credibility for choosing AD over M, as discussed above. The outcome also depends on the relative sizes of parties A and D. If party D is much larger than party A, party D will pull the policy away from M and toward AD. If, however, party A is much larger than party D, party A might care more about reaching toward the median voter, and in this case it might leave the policy at M. This scenario happened in Latvia in which a broad-spectrum six-party government adopted reform as a consensual solution, which has proven sustainable in the face of two rounds of elections, seven government reshuffles, and growing public discontent. The above analysis suggests the following:

> **Proposition 5**. When a party system contains a large party that opposes both diffuse and concentrated costs of pension reform, there is a high risk of reform reversal.
>
> **Proposition 6**. Sustainability of reform in the medium term is more likely when reform is a consensual solution among multiple parties than when it is adopted by a two-party coalition on its contract curve.

From propositions 4 and 6 it follows that, while consensus is not necessary to adopt reform, a more consensual reform has a better chance to endure.

This chapter developed a two-dimensional framework for analyzing the politics of pension reform based on the distinction between the diffuse and concentrated costs of reform that will serve as theoretical support for the following empirical chapters. Political parties' ideologies, connections with interest groups, and strategic interactions with other parties define the available options for coalition formation. The strongest supporters of reform are liberal parties because of their right orientation and lack of connections with interest groups. On the contrary, the strongest opponents are nationalist and unreformed communist parties because of their left orientation and connections with interest groups. Social democrats and Christian democrats may participate in pro-reform coalitions, but their support for reform is conditional on strategic calculations. The sustainability of reform depends on the configuration of the party system and the outcome of reform: consensual reforms are more likely to endure; however, once adopted, reforms change the status quo against which parties assess alternative policies and they tend to be "sticky," even in the absence of consensus.

CHAPTER 4

Political Parties and Pension Reform in Comparative Perspective

In this chapter, I provide a comparative cross-national analysis of pension reform processes in Central and Eastern Europe (CEE). The four cases compared are Poland, Hungary, Romania, and Slovakia, which present substantial variation on the independent variables of interest: configuration of the party system and coalition formation (Table 4.1). The timing and outcome of pension reform also varies considerably across these cases. Hungary and Poland accomplished major pension reform early, although with notable differences that highlight the importance of the outcome of reform for reform sustainability. Romania and Slovakia have attempted to catch up with Hungary and Poland after a long stalemate. Three of the cases—Romania, Hungary, and Slovakia—present different variations of reform reversal. Romania experienced a dramatic reversal of the second pillar reform, which contributed to the deferral of further reforms for several years, while Hungary and Slovakia had reductions in the size or scope of the second pillar. The four cases also show substantial variation in the extent to which previous occupational categories have been exempted from reform, with Poland and Romania providing evidence for the high resilience of inherited pension privileges.

The detailed case study information presented in this chapter also serves as a background for subsequent chapters. Following a brief overview of the data and method, the subsequent sections of the chapter discuss the cases in turn, and the last section analyzes the emerging patterns of pension reform in Central and Eastern Europe.

Data and Method

I focus on Poland, Hungary, Romania, and Slovakia, which present substantial variation on the independent variables of interest: the configuration of the party system and the characteristics of the pro-reform coalition. The party systems examined differ in the relative salience of the major divides, as well as the party positions with respect to these divides. For example, Hungary is a case where the major divide concerns nationalist and religious values, while in the other three cases the major divide is economic. Romania shows a changing pattern from a dominant economic divide prior to 2006 to a noneconomic divide during the period 2006–2008. In Hungary and Slovakia the postcommunist/anti-communist divide has a low profile, while in Poland and Romania it has been highly salient, but is declining. In Hungary and Poland the ex-communist party has modernized early; in Romania it has suffered a late modernization; while in Slovakia it split between a reformed and an unreformed communist party. The cases also vary regarding the characteristics of the coalitions that adopted pension reform. In Slovakia only center-right coalitions supported reform; in Romania and Poland both center-right and center-left coalitions participated in pension reform; while in Hungary the pro-reform coalition was cross-spectrum (socialist-liberal; see Table 4.1).

The outcome of pension reform also varies considerably across cases (the dependent variable). Hungary and Poland accomplished major pension reforms early, in the first decade of postcommunist transition, while Romania and Slovakia had reforms blocked until after the mid-1990s and completed their reforms in the second decade of postcommunist transition. Reforms in Hungary and Slovakia and the early reforms in Romania were adopted unilaterally by the governing coalition, without the inclusion of the opposition parties in the process, and the consequence was a major reversal in Romania and a scaling back of the second pillar in Hungary and Slovakia. Reforms in Poland and the late reforms in Romania were more consensual and therefore the chances for long-term sustainability of reform are good.

The four cases are very similar with respect to other characteristics that could influence pension outcome, such as similar pension systems inherited from the communist regime and the existence of pension crises, external debt, and pressures from international financial institutions (control variables). All four countries started with pension systems that provided universal coverage, generous benefits, and a loose connection between contributions and benefits in order to fulfill a redistributive function. They had low retirement ages that were common throughout the region, 53–57 for women and 60–62 for men; low contributory periods; provisions for early retirement;

and special pensions for numerous occupational categories, such as civil servants, uniformed forces, and workers in heavy industry, that provided generous benefits. These countries were all experiencing a process of population aging, which was putting increased pressure on the pension budget, with system dependency ratios[1] ranging from 53 to 57 pensioners per 100 contributors for Poland, Romania, and Slovakia to as high as 78 pensioners per 100 contributors for Hungary in the mid-1990s (Palacios and Pallarès-Miralles 2000).

In all four countries, the adverse demographic trends were compounded early in the postcommunist transition by adverse economic trends, leading to an increase in unemployment that ran in the double digits throughout most of the 1990s in Poland and Slovakia, an increase in the size of the informal sector of the economy, and decreasing contributions to the pension fund. By the mid-1990s all four cases had experienced deficits in their pension funds of 1, 2, or even 3 percent of the GDP, which were covered by transfers from the state budget (Palacios and Pallarès-Miralles 2000). In addition, they all had external debt, which was particularly high in Hungary—an inheritance from the previous communist regime that the first Hungarian postcommunist governments did not make a priority to address.

When pension reform came on the agenda, all four countries were in the process of reforming their economies with support from international financial institutions and were trying to be accepted into the North Atlantic Treaty Organization (NATO) and the European Union (EU). The effectiveness of the pressures for pension reform exerted by international financial institutions depended to a large extent on domestic factors. During the early years of postcommunist transition, the international financial institutions did not find in Romania and Slovakia governments responsive to their influence, despite the suspension on their loans. The role of the EU is more complex. The preparation for the accession to the EU created incentives for the adoption of pension reform both in Hungary and Poland, which passed pension reform early and joined the EU in the first wave of the 2004 eastern enlargement, as well as in Romania and Slovakia, which adopted pension reform late and joined the EU in the second wave of the 2007 expansion. However, it is difficult to disentangle the role played by the EU in pension reform from the role of domestic political factors. As the evidence in this book will show, the same domestic political factors that caused Romania and Slovakia to be rejected by the EU the first time around are also responsible for blocking pension reform throughout the 1990s. Only after the domestic political configuration in these two countries shifted at the end of 1990s did their governments become susceptible to international influences, making possible both pension reform and access to the EU.

Overall, demographic, economic, and international factors are relatively similar across the four cases. Hungary stands out as a case in which a deep pension crisis coupled with a high external debt, and the prospect for joining the EU in the first wave of eastern enlargement, might explain the early adoption of pension reform. However, Poland is also an early reformer and it had only one of these conditions present, the accession to the EU, which suggests a need to examine domestic factors in order to account for the similarities and differences across cases.

The four-case comparison evaluates the national processes of pension reform in an attempt to identify general patterns within the region. It examines the long-term processes of the development of political parties and the formation of the divides that structure the party system and constrain present choices, taking into account the broader cultural milieu in which this process is embedded. This analysis helps uncover the causal mechanisms that underlie the politics of pension reform and generates new research hypotheses that could be further explored with other research methods. Within each case, I look at several coalition governments over time (Table 4.1), combining a most-similar research design with longitudinal analysis within cases.

The measures of the independent and dependent variables are explained in detail in Appendix A. Appendix D provides details on the public opinion surveys used to spatially position party constituencies.

POLAND: DEEP DIVIDES AND PRAGMATIC APPROACHES

Similar to Hungary, Poland was at the forefront of pension reform in the postcommunist region. The Polish Sejm passed laws that created the second pillar in the summer of 1997, the public system reform in November 1998, and the third pillar in April 2004. By the time the two main pillars of the pension system were adopted and implemented in Poland and Hungary, pension reform had not even begun in Romania and Slovakia. Pension reform in Poland was characterized by a two-stage adoption by two different governing coalitions because of the persistence of a deep postcommunist/anti-communist divide that precluded the formation of cross-spectrum coalitions. The main political parties agreed, however, with the basic reform design, and there were no major attempts at reversal.

As in the other three cases examined in this book, Poland followed the World Bank's three pillar model of pension reform (World Bank 1994). The second and third pillar laws, which established private pension funds, were adopted in August 1997 as the Act of 28 August 1997 on organization and operation of pension funds[2] and the Act of 22 August 1997 on employee pension programs,[3] respectively by the coalition of the SLD (Democratic Left Alliance) and the PSL (Polish People's Party). Later, a new law called the Act of 20 April 2004 on individual pension accounts,[4] adopted by the center-left coalition of the SLD, the UP (Labor Union), and the PSL established voluntary private pension funds in addition to the occupational schemes of the third pillar. The first pillar (public system) reform was voted by the Sejm on 26 November 1998 and was adopted as the Act of 17 December 1998 on pensions from the Social Insurance Fund.[5] This law was adopted by a center-right coalition of the AWS (Solidarity Electoral Action) and the UW (Freedom Union).

In the first years following the collapse of communism, Poland faced a pension crisis manifested by a rapid increase in the system dependency ratio from 40 pensioners for every 100 workers in 1989 to around 55 pensioners for every 100 workers in the mid-1990s and almost 70 pensioners for every 100 workers toward the end of the decade (Palacios and Pallarès-Mirales 2000). The increase was mainly due to economic and political factors, and to a lesser extent to demographic trends. Compared to the other Central and Eastern European countries, Poland had a relatively favorable demographic situation (Orenstein 2000), with an old-age dependency ratio[6] of less than 30 people over 60 years of age to 100 people under 60 years of age in the mid-1990s, while many countries reached values higher than 35 and some close to 40, e.g., Bulgaria (Palacios and Pallarès-Mirales 2000). The large difference between the two ratios is due to the numerous pensioners under age 60, many of who retired during the first years of the transition.

In an attempt to counter the adverse effects of the shock therapy, which was launched by the first postcommunist government of Tadeusz Mazowiecki to transition rapidly from a state-owned to a free-market economy, the early postcommunist governments extended the provisions for early retirement and relaxed the requirements for granting disability pensions. For instance, in the first half of 1990s the number of disability pensioners more than doubled to

37 percent, one of the largest in the world (World Bank 1997). As a result of these trends, the number of contributors to the pension system significantly declined while the number of beneficiaries dramatically increased, leading to a financial imbalance of the public pension fund. At the same time, the replacement ratio, representing the value of the average pension relative to the average wage, increased from 53 percent in 1989 to 73 percent in 1993, further contributing to the deterioration of the balance between revenues and expenditures in the public pension fund. According to the World Bank (1997), the combined pension expenditures more than doubled during the early transition, from 7 percent of GDP in 1988 to 15.5 percent in 1995. The excess that the pension fund had at the beginning of the transition was rapidly exhausted. Poland's pension fund experienced deficits ranging from 0.4 percent to 1.6 percent of GDP before 1993, which were covered by subsidies from the state budget and led to a high budget deficit (Muller 2002, Orenstein 2000).

Similar to Hungary, Romania, and Slovakia, Poland used IMF loans during the first years of the transition, which exposed it to international pressures for a neo-liberal type of pension reform. Like Hungary, Poland was considered for the first wave of NATO and European Union eastern enlargement, which created incentives for pursuing a reform agenda. In retrospect and compared to the reform process in the other three countries, where the entire reform package or parts of it have been adopted unilaterally without the participation of the opposition, pension reform in Poland looks relatively uncontroversial.

The Party System

Compared to Hungary, Poland was at a disadvantage in terms of its chances for accomplishing reform because of the persistence of a deep postcommunist/anti-communist cleavage between the SLD (Democratic Left Alliance, Sojusz Lewicy Demokraticznej) and the PSL (Polish People's Party, Polskie Stronnictwo Ludowe) on the one hand and the AWS (Solidarity Electoral Action, Akcja Wyborcza Solidarność) and the UW (Freedom Union, Unia Wolności) on the other. This division precluded the formation of coalitions across the cleavage, despite the existence of ideological affinities and convergent interests between the parties. Because of this cleavage, a socialist-liberal coalition similar to that of Hungary was not possible in Poland. The SLD originated in the former communist party the PZPR (Polish United Workers' Party, Polska Zjednoczona Partia Robotnicza) and was the main left alliance, later transformed into a party, until 2004 after which it declined. The communist PZPR lacked legitimacy in the eyes of nearly all Poles because it was perceived as being imposed by the Soviet Union (Ishiyama 1995). In addition, the party never really penetrated the society and was unable to build a reliable party organization (Grzymała-Busse 2002). Repeated popular protests in 1956, 1968, 1970, and 1976 and the formation of the anti-communist Solidarity movement, based on the trade unions, led to dramatic clashes between the communist party and the society, culminating in the imposition of Martial Law in 1981. After several years of relative quiet, during which Solidarity continued its activity underground and many of its activists were imprisoned, new waves of popular protests emerged in 1988.

The PZPR's lack of legitimacy induced the party leadership to accept some measure of intraparty pluralism and moderate economic reform, which was meant to legitimize the party rule in the face of acute economic problems (Ishiyama 1995; Markowski 2002). The PZPR contained internal factions, which surfaced during the anti-communist revolts and employed, for the most part, a collective leadership in which the functions of party leader, prime minister, and president were separated (Markowski 2002). The strikes of 1988 and the party's engagement in the roundtable negotiations with Solidarity created an impetus for the reformist factions within the PZPR to propose a democratization of the party. The reformists got their chance after the dramatic defeat of the party in the semi-free elections on 1989 in which the communists lost every contested seat. Their mobilization culminated in the election of the young party activist and former youth minister Aleksander Kwaśniewski as leader of the party, paving the way for the ascension of reformists to the top of the party hierarchy. Although the party did not formally repudiate its communist past, it changed its name to SdRP (Social Democracy of the Republic of Poland, Socjaldemokracja Rzeczpospolitej Polskiej) and abandoned all the PZPR symbols. Some of the factions within the party left to form separate parties, among them the hardliners, who established the ZKPP (Union of Polish Communists "Proletariat", Związek Komunistów Polskich "Proletariat"). The SdRP maintained its close ties with the successor communist trade unions, the OPZZ (All-Polish Alliance of Trade Unions, Ogólnopolskie Porozumienie Związków Zawodowych), with which it formed the SLD. Initially, the SLD was a loose alliance of several left parties, civic organizations, and trade unions led by the SdRP. Over time it became a political party with the same name under the leadership of Leszek Miller.

A close communist-era ally of the Polish United Workers' Party was the Polish People's Party, which was more successful than the PZPR in penetrating the society in rural areas in which it developed extensive local networks (Grzymała-Busse 2002). These networks were essential for the party's survival in the postcommunist period and contributed to its transformation into a clientelistic party.

On the other side of the postcommunist/anti-communist cleavage were the political parties originating in the Solidarity movement, the AWS (Solidarity Electoral Action) and the UW (Freedom Union). The roots of the AWS can be traced back to the Trade Union Solidarity formed in Gdansk in 1980 under the leadership of Lech Wałęsa. During the 1980s Solidarity had an estimated membership of 10 million workers, about half the size of the workforce, and was responsible for the numerous revolts against the communist government (Bugajski 2002). With the imposition of Martial Law by General Wojciech Jaruzelski in 1981, Solidarity was banned and its leaders, as well as thousands of its sympathizers, were imprisoned. Solidarity continued to function underground for the rest of the decade until the roundtable negotiations of 1989 in which the communist government re-established it as a legal trade union. It also became the leading opposition force in the semi-free elections of 1989, in which Solidarity candidates won all contested seats but one in the Sejm and Senate (Wiatr 1997). A major split within Solidarity occurred with the call for early presidential elections meant to replace General Jaruzelski, in which Solidarity presented two candidates: Lech Wałęsa and Tadeusz Mazowiecki, who was Wałęsa's advisor and the first postcommunist prime minister. Wałęsa was mostly supported by trade unionists while the intellectuals in Solidarity, including such prominent figures as Bronisław Geremek, Jacek Kuroń, and Adam Michnik, supported Mazowiecki. Wałęsa won the presidency, but the Solidarity groups sustaining him performed poorly in the subsequent 1991 and 1993 parliamentary elections, which led them to unite in the AWS (Kaminski, Grzegorz, and Swistak 1998). In the 1997 elections, the AWS gained the largest share of the seats and formed the government with the UW. The Solidarity splinters supporting Mazowiecki performed well in the 1991 elections and participated in the government of Hanna Suchocka, later uniting in the UW, which became the third largest party after the 1997 elections (Wiatr 1997).

This history of conflict and repression between the communists and Solidarity left deep marks on the configuration of the party system that emerged and precluded the formation of coalitions that crosscut the postcommunist/anti-communist cleavage, despite obvious policy affinities between parties across the cleavage, which was consequential for the fate of pension reform in Poland. When the SLD won the 1993 elections, its first choice for coalition formation was the UW. The two parties already had a history of cooperation at the local level, but the UW refused to make an alliance at the national level. The UW feared that a coalition with the SLD would cause the party to lose the only thing that clearly distinguished it, i.e., its Solidarity roots, which might eliminate it from the political scene (Grzymała-Busse 2002). The SLD had no other choice but to turn to its former ally, the PSL.

Role of Political Parties and Coalitions in Pension Reform

The coalition of the SLD and the PSL experienced numerous internal tensions because of diverging views on a number of issues, such as agricultural policy, local administration reform, privatization, and the role of the church (Grzymała-Busse 2002). The PSL wanted to make sure that its rural constituents would be protected from privatization and international competition and attempted to block the reforms proposed by the SLD. When pension reform came to the agenda, the Ministry of Finance, the Ministry of Labor, and Solidarity unions advanced competing proposals for reform, which led to a deadlock that lasted for more than a year. To resume the reform process, Prime Minister Włodzimierz Cimoszewicz of the SLD centralized the process of designing a comprehensive reform by creating the Office of the Plenipotentiary for Social Security Reform, which was directly accountable to the prime minister (Müller 1999; Orenstein 2000). A World Bank official was appointed head of the office, thus opening the door to direct World Bank involvement and paving the way toward a radical pension reform.

With the input of experts from the opposition UW, by February 1997 the Office of Plenipotentiary prepared the reform proposal called *Security through Diversity*, which envisaged a fundamental restructuring of the public system (first pillar) and the creation of mandatory and voluntary pension funds (second and third pillars) (Aleksandrowicz 2007; Chłoń at al. 1999; Chłoń-Dominczak 2004; Góra 2001; Guardiancich 2004; Müller 1999; Orenstein 2000). In order to induce the PSL to support the reform proposal, the heavily subsidized farmers' pension system, Kasa Rolniczego Ubezpieczenia Społecznego (KRUS), was excluded from the reform. Before the elections scheduled for September 1997, the center-left coalition of the SLD and the PSL passed in August 1997 the laws establishing the second and third pillars, which represented the least controversial part of pension reform. The opposition parties also voted overwhelmingly in favor of the two bills, which passed with support of over 90 percent of the deputies.[7]

The task of passing the unpopular reform of the public pension system fell to the center-right coalition of the AWS and the UW, which came to power during the following term (1997–2001). The disagreements between the AWS and the UW on the one hand and the government and the trade unions on the other led to a series of compromises that required numerous alterations to the initial reform proposal. While the UW was committed to the *Security through Diversity* project, to which it had directly contributed during the previous term, the AWS supported the initial Solidarity trade unions' proposal, which was less radical (Guardiancich 2004: 50; Orenstein 2000: 52). Meanwhile, both Solidarity and postcommunist OPZZ (All-Poland Alliance of Trade Unions, Ogólnopolskie Porozumienie Związków Zawodowych) trade unions mobilized against some of the more controversial provisions, such as the elimination of previous pension privileges; the incorporation of occupational schemes for miners, railroad employees, and uniformed forces into the general public system; and increasing the retirement age (Aleksandrowicz 2007; Orenstein 2000; Wenzel 1998). In addition, a change of leadership in the SLD brought to the forefront the former Labor Minister Leszek Miller, a strong opponent of pension privatization, which shifted the SLD's position against the government proposal.

The rewriting of the public system rules by the AWS was followed by splits within both the AWS and the opposition SLD between the wings committed to radical reform and the more conservative groups associated with Solidarity and post-communist OPZZ unions, respectively. Despite a series of concessions by the government, the differences were not reconciled. They surfaced powerfully during the parliamentary debates of the public system reform bill, during which voting coalitions on amendments often crosscut party and coalition lines.[8] After prolonged negotiations, the governing coalition of the AWS and the UW passed the two laws of the public system reform with the opposition of the SLD and the PSL. The most radical element of the reform was the introduction of a notional defined contribution (NDC) system, setting up a new formula for the calculation of benefits that strictly ties contributions and benefits and therefore eliminates redistribution. In contrast, reform failed to raise the retirement age, which remained at 60 for women and 65 for men, and to eliminate previous occupational privileges.

Compared to Hungary, pension reform in Poland has been more limited, excluding the farmer's pension system and allowing other occupational groups to draw special privileges under the new system, mainly due to the fact that the most committed pro-reform parties, the SLD and the UW, could not participate in government together. At the same time, pension reform has been more consensual because of the participation of all four major parties at different stages in the reform process and also because of the compromises reached between them and with the trade unions, which minimizes the chances of reform being overthrown by subsequent governments.[9]

Figure 4.1 illustrates the relative positions of party constituencies using public opinion data from the *Central and Eastern*

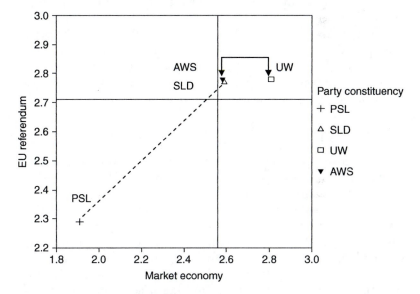

Figure 4.1 Poland, 1997. Party constituencies and attitudes toward a free market economy and European integration

AWS=Solidarity Electoral Action (43.69%), SLD=Democratic Left Alliance (35.65%), UW = Freedom Union (13.1%), PSL = Polish People's Party (5.86%).

The governing coalition of AWS and UW passed the public pension system reform (1997–2001).

--- The coalition of SLD and PSL passed the bill establishing private pension funds (1993–1997).

Numbers in parentheses represent the percentage of seats won by each party in 1997 elections.

Scale on each axis range from 1 = strongest opposition to 3 = strongest support.

Source of public opinion data is the *Central and Eastern Eurobarometer 8: Public Opinion and the European Union, October–November 1997* and source of election data is *Project on Political Transformation and the Electoral Process in Postcommunist Europe,* http://www.essex.ac.uk/elections/

Eurobarometer 8: Public Opinion and the European Union, October–November 1997, conducted in October–November 1997 during the term when the center-right coalition of the AWS and the UW passed the public pension system reform (details about the particular questions asked are provided in Appendix D and representations of the Polish party system based on roll call analysis and expert survey are offered in chapter 5). The reference lines are drawn at the mean of responses on each axis. Figure 4.1 shows that the constituencies of the two major parties, AWS and SLD, overlap and that they are both relatively close to the UW constituency, forming a liberal pole that opposes the left nationalist pole of the Polish People's Party. In light of the theoretical framework developed above, the spatial configuration depicted in Figure 4.1 suggests that all three parties, AWS, SLD, and UW, are likely reformers while the PSL is an enemy of reform. The spatial closeness of the AWS, SLD, and UW explains the participation of each of the three parties at different stages of the reform process and the collaboration between the SLD and the UW in the preparation of the reform proposal despite the deep postcommunist/anti-communist divide that separates them.

Main Features of the Polish Pension Reform

The legislative framework for the first pillar is the Act of 17 December 1998 on pensions from the Social Insurance Fund,[10] which went into effect on 1 January 1999. The public system is based on a notional defined contribution (NDC), meaning that while in practice it is a PAYG-type system similar to that of Hungary, Romania, and Slovakia, which is financed by the contributions of the current generations of workers, the benefits are calculated using a formula that considers an individual's lifetime contributions indexed according to wage growth as if they were deposited into an individual account. The first pillar is financed by contributions from both the employer and the employee and is administered by the Social Insurance Institution (*Zakład Ubezpieczeń Społecznych*, ZUS). Those born after 31 December 1969 were required to join, while participation was voluntary for those born between 31 December 1948 and 1 January 1969 (Ministry of Labour and Social Policy n.d.). The current total pension contribution is 19.52 percent of taxable income, of which the employer pays half (9.76 percent), all of which is directed into the first pillar. The employee pays the other half, which may go entirely into the public system or 7.3 percent of it is transferred to a mandatory pension fund (second pillar) for those who join the second pillar. The retirement age is 60 for women and 65 for men and the contributory periods are 20 and 25 years, respectively. The legislation has provisions for early retirement of five years for both men and women and for individuals who had worked at least 10 or 15 years in special conditions or doing work of a special nature, if they were born before 1949, and also for many born between 1949 and 1969 (Ministry of Labour and Social Policy n.d.).

The second pillar law was established by the Act of 28 August 1997 on organization and operation of pension funds.[11] Participation in the second pillar is mandatory for those under the age of 30 as of 1 January 1999 and for new entrants in the labor market, and it is voluntary for those between the ages of 30 and 50. Those aged 50 or over will remain insured exclusively by the public system and will not be affected by the reform. Contributions are paid exclusively by the employee and represent 7.3 percent of taxable income.

Individuals qualify for benefits paid from the second pillar when they reach the retirement age. Benefits paid from the second pillar are subject to certain protections and guarantees by the government. There is a minimum benefit guarantee that applies in case an individual's total pension is lower than the minimum pension. The difference is covered through the state budget. There is also a minimum return guarantee for each pension fund, which should be at least half of the rate of return for all the funds in a given year. If the return is lower, the pension fund is required to cover the difference from its own reserve fund. In case of bankruptcy of a fund, the state will cover the difference through the state budget. In the future it is expected that approximately 60 percent of the pensions will be paid from the first pillar and 40 percent from the second pillar.

In 2010, the number of participants in the second pillar reached over 14.5 million. In mid 2010 there were 14 registered open pension fund companies who managed approximately US$57.1 billion (Polish Financial Supervision Authority 2010). Similar to Hungary, Romania, and Slovakia, the market is concentrated and dominated by international companies. The top four large companies together have a market share of over 70 percent: the British Aviva and the Dutch Internationale Nederlanden Groep or ING dispute the top positions, each with a market share around 24 percent, followed by the Polish Powszechny Zakład Ubezpieczeń or PZU (market share 14 percent), and the American International Group or AIG, renamed since September 2009 Amplico (market share 8 percent) (Polish Financial Supervision Authority 2010).

The third pillar was adopted initially as the Act of 22 August 1997 on employee pension programs,[12] but it did not attract a lot of participants because of the unfriendly regulatory framework. Less than 1 percent of the active population was covered in 2006 (International Organisation of Pension Supervisors 2008b). In order for an employee to participate, the employers must offer a plan to more than 50 percent of the employees in the company. When the employee left the company, it was difficult to transfer the capital if the new employer did not offer an occupational plan, which made the plan very unpopular. The employee could not receive benefits before reaching retirement age. The pension funds did not provide a minimum return guarantee and there were no caps on fees, which could vary widely (International Organisation of Pension Supervisors 2008b). For these reasons, this act has been replaced by the new Act of 20 April 2004 on occupational pension schemes.[13] Under the new law, an employee may leave the plan and transfer his or her accumulated capital into another occupational plan or into an individual retirement account; the employee may also transfer the capital from an individual account into an occupational retirement scheme. In 2010 the number of members remained very small, around 58,000 and the total value of the assets accumulated in the occupational pension funds was approximately US$504.5 million (Polish Financial Supervision Authority 2010). Pension companies who administer occupational pension plans are required to be based in Poland (International Organisation of Pension Supervisors 2008b). In 2010 there were five registered pension companies administering occupational pension plans (Polish Financial Supervision Authority 2010).

In addition to the occupational pension schemes, the Act of 20 April 2004 on individual retirement accounts[14] allows Polish people to set up individual pension accounts, known by their acronym IKE (indywidualne konta emerytalne), starting in September 2004. IKE savings can be withdrawn at age 60 tax-free. If they are withdrawn before age 60, they are subject to taxation and penalties (International Social Security Association n.d.b). There is a cap on the amount that is tax exempt, which is limited to 150 percent of the average wage. Benefits are tax exempt. Individuals may switch from one IKE to another, but they have to pay a fee.

The Aftermath of the Reform

The deep disagreements regarding pension privileges in Poland persisted well into the 2000s. Particularly problematic has been the issue of early retirement. The new system introduced new types of pre-retirement benefits and, as a result, the number of people below retirement age receiving some form of long-term benefits has in fact increased (Chłoń-Dominczak 2007). Not only did every post-transition government avoid dealing decisively with the issue, but also the incomplete reform in this area opened the gate for expanding the already existing pension privileges. Faced with pressures from the miners who went on strike in 2005, the center-left governing coalition dominated by the SLD amended the law on public pensions. The new Act of 27 July 2005 amending the law on pension from ZUS and the law on Teacher's Charter,[15] prolonged early retirement for miners and extended the benefits to other categories of workers in mining (Aleksandrowicz 2007). The act passed with large support from both the left and the right; the only party who opposed it was the center right Civic Platform (Platforma Obywatelska).[16]

The issue continues to be divisive, as suggested by the high absenteeism at this vote (over 26 percent) and by the long-standing debate over the "bridging pensions." Since the 1999 reforms, the bridging pensions have been proposed as a means to replace early retirement for certain categories of workers, thus in fact prolonging early retirement privileges well into the future (Aleksandrowicz 2007: 22; Chłoń-Dominczak 2004: 265). The center-right governing coalition of Civic Platform and Polish People's Party eventually passed in November 2008 the Act of 19 December 2008 on bridging pensions,[17] drastically cutting to one-fourth the number of beneficiaries and introducing provisions for gradually lifting the bridging pensions (Polska Agencja Prasowa 2008). The measure was strongly opposed by the left parties, whose deputies all voted against the bill. Most likely the issue will resurface again in the future. Approximately 1 million people benefited from early retirement under the previous legislation, leading to an average retirement age of 57 years for both sexes and an employment rate below 55 percent (International Social Security Association n.d.b). Beginning in January 2009, the legal retirement age of 65 for men and 60 for women applied to most categories of workers, with the exception of those working in special or hazardous conditions, such as underground or underwater, who can still retire early.

The politics of pension reform in Poland reveal the most consensual pattern of all four cases examined in this book. The major political parties have agreed with the basic design of pension reform, which has remained largely unchanged for more than a decade. The case of Poland also shows that those areas that were sheltered from reform because of a lack of agreement between the major political actors continue to be divisive. Specifically, occupational privileges have been a thorny issue for every single government, and these privileges have been gradually scaled back while providing compensation along the way to the groups adversely affected. How Poland has chosen to deal with occupational privileges illustrates the difficulty of cutting back acquired entitlements, which are likely to cast a long shadow into the future.

HUNGARY: PARTIAL CONSENSUS AND THE RISK OF REVERSAL

Hungary, like Poland, was an early reformer in the postcommunist region. Hungary had introduced voluntary private pension funds (third pillar) since 1993, while these where adopted much later in a majority of the other countries in the region. Hungary also adopted relatively effortlessly the first and second pillar reforms in 1997, in sharp contrast with the other three cases in which reform suffered long delays or controversies among the main political parties, leading to the adoption occurring in several stages by successive governing coalitions. Despite ongoing disagreements between the major parties and several alterations of the reforms, the general World Bank three-pillar model initially adopted has remained in place.

The reforms of the first pillar (public system) and second pillar, which established mandatory private pension funds, were adopted in July 1997 by the socialist-liberal coalition of MSzP (Hungarian Socialist Party, Magyar Szocialista Párt) and SzDSz (Alliance of Free Democrats, Szabad Demokraták Szövetsége). They were both amended by the next center-right coalition of the Fidesz (Federation of Young Democrats, Fiatal Demokraták Szövetsége), the FKgP (Independent Smallholders Party, Független Kisgazdapárt), and the MDF (Hungarian Democratic Forum, Magyar Demokrata Fórum), and again by the subsequent socialist government.

Similar to Poland, Romania, and Slovakia, by the mid-1990s Hungary was experiencing a pension crisis due to adverse demographic trends coupled with high unemployment. Many of those hit by unemployment chose early retirement or disability pensions, which led to an increase in the number of pensioners. Augusztinovics and Köllő estimate the number of unemployed who chose to retire early to be in the hundreds of thousands, which led to the abnormal situation of having more disability than old-age pensioners among the new retirees (2009: 93–94). The system dependency ratio, representing the number of pensioners divided by the number of contributors to the pension system, increased from 50 pensioners for every 100 workers in 1989 to over 70 pensioners for every 100 workers in the mid-1990s as a direct consequence of a rapid increase in the number of pensioners during the early transition (Palacios and Pallarès-Mirales 2000). The national pension fund registered deficits throughout the first half of the 1990s of as much as 2 percent of the GDP, which were financed through transfers from the state budget (Orenstein 2000).

Long-term projections showed a demographic structure that made the existing pension system unsustainable in the long term because of adverse demographic trends similar to those in Poland, Romania, and Slovakia (The World Bank). In early 1990s, the demographic structure of Hungary showed more adverse trends compared to its neighboring countries, with the population at age 60 and over representing about 26 percent of the total population and about 35 percent of the working age population (Palacios and Pallarès-Mirales 2000). Long-term projections also showed these numbers to be on the rise due to a decline in the fertility rate and population aging. The expectation was that the percentage of the population aged 60 and over would rise to 38 percent of the total population and would surpass 60 percent of the working age population by 2040 (Palacios and Pallarès-Mirales 2000). The disproportion of the aged in the total population would have put enormous strain on the pension system in the absence of major reforms. The system dependency ratio was already at a very high of 78 pensioners for every 100 contributors in the mid-1990s, and further increases were virtually untenable (Palacios and Pallarès-Mirales 2000). This inevitably led to an increase in pension expenditures as a percentage of the GDP, pension fund deficits, and a decline in the replacement rate (average pension/average wage) from 40.4 in 1994 to 36.5 in 1996 (International Labour Organization [ILO] 1997; Palacios and Pallarès-Mirales 2000).

Similar to a majority of Central and Eastern European countries, Hungary had external debt and used IMF and World Bank loans for economic restructuring. Hungary's debt was larger compared to the other three cases analyzed in this book, averaging 10 percent of its gross national product (GNP) for the period 1990–1999, and the average IMF credit was 1.7 percent of the GNP for the same time period, which created an opportunity for these institutions to exert pressures for the restructuring of the pension system. When pension reform came on the political agenda, Hungary was also preparing to join NATO and the European Union, which might have strengthened the commitment of the socialist-liberal government to pursue the reforms.

The Party System

Unlike most of the other former communist countries, the postcommunist/anti-communist divide has not been salient in postcommunist Hungary, mainly due to the comparative mildness of the former communist regime in this country after Janos Kadar's pro-market reforms in the 1960s, which for this reason was dubbed "goulash communism." The literature emphasizes Hungary's exceptionalism as the most liberal among the former communist countries (Agh 1995). The communist party, the MSzMP (Hungarian Socialist Workers' Party, Magyar Szocialista Munkáspárt) had pursued economic reforms and encouraged intraparty political pluralism and the ascension of a young technocratic intelligentsia within the party hierarchy (Ishiyama 1995; Kitschelt et al. 1999). This has paved the way for the victory of the reformers, led by Miklós Németh, Imre Pozsgay, and Reszô Nyers, over the hardliners (Grzymała-Busse 2002). In 1989 the MSzMP renamed itself MSzP (Hungarian Socialist Party) and was the first ex-communist party to modernize, becoming a social-democratic party similar to modern European left parties, which has since accepted the basics of a free-market economy and the country's membership in international organizations. The hardliners in the MSzMP, led by Károly Grósz, left the party and formed the Hungarian Socialist Workers' Party (Munkáspárt). The MSzP leadership welcomed the formation of the Munkáspárt because it allowed the party to make a clean break with its past and at the same time created a radical left from which the MSzP could differentiate itself as a social democratic alternative (Grzymała-Busse 2002).

Due to the absence of a history of repression and its moderate stance, the Socialist Party has been an acceptable coalition partner to other parties during the early postcommunist transition. When it entered government between 1994 and 1998, the MSzP formed a coalition with the liberal SzDSz (Alliance of Free Democrats) and pursued a neo-liberal agenda with radical economic reforms meant to revitalize the economy. The more conservative factions within the party opposed the austerity program known as the "Bokros package" after the former Minister of Finance Lajos Bokros, but the liberal factions, which held the leadership positions, prevailed in this conflict (Bugajski 2002).

The Fidesz (Federation of Young Democrats), which developed into the main center-right party, followed an almost reverse trajectory. Originating in the youth anti-communist movement, the Fidesz was initially a center-right liberal party that took an active role in the roundtable negotiations of 1989 and the subsequent collapse of communism in Hungary. The Fidesz wanted to be a party of the youth and set an initial age limit of 35 for its membership, which it later repealed as its leadership approached the limit (Bugajski 2002). In 1992, the Fidesz entered the Liberal International, and its young leader, Viktor Orbán, became vice president of the organization (Bugajski 2002). In the 1994 elections, the Fidesz formed a liberal electoral bloc with the Alliance of Free Democrats (SzDSz) and two other parties that did not enter the parliament with the goal to propose a liberal alternative to the Hungarian Socialist Party. The Fidesz barely surpassed the 5 percent threshold and the alliance broke up as a consequence of the party's poor electoral performance. The SzDSz's entrance into a coalition with the Socialists marked the end of the Fidesz's aspirations toward liberalism and the beginning of divergent pathways between the Fidesz and the SzDSz. While the latter remained committed to liberalism, the Fidesz took a sharp turn toward right nationalism, and the dividing line between the Fidesz and the Socialists changed from right versus left to nationalist-conservative versus cosmopolitan-libertarian. The Socialists in coalition with the smaller liberals became the promoters of economic reforms and European integration, an alliance they maintained for 14 years during several terms in office, while the Fidesz in coalition with smaller nationalist parties became the defenders of nationalism and traditional values. The Fidesz quit the Liberal International and joined the European People's Party in 2000. The Party's turn toward conservatism caused a split within its ranks, and several prominent leaders left to join the Alliance of Free Democrats, such as Gábor Fodor, who later became president of the SzDSz.

Role of Political Parties and Coalitions in Pension Reform

Pension reform was on the agenda of the socialist-liberal government of Gyula Horn (Table 4.1), which enjoyed the legislative support of the MSzP (Hungarian Socialist Party) and the SzDSz (Alliance of Free Democrats). The numerous conflicts within the governing coalition over the reform package and the opposition of the former communist unions MSzOSz (National Confederation of Hungarian Trade Unions, Magyar Szakszervezetek Országos Szövetsége), which were affiliated with the Hungarian Socialists, resulted in a compromise that included a reduction in the size of the second private pillar from 10 percent of the payroll to an initial 6 percent that would gradually increase to 8 percent, a deferral of the new indexation rules until 2001 and of the new benefit formula until 2013 (Müller 1999).

Reform was passed on 15 July 1997, with the exclusive support of the governing coalition of the MSzP and the SzDSz and the opposition of the Fidesz, the Hungarian Democratic Forum (MDF), the Christian Democratic People's Party (KdNP, Kereszténydemokrata Néppárt), and the Independent Smallholders Party (FKgP). The package contained a reform of the public system comprising a gradual increase in the retirement age from 55 for women and 60 for men to 62 for both by 2008, a new formula for the calculation of benefits that would closely tie the contributions and benefits (from 2013), and a mixed indexation of benefits based on the Swiss model that combines an increase based on prices with an increase based on wages[18] (Müller 1999). In addition to the rationalization of the public system, the package also included the creation of a second mandatory fully funded pillar that would absorb 6 percent of the payroll, representing 25 percent of the total pension contribution that would later increase to 8 percent of the payroll.

Despite a large majority enjoyed by the government (72 percent of the seats in the parliament) and its sustained efforts to create a broad consensus over the reform package, especially by including the trade unions in the deliberation process, the main right opposition party, the Fidesz, did not give its consent. When the Fidesz came to power following the May 1998 general elections, in coalition with the FKgP and the MDF, it attacked the second pillar in an attempt to reduce its size and scope, although the general framework of the three pillar system remained in place. The new government cancelled the projected increase in the size of the second pillar from 6 percent to 8 percent of the payroll; made membership of the new entrants voluntary; opened up the second pillar, allowing those already in the private pillar to return to the public system over a period of one year; and eliminated the independent pension administration, bringing it under direct government control (Impavido and Rocha 2006; Orenstein 2000).

These reform alterations are in line with the Fidesz's increasing nationalist-conservative and anti-liberal orientation and help to explain the major puzzle of the Hungarian pension reform, which is why a neo-liberal reform was adopted under a socialist-dominated government only to be subsequently scaled down by a right coalition. The MSzP, although a center-left party, favors a free-market economy and is one of the most cosmopolitan Hungarian parties. In contrast, the Fidesz, the major right party, is nationalist and adopts a more reserved attitude toward a free-market economy than the MSzP and SzDSz, making observers of the Hungarian political system wonder which one of the two parties is the right and which one is the left.[19] The strength of the socialist-liberal coalition explains how it was possible for Hungary to accomplish both first and second pillar reforms in one shot, while most other countries spaced them in order to make them more palatable to the public. The downside of the Hungarian reform is that the government did not secure the consent of the opposition, which subsequently exposed the reform to the risk of reversal.

A spatial representation of parties' positions on the two main axes of the Hungarian political space, left versus right and nationalist-conservative versus cosmopolitan-libertarian, helps ease the understanding of the peculiarities of the Hungarian pension reform. Chapter 5 is specifically concerned with obtaining spatial representations of political parties based on roll call analyses of voting in legislatures and surveys of country experts, while this chapter presents parties' constituencies in a two-dimensional space, which provides some idea of parties' relative positions (Figure 4.2). The data come from the *Central and Eastern Eurobarometer 6: Economic and Political*

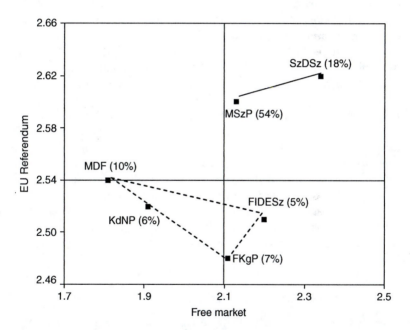

Figure 4.2 Hungary, 1995. Party constituencies and attitudes toward a free market economy and the referendum on EU accession

MSzP = Hungarian Socialist Party (54.15%); SzDSz=Alliance of Free Democrats (17.88%); MDF = Hungarian Democratic Forum (9.84%); FKgP=Independent Smallholders Party (6.74%); KdNP = Christian Democratic People's Party (5.7%); Fidesz=Alliance of Young Democrats (5.18%).

——— The pro-reform coalition of MSzP and SzDSz passed first and second pillar reforms (1994–1998).

----- The anti-reform coalition of Fidesz, FKgP, and MDF partially reversed reform (1998–2002).

Numbers in parentheses represent the percentage of seats won by each party in 1994 elections. Scale on each axis range from 1 = strongest opposition to 3 = strongest support.

Source of public opinion data is the *Central and Eastern Eurobarometer 6: Economic and Political Trends, October–November 1995 and source of election data is Project on Political Transformation and the Electoral Process in Postcommunist Europe*, http://www.essex.ac.uk/elections/

Trends, October–November 1995, conducted in October–November 1995 during the term when the socialist-liberal coalition passed the pension reform package (details about the particular questions asked are provided in Appendix D).

The reference lines are drawn at the mean of responses on each axis. Figure 4.2 shows that the constituencies of the two governing parties, the MSzP and the SzDSz, are relatively close to one another and constitute a liberal pole. In contrast, constituencies of the opposition parties, the Fidesz, the FKgP, the MDF, and the KdNP form a nationalist-conservative pole. The socialist-liberal coalition, which adopted pension reform in Hungary, is both pro-market and cosmopolitan, thus bringing support to the theoretical argument of this study. The theory also suggests that, in addition to the socialist-liberal coalition, a center-right coalition of the Fidesz and the SzDSz could also have supported pension reform, though the latter is a less likely pro-reform coalition because of the Fidesz's nationalist stance.

To use a counterfactual, one can imagine a scenario in which the Fidesz won more seats and the MSzP fewer seats in the 1994 elections. Under such circumstances, the liberal electoral alliance of the Fidesz and the SzDSz would have been likely to endure and form the government and, consequently, adopt pension reform with or without the support from the MSzP. The Fidesz was not a natural enemy of reform, but was forced into this position as a result of its rejection by the SzDSz following its poor 1994 electoral performance. If their alliance had lasted, the Fidesz and the SzDSz might have followed similar trajectories, leading to the creation of a center-right alternative to the MSzP, and the configuration of the Hungarian party system might have been less atypical.

Main Features of the Hungarian Pension Reform

The legislative framework for the public pension system (first pillar) are Act LXXX/1997 on the scope of eligible individuals to social security benefits and the financing of these benefits and Act LXXXI/1997 on social security benefits.[20] The public system is a PAYG mandatory scheme for everybody, which has tightened the link between contributions and benefits relative to the old pension system. Contributions are paid by both the employer (18 percent of the gross wage) and the employee (1 percent of the gross wage, which was raised in 2003 to 1.5 percent). Retirement age was gradually increased from 60 years for men and 55 for women to 62 for both sexes until 2009. The contributory periods required to receive a pension increased to 20 years

(International Organisation of Pension Supervisors 2008a; Müller 1999). The redistributive elements still in effect in 2010, such as the possibility to retire with only 15 years of contribution, the minimum pension guarantee, and the degressive method of calculating pensionable earnings, will be phased out by 2013 (Augusztinovics and Köllő 2009). Since 2001, pension indexation has changed from wage indexation to Swiss indexation, which is based half on wages and half on prices and keeps pensions down during times of economic growth when wages grow faster than prices. Pension benefits are not taxed, but under the current legislation they may become taxed in 2013.

The second pillar was established through Act LXXXII/1997 on the private pension and the private mutual pension funds,[21] adopted in July 1997, and went into effect on 1 January 1998. The size of the second pillar was initially 6 percent of the total pension contribution, paid entirely by the employee, and increased to 7 percent in 2002 and to 8 percent in 2004. All new entrants to the labor market after 30 June 1998 are required to join. Those already in the labor market may join the second pillar if they are younger than 47 (International Social Security Association n.d.a.). The retirement age and contributory period to receive a full pension are the same as for the public system. The law provided a minimum return guarantee for those who contributed at least 15 years to the second pillar, to be provided from the public system. Subsequent legislation removed this minimum guarantee, maintaining it only for cases of fraud in the pension fund. The fees for administering the pension funds have increased over time; in 2004 they ranged from 7.6 to 10 percent of contributions, depending on the type of institution managing the funds (Impavido and Rocha 2006: 19). The benefits and investment income from the second pillar are currently tax exempt, but the benefits will be taxed beginning in 2013 (International Social Security Association n.d.a.).

As of 1998, 38 pension fund administrators were licensed to operate by the Pension Fund Supervision Agency. In 2010, their number had decreased to 19 to manage the accounts of approximately 3 million members and assets amounting to US$14.2 billion (Hungarian Financial Supervisory Authority 2010). The five largest pension administrators administer about 80 percent of the total assets, a concentration of the market that is common to the other three cases examined in this book (International Organisation of Pension Supervisors 2009). Because of the very high concentration of the market, and in order to prevent further concentration, the Hungarian Financial Supervisory Authority only reports aggregate data on the mandatory and voluntary pension funds in terms of market share, membership, and assets.

The Hungarian mandatory private pillar was one of the first pension schemes to be adopted in Central and Eastern Europe and the first participants are expected to retire around 2020. Due to the fact that many older workers had joined the private scheme without having long enough contributory periods, the private system is likely to provide them lower benefits than if they had stayed in the public system. Also taking into account the very high unemployment rates in Hungary in the first two decades of postcommunist transition and the fact that many people are not employed in the formal economy and do not pay pension contributions, when these workers will retire in the next 10–15 years under the new system they will be left without an old-age pension. Augusztinovics and Köllő (2009) estimate that number to be between 250,000 and 500,000 Hungarians, or 10–20 percent of the cohorts that will retire until 2020.

In Hungary, the third pillar was created early compared to the other countries in the region. It was established through Act XCVI/1993 on voluntary mutual funds[22] and later amended by Act XV/1996 amending the 1993 act on voluntary mutual funds.[23] Contributions can be paid by both the employee and the employer. The benefits and the investment income are tax exempt, and both employee and employer contributions are partially tax exempt. In 2010 the number of voluntary pension funds was 62, the value of the assets managed was approximately US$4.2 billion, and the membership was approximately 1.3 million (Hungarian Financial Supervisory Authority 2010; International Organisation of Pension Supervisors 2009). Similar to the second pillar, the market for the voluntary pension is characterized by high concentration: the top five pension administrators manage the savings of 64 percent of the members, representing 56 percent of the assets (Hungarian Financial Supervisory Authority 2009). There is no minimum return guarantee for the voluntary pension funds.

The Aftermath of the Reform

The Fidesz government in power during 1998–2002, which was supported by a coalition of the FKgP (Independent Smallholders Party) and the MDF (Hungarian Democratic Forum), attacked both the reform of the public pension system and the mandatory private pillar that had just begun to operate in January 1998. The government deferred the increase in the size of the second pillar from 6 to 8 percent, made entrance to the second pillar voluntary, and increased pensions in the public system across the board. The government decree 165/2000, which was issued in September 2000 and took effect in November 2000, increased all old-age, survivors, and disability benefits by 2.6 percent (International Social Security Association n.d.a). This measure limited the effects of the 1997 public system reform, which attempted to more closely tie contributions and benefits and reduce the fiscal deficit of the pension fund. The parliament also passed legislation that came into effect in January 2002 that limited the scope of the mandatory private pillar. The second pillar was opened up for a period of one year (January to December 2002), during which people who had previously joined the second pillar could opt out and return to the public PAYG system. In addition, under the new legislation new entrants to the labor market were not required to join the second pillar, but instead had the option of becoming insured exclusively with the public system. Those who joined the second pillar after 1 January 2002 could reverse their decision and fully return to the public system until the end of 2003 (International Social Security Association n.d.a). The minimum return guarantee previously provided by the public system to those who had contributed to the second pillar for 15 years was removed by the new legislation.

A new reform of the public pension system passed under the socialist minority government on 11 May 2009. Overall, the package attempted to reduce the costs of pensions paid from the public system, given the economic decline of the Hungarian economy of up to 6 percent per year. The specific measures include a gradual increase in the retirement age from 62 to 65 from 2012 to 2017. The indexation rules were also changed from an indexation based equally on prices and wages to an indexation based on prices when GDP growth is below 3 percent a year and an indexation based on both prices and wages when GDP growth is higher than 3 percent—in the following proportions: 80 percent to 20 percent for GDP growth between 3 and 4 percent; 60 percent to 40 percent for GDP growth between 4 and 5 percent; and equal proportions for GDP growth higher than 5 percent. The new indexation rules make the indexation of pension benefits contingent on economic performance. The change in the rules leads to an overall decline in pension benefits compared to the previous indexation system, because the price-based indexation is less generous than the wage-based indexation. In addition, the so-called "13th month pension" granted in addition to the 12 monthly pension payments was eliminated and replaced with a pension bonus ranging from US$100 to $400 to be paid only when the GDP is above 3.5 percent (International Social Security Association n.d.a).

The divisions that characterized the initial adoption of pension reform in Hungary have persisted well into the second decade of post-communist transition, leading to several successive modifications of reforms. The Fidesz-led center-right government attempted to limit the scope of the second pillar and to increase the benefits under the public system. Upon returning to office the socialist government took the opportunity to reverse to the initial path of reforms, trying to limit the deficit in the public scheme and strengthen the second private pillar. Despite these steps back and forth, the main three-pillar structure of the new pension system has not been challenged, and thus chances for long-term sustainability of pension reform in Hungary remain good. The politics of pension reform in Hungary largely resembles that of Slovakia, in which reforms were also unilaterally adopted and then altered when the opposition came to power, particularly the second pillar, but the basic organization of the new system was left in place.

ROMANIA: THE UNREFORMED LEFT AND DRAMATIC REVERSALS

In contrast with Hungary and Poland, who were at the forefront of pension reform in the postcommunist region, Romania has been a late reformer. Although reforms were virtually complete in Hungary and Poland by the end of 1990s, the reform process in Romania has been characterized by its near absence in the first postcommunist decade. The second decade witnessed an uneven reform process, marked by a partial reform and a major reversal, followed by a completion of reforms in parallel with countless revisions of the reforms adopted. The overall pattern was one of irreconcilable disagreements between the center-right, center-left, and nationalist political parties in the first decade, which led to a stalemate despite the pressures for reform from the World Bank and the IMF. This pattern abruptly changed to one reflecting compromise between the major political parties in the second decade, prompted by Romania's accession to NATO in 2004 and the European Union in 2007. The continuing differences between the parties resurfaced as endless delays, missed opportunities, hasty adoptions when deferral was no longer an option, and recurring alterations of the reforms adopted.

Romania eventually followed Hungary and Poland in adopting the World Bank model of a three-pillar pension system (World Bank 1994). The first pillar (public system) reform took place on 17 March 2000, as Law 19/2000 on the public pension system and other social insurance benefits.[24] This law was adopted by a center-right coalition of the CDR (Democratic Convention of Romania, Convenţia Democrată Română), the PD (Democratic Party, Partidul Democrat), and the party of the Hungarian minority UDMR (Democratic Alliance of Hungarians in Romania, Uniunea Democrată a Maghiarilor din România). In the decade following the adoption Law 19/2000 suffered approximately 40 alterations[25] by every new governing coalition coming to power.

The second pillar law, which established mandatory private pension funds, was initially adopted as an emergency ordinance by the outgoing center-right government of Mugur Isărescu of the CDR. The ordinance was cancelled by the incoming center-left government of Adrian Năstase of the PSD (Social Democratic Party, formerly PDSR [Party of Social Democracy of Romania, Partidul Democraţiei Sociale din România]) before it took effect. It was eventually adopted on 18 October 2004 as Law 411/2004 on private pension funds[26] under the government of Năstase at the end of the 2000–2004 legislative term, supported by a center-left coalition of the PSD/PDSR, the PUR/PC (Romanian Humanist Party [Partidul Umanist Român], renamed the Conservative Party [Partidul Conservator] in 2005), and the UDMR. This law suffered three alterations until March 2010, all by the center-right government that was in power during the 2004–2008 term.

The third pillar law, which created voluntary private pension funds, was adopted on 22 May 2006 as Law 204/2006 on voluntary pensions[27] by the center-right coalition of the PNL (National Liberal Party, Partidul Naţional Liberal), the Democratic Liberal Party (Partidul Democrat Liberal, PD-L)/PD, the PUR/PC, and the UDMR. This law had been subject to one modification until the time of writing.

Similar to Hungary and Poland, by the mid-1990s Romania was confronted with a pension crisis due to the combined effect of demographic, economic, and political factors. An aging population coupled with high unemployment, fiscal evasion, and early retirement led to an increase in the system dependency ratio from about 30 pensioners for every 100 workers in 1989 to 55 pensioners for every 100 workers in 1995, and to almost 85 pensioners for every 100 workers toward the end of the decade (Casa Naţională de Pensii şi Alte Drepturi de Asigurări Sociale n.d.). The initial surplus of the pension fund was rapidly exhausted, and by 1995 the pension fund ran into a deficit. The deficit quickly reached a peak of 1.6 percent of the GDP in 1998 and continued at high levels approaching 1 percent of the GDP until the middle of 2005 (Casa Naţională de Pensii şi Alte Drepturi de Asigurări Sociale n.d.), which required state subsidies and treasury loans and forced pension reform on the political agenda. In addition, long-term projections showed that the pension system was unsustainable in its existing form because of adverse demographic trends similar to those in Hungary, Poland, and Slovakia (The World Bank n.d.). In the early 1990s, the demographic structure of Romania was comparable to that of its neighboring countries, with the population aged 60 and over representing about 17 percent of the total population and about 30 percent of the working age population (Palacios and Pallarès-Mirales 2000). Long-term projections, however, showed that these numbers were on the rise due to a decline in the fertility rate and population aging. The expectation was that the percentage of the population aged 60 and over would rise to 30 percent of the total population and would surpass 60 percent of the working age population by 2040 (Palacios and Pallarès-Mirales 2000). The disproportion of the aged in the total population would have put enormous strain on the pension system in the absence of major reforms. While the system dependency ratio, representing the number of pensioners divided by the number of contributors to the pension system, in Romania was 38 in 1991, it increased to 58.3 in the mid-1990s (Palacios and Pallarès-Mirales 2000). This inevitably led to an increase in pension expenditures as a percentage of GDP, pension fund deficits, and a decline in the replacement rate (average pension/average wage) from 43.1 in 1994 to 39.2 in 2000 (ILO 1997; Palacios and Pallarès-Mirales 2000).

Using the dire straits of the pension system as political leverage, the IMF and the World Bank conditioned their loans on the adoption of a comprehensive pension reform. Every government since 1996 had pension reform on the agenda, yet reform has been a very difficult and protracted process that was still not completed in 2010, a decade after its inception. Although the three pillars of the World Bank basic reform model were adopted by 2006, numerous modifications, particularly to the public pension system (first pillar), have taken place in the meantime. Unlike Hungary and Poland, where the adoption process in retrospect seems unusually brief and uncomplicated, in Romania the lack of a basic consensus between the major political actors, particularly in the first decade of postcommunist transition, has been responsible for numerous setbacks. Six cabinets during four legislative terms have been involved with the pension reform process (Table 4.1).

The Party System

The Romanian party system has suffered profound transformations in the two decades of postcommunist transition, which are characterized by three main features. First, similar to other countries in the region, Romania has seen a reduction in the number of political parties that mushroomed immediately following the collapse of communism and a consolidation of the party system into a center-left, a center-right, a nationalist pole and the ethnic UDMR (the Democratic Alliance of Hungarians), which has maintained a distinct position. Each of the poles of the party system underwent substantial alterations, but they all maintained some continuity over time with their original political formations (political parties, alliances of parties, fronts, and social movements) despite numerous splits, mergers, name changes, and even major ideological shifts from one pole of the party system to another.

Second, the former communist party has undergone a late process of modernization, unlike its counterparts in Hungary and Poland. During the first decade of postcommunist transition, the PDSR/PSD (Party of Social Democracy in Romania/Social Democratic Party, formerly the Democratic National Salvation Front [Frontul Democrat al Salvării Naționale], FDSN), the main successor to the former communist party, despite its social-democratic label remained largely unreformed. The PDSR/PSD dominated Romania's political life until after the mid-1990s and delayed significant economic and political reforms (Gross and Tismăneanu 2005). The PDSR/PSD slowly modernized and began following a similar path to the Hungarian and Polish former communist parties in the second decade of postcommunist transition, though it has remained plagued by a considerable amount of corruption.

Third, the political right in Romania has remained divided despite its growth in strength due to an increase in its constituency and the ideological shift of the PD/PD-L (Democratic Party/Democratic-Liberal Party, formerly National Salvation Front [Frontul Salvării Naționale], FSN), from a social-democratic to a center-right position following CDR's (Democratic Convention of Romania) victory in the 1996 elections. The divisions within the right have contributed to the difficulties in advancing the right's political agenda during its three terms in office from 1996 to 2000, 2004 to 2008, and 2008 to present.

The Center-Left
Romania has emerged from a patrimonial communist system (Ishiyama 1997, 2006; Kitschelt 1995) that was characterized by powerful "hierarchical chains of personal dependence between leaders and followers, [...] low levels of interelite contestation, popular interest articulation, and rational-bureaucratic professionalization"

(Ishiyama 1997: 302). The Romanian Communist Party (Partidul Comunist Român, PCR) was one of the most repressive in the region. The party had distanced itself from the Soviet Union after Stalin's death and established an anti-Soviet nationalist-communism. The limited liberalization that took place across Central and Eastern Europe in the 1960s, prompted by the reforms of Nikita Khrushchev, left out Romania (Tismăneanu 2003). Two decades later, political and economic liberalization set in motion by the reforms of Mikhail Gorbachev in the Soviet Union also did not touch the PCR. The party, under its leader Nicolae Ceauşescu, chose not to reform and instead repressed popular protests that followed the collapse of communism in the neighboring countries.

The ex-communist party coming out from a patrimonial regime had a tremendous advantage over its competitors on both the left and the right. Of the nine patrimonial regimes in the postcommunist region, in only one case the former communist party had a left competitor that was able to gain more than 5 percent of the seats in the lower house in the first postcommunist election (Ishiyama 1997: 313–314). In Romania the FSN (National Salvation Front), the Communist successor party (Ishiyama 1995, 1997; Pop-Elecheş 1999, 2008), faced practically no competition from other left parties (Ishiyama 1997: 314; Mihuţ 1994), winning 66.41 percent of the seats in the lower house in the 1990 elections, while its candidate, Ion Iliescu, won the presidency with an astounding 85.07 percent of the vote (Project on Political Transformation and the Electoral Process in Postcommunist Europe 2002).

The FSN under the leadership of Ion Iliescu adopted a reformist facade but did not try to break with its communist past. The younger reformist premier Petre Roman attempted some moderate economic reforms but quickly clashed with president Iliescu, who opposed any attempt at political and economic liberalization. Divisions within the FSN became evident between the reformist wing led by Prime Minister Petre Roman and the hard-liners led by President Ion Iliescu, leading to the prime-minister's removal from power following the September 1991 *mineriad*, during which several thousand miners violently attacked the capital city (Stan 2005b). The tensions between Ion Iliescu and Petre Roman also led to departure of Ion Iliescu's hard-line faction from the FSN to create the FDSN (Democratic National Salvation Front, which after several mergers renamed itself the Socialist Democratic Party of Romania, PDSR, and later the Social Democratic Party, PSD). Petre Roman remained the leader of the smaller FSN (renamed

Democratic Party, PD, and later Democratic Liberal Party, PD-L). Although the literature consistently identifies the FDSN/PDSR as a Communist successor party, opinions are divided about whether the FSN also deserves this label (Pop-Elecheş 2008: 468). Despite the fact that the FSN inherited the name of the institutional successor of the former Communist Party, most scholars see the FDSN/PDSR as the successor party because of its institutional, leadership, and ideological continuity with the Romanian Communist Party (Pop-Elecheş 2008: 469).

During its term in office, the FSN under Ion Iliescu blocked all major reforms. By the end of 1992, less than 1 percent of the state's overall assets had been privatized, there was no privatization of large state-owned companies or state farms (Freedom House 1995), and the foreign direct investment was a modest US\$73 million, which represented the equivalent of 0.3 percent of the GDP (Voinea 2003).

Following the 1992 parliamentary elections, Ion Iliescu's FDSN/PDSR remained the dominant political party on the Romanian political scene, winning 35.67 percent of the seats in the lower house (Project on Political Transformation and the Electoral Process in Postcommunist Europe 2002), almost three times more than Petre Roman's FSN and about 40 percent more than its closest right competitor, the CDR (Democratic Convention of Romania). The FDSN/PDSR formed a minority government supported by the nationalist PRM (Greater Romania Party, Partidul România Mare) and PUNR (Romanian National Unity Party, Partidul Unității Naționale a Românilor), and the nationalist-socialist PSM (Socialist Labor Party, Partidul Socialist al Muncii). Meanwhile, Petre Roman's FSN was in opposition. The FDSN/PDSR pursued a gradualist approach to reform (Freedom House 1997; Pop-Elecheş 2008: 469) for fear of alienating its constituency that was largely based in rural areas, blue collar workers and generally low-educated and low-income individuals (Feşnic and Armeanu 2008). By the end of 1996 the privatization of state-owned companies proceeded with caution: fewer than 50 large companies had been privatized and only a few inefficient, large state-owned enterprises had been restructured or closed (Freedom House 1997; International Monetary Fund [IMF] 1998). The government was plagued by widespread corruption and attracted little foreign investment because of cumbersome bureaucracy and corruption, and there was little or no reform in key economic sectors, such as energy in which the state continued to have a monopoly over production and distribution and controlled the energy prices (Freedom House 1997; IMF 1998).

The PDSR and its candidate Ion Iliescu's electoral defeat in the 1996 parliamentary and presidential elections marked a major turning point in the evolution of the party system and paved the way for two subsequent long-lasting and interconnected developments. On the one hand it put an end to the FDSN/PDSR domination of the party system, leading to more balance between the left and the right and thus creating an opening for future alternation in power, which was absent in Romania for the first two postcommunist elections. On the other hand it forced the FDSN/PDSR to undertake a major process of internal transformation in order to redefine its postcommunist identity. While the PSDR's distance from its previous hard-line stance has been a long and slow progression, it became evident during the legislative term of 2000–2004, which brought the PDSR/PSD back in power (Pop-Eleches 2008: 470), and again during the term of 2008–2012, during which the PSD participated in a liberal-conservative–socialist coalition with the PD-L (Liberal Democratic Party, formerly FSN), that the party had been pursuing a significant process of change.

During its 2000–2004 term in power, the PDSR/PSD formed a minority government supported by the Hungarian UDMR. Its former ally, the PRM (Greater Romania Party), came in second with 24.35 percent of the seats in the lower house (Project on Political Transformation and the Electoral Process in Postcommunist Europe 2002), but was not invited into the coalition. The PDSR/PSD continued the economic reforms and pro-Western orientation of the previous center-right government, and in 2004 Romania joined NATO and signed the accession treaty to join the European Union (Downs and Miller 2006; Gross and Tismăneanu 2005: 151–152). The 1991 Constitution was significantly amended in 2003, providing better protection of property rights, better guarantees of minority rights, and an independent judiciary (Mungiu-Pippidi 2004). The PDSR/PSD government privatized key state-owned companies, such as the oil company Petrom, the utility providers Distri Gas and Electrica, the Sidex Steel Mill, and the Commercial Bank of Romania (Gross and Tismăneanu 2005). The private sector share of GDP continued to increase from 55 percent in 1996 to 69 percent in 2003 (IMF 2004), and in 2003 the government passed a new anticorruption law (Mungiu-Pippidi 2004). It seemed at the time that the PDSR/PSD was renouncing its previous anti-liberal policies and was following in the footsteps of its Hungarian and Polish counterparts. However, the party was plagued by allegations of corruption, and Romania was ranked one of the most corrupt countries in Europe and considerably more corrupt than Bulgaria, another European Union accession country, according to the Transparency International *Corruption Perceptions Index* (Transparency International 2009).

In the next term, 2004–2008, after the breakdown of the PNL-PD-UDMR-PUR governing coalition, the PSD supported the new minority government of PNL-UDMR(Popescu 2009; Young 2009). The informal coalition of PNL-PSD, labeled pejoratively by the Romanian media the "monstrous coalition" (Cornea 2007), was instrumental in passing several memorable decisions, including the suspension of the Romanian president, Traian Băsescu[28] (BBC News 2007; Condon and Wagstyl 2007; Young 2009), and rejected the request by the National Anticorruption Department to pursue a case of corruption against the former PSD prime minister Adrian Năstase.[29] The PNL-PSD informal coalition also attempted to close down the National Anticorruption Directorate; tried to change the Criminal Code in order to reduce the power of the prosecutors and introduce more severe punishments against the journalists; and centralized power in the executive, legislating by emergency ordinances (there were 130 ordinances emitted only in 2007) and thus circumventing the Parliament. Meanwhile corruption ran rampant, forcing the resignation of two deputy prime ministers, among other top political figures (Mungiu-Pippidi 2008; Young 2009). Romania became ranked as the most corrupt country in the European Union, equal with Greece and Macedonia, according to the *Corruption Perceptions Index* (Transparency International 2009).

At the end of 2008, the PSD again had a chance to come back to power, this time in a grand coalition with the PD-L. This coalition, however, was short-lived and by October 2009 it succumbed as a result of tensions between the two parties, which were amplified by the contentious November 2009 presidential elections. The incumbent PD-L candidate Traian Băsescu won a second term by a narrow margin (50.33 percent vs. 49.66 percent for the PSD candidate Mircea Geoană [Biroul Electoral Central 2009]) amid accusations of electoral fraud by the PSD (Pora 2009). The two fleeting cross-spectrum coalitions that the PSD formed with the PNL during the 2000–2004 term and with the PD-L during the 2008–present term show the significant transformation that the successor communist party has undertaken, compared to the previous decade, toward abandoning its previous hard-line stance, more moderation, and increased ability to compromise with center-right parties. The pro-market and pro-Western policies the PSD adopted during its 2000–2004 term in office point in the same direction. However, the party's swing toward modernization is confounded by its poor corruption record.

The Center-Right

The Romanian center-right has undertaken massive transformations in the two decades following the collapse of communism, characterized by a demise of almost all of the early political parties and a gradual process of consolidation into fewer, stronger parties. However, the political right has not been able to overcome its internal divisions and has never been able to offer a coherent alternative to the stronger social-democrats on the left. The political right's three terms in power from 1996 to 2000, 2004 to 2008, and 2008 to present have tarnished its image and left its constituents bitterly disappointed.

Opposition to the FSN and its candidate Ion Iliescu began to form early in 1990, represented by several reconstituted historical political parties, such as the PNL (National Liberal Party), the PNȚCD (National Peasant Christian-Democratic Party, Partidul Național Țărănesc Creștin Democrat), and the PSDR (Romanian Social Democratic Party), together with new political parties: the PER (Ecologist Party of Romania), the PAC (Civic Alliance Party), and the PAR (Alternative for Romania Party), among many others. The early opposition was highly fragmented with weak political parties. In the first postcommunist elections of 1990, the center-right parties together (excepting the parties of ethnic minorities) gained fewer than 60 of the 396 seats in the lower house (Project on Political Transformation and the Electoral Process in Postcommunist Europe 2002). Among them, the PNL gained the largest number of seats (29 seats), followed by the PNȚCD with 12 seats (Project on Political Transformation and the Electoral Process in Postcommunist Europe 2002). A slow process of consolidation was noticeable with the 1992 elections in which the center-right, although still weak and fragmented, managed to come in second after the FDSN under the umbrella of the CDR (Romanian Democratic Convention), gaining 82 of the 341 seats in the lower house (Project on Political Transformation and the Electoral Process in Postcommunist Europe 2002). The CDR also did well in the local elections of 1992 in which it won in Bucharest and other large cities.

During 1992–1996 the CDR represented the main opposition to Ion Iliescu's FDSN. Petre Roman's FSN was also in opposition at the time, but its position was less clearly defined. Only later on did the FSN moved more decisively toward center-right. The CDR was a loose center-right coalition of several parties and civic organizations brought together by the opposition to the FDSN and contained a variety of ideological strands, from Christian democrats to social democrats, liberals, and greens. The diversity within the coalition was difficult to manage and led to a split in early 1992 when the PNL left the

CDR, while a small splinter of the PNL remained in the coalition. As a result of the PNL leaving the coalition, PNȚCD became the dominant party. Tensions between the members of the coalition led several other parties to leave the CDR before the 1996 general elections.

The 1996 election brought the first postcommunist victory of the right, with the CDR coming in first followed by Ion Iliescu's PDSR (formerly FDSN) and Petre Roman's PD (formerly FSN). The CDR formed a governing coalition with Petre Roman's PD and the Hungarian UDMR. In presidential elections held concomitantly, CDR candidate Emil Constantinescu gained the presidency. The right's term in power was fraught with internal disagreements and was marked by a succession of three prime ministers, the last of which was an independent (Mugur Isărescu, the National Bank Governor), leading to a mixed policy record (Stan 2004). Mainly, the CDR-led coalition was accused of delaying economic reforms and failing to fight corruption. Major economic reforms did not start until later into the term. To accelerate privatization, the government created a Privatization Ministry in December 1997. However, only 4 percent of the companies that privatized in 1997 were large, 83 percent were small, and 13 percent were medium sized (Freedom House 1999).

Privatization took off in the second half of the term, during which some of the most important state-owned companies such as Romtelecom, the state telecomunications provider, the Romanian Postal Service, and Romania's largest car manufacturer Dacia were privatized (Freedom House 1999). By the end of 2000 the private sector share of GDP had increased to 65 percent, from 39 percent in 1994 and 55 percent in 1996 (IMF 2004). Subsidies to state-owned enterprises continued but were made transparent in the state budget. A decision by the government to close down about 100 inefficient coal mines that would have led to the loss of approximately 90,000 mining jobs resulted in strikes and a violent march by the miners toward Bucharest, known as the 1999 *mineriad*, prompting the government to re-open two of the closed mines and channel part of the European Union development funds toward the Valea Jiului mining region (Gongwer 2000). Government attempts to fight corruption were marginally successful, resulting mostly in the prosecution of low-level officials (Freedom House 1999). Reform in all areas accelerated, particularly in 2000, but by the end of the term a series of reforms remained incomplete. Romania's application to NATO was rejected in 1997, adding to the widespread dissatisfaction with the performance of the right and contributing to its electoral loss in the 2000 elections. PNȚCD, the party supporting president Emil

Constantinescu and two of the CDR prime ministers, all but disappeared from the political scene.

The right came back into power after the 2004 elections, although the Justice and Truth center-right alliance (Alianţa Dreptate şi Adevăr, known as Alianţa DA) of PNL and PD came in second with 112 seats (33.73 percent) in the lower house after the National Union PSD+PUR, formed by the PSD and the PUR (Humanist Party of Romania), which gained 132 seats (39.75 percent) (Biroul Electoral Central 2004). However, the newly elected president, Traian Băsescu of the Justice and Truth Alliance, in the concomitant presidential elections designated Călin Popescu-Tăriceanu of the PNL to form the government. The government included PNL, PD, UDMR, and PUR (which switched sides) and also relied on the seats reserved for ethnic minorities (Downs and Miller 2006). The narrow majority has been a source of government instability, leading to a series of significant political crises, thus severely limiting the ability of the governing coalition to advance its political agenda and tarnishing its reputation.

The first crisis was the proposal by the government in 2005 to call for early elections in the hope of strengthening its parliamentary support. The prime minister soon abandoned the idea for fear of what the elections might bring to his party, which paved the way for a prolonged conflict between the prime minister and the president, who supported early elections. The second crisis was a conflict between Prime Minister Tăriceanu's PNL and President Băsescu's PD, the two major parties in the governing coalition. The PSD took advantage of this conflict and supported PNL's efforts to remove the PD from the governing coalition. The coalition broke down in April 2007 and was succeeded by a new government under Tăriceanu, formed by the PNL and UDMR alone, with parliamentary support from the PSD (Popescu 2009). The final crisis was the vote by the reunited chambers of the Romanian parliament to suspend president Băsescu.

Government instability, its weakness, and its need to rely on the parliamentary support of the PSD and even the PRM led it to renounce some of its previous policies. Fighting corruption is one such famous policy area, in which the president was left to fight corruption alone while Prime Minister Tăriceanu and his government, supported by the PSD, replaced the PD Minister of Justice, who was actively involved in the anti-corruption campaign, with a new minister who, disregarding the advice of the European Commission, attempted to close down the National Anticorruption Directorate (Mungiu-Pippidi 2008; Young 2009). Of the package of bills that the government intended to put up for vote by the end of the term, many important bills remained blocked at various stages of adoption and were deferred to the next government, such as the health care reform, constitutional reform, educational reform, and reform of the wage system (Revista 22 2009). Romania's joining of the European Union in 2007 helped improve the reputation of Tăriceanu's government, although the process had started during the previous PSD government.

Despite the poor record of the center-right government, center-right parties did well in the 2008 elections, together gaining 180 seats (53.89 percent) in the lower house (Biroul Electoral Central 2008). PD-L came first with 115 seats, followed by the PSD with 110 seats and the PNL with 65 seats. The incumbent president, Traian Băsescu of PD-L, was reelected by a narrow margin in the 2009 presidential election. This time the right had a majority of its own. Despite expectations by constituents of the right that the PD-L and PNL would overcome their past disagreements and join together in a stronger government, PD-L chose instead to form the government with the PSD. This government collapsed in less than a year and was replaced by a minority government of the PD-L and the Hungarian UDMR, which relied on the support of independents and the seats reserved for ethnic minorities.

The right's trajectory shows a consolidation from the initial fragmentation into two stronger political parties and the disappearance of many early parties, including the virtual disappearance of the PNȚCD. After being the main party in the CDR and providing one president and two prime ministers, the PNȚCD has all but disappeared from the political scene because of its failure to broaden its ideological appeal, to diversify its electoral base, and de-centralize its rigid organizational structure (Stan 2005a). The largest parties on the right are now PD-L (formerly PD), which had shifted from social democracy to a center-right position, followed by the PNL. According to the party platforms, the PD-L and the PNL are hard to distinguish in their economic and foreign policy. The more conservative and populist views of the PD-L versus the more liberal views of the PNL on social issues is what sets the two parties apart (PD-L n.d.; PNL n.d.). It is difficult for an observer to identify programmatic differences between the two parties that would explain their difficulty in governing together. Rather, it is the other way around: PD-L and PNL are very much alike and they compete against each other for the same center-right electorate. The problem for each is not so much how to attract votes from the leftist PSD, which has an entirely different constituency, but rather how to attract votes from one another and to maintain their constituencies at the same time. The PD-L has come a long way from being the reformist wing of the FSN (National Salvation Front) to becoming the main party on the right. The challenge it faces is how to present itself as an alternative to the PNL without distancing itself too much from the core values that the constituents of the right support: free-market economy, pro-Western policies, and individualism.

The Nationalists

Nationalist parties have been represented by the PRM (Great Romania Party), PUNR (Romanian National Unity Party), and the nationalist-socialist PSM (Socialist Labor Party). Nationalist parties in Romania have been stronger compared to those in Hungary and Poland, but weaker than Mečiar's HZDS (Movement for a Democratic Slovakia) in Slovakia. The nationalists in Romania have never been in a position to form the government or to win the presidency as they were in Slovakia, though they participated in the government during the 1992–1996 term, and the PRM's candidate Corneliu Vadim Tudor came in second in the presidential elections of 2000. Unlike the center-left and the center-right, the fortunes of the nationalist parties have fluctuated to a much larger extent, eventually leading to the demise of the PSM and the PUNR, and the failure of the PRM to pass the electoral threshold in the 2008 elections. Although the nationalists were very influential in the politics of Romania during the first 15 years after the collapse of communism, their strength has diminished. However, given the abrupt electoral changes suffered by the PRM over a single legislative term, a reemergence of this party is still possible.

The first nationalist party established was the PUNR, based in Transylvania. Gheorghe Funar, the charismatic mayor of Cluj-Napoca, was the leader of the PUNR for most of its existence. The PUNR's discourse was directed against the Hungarian minority in Romania, which is mainly concentrated in Transylvania. The PUNR called for banning the Hungarian UDMR alliance, excluding ethnic Hungarians from the Armed forces, and prohibiting them from studying in their own language (Economist 1995). One famous episode was the decision of Gheorghe Funar to have the benches in Cluj-Napoca's public parks painted in red, yellow, and blue, the colors of the Romanian flag. Together with the PRM and the PSM, the PUNR participated in the PDSR-led government during the 1992–1996 term in which it held four cabinet posts. The poor electoral performance of the PUNR in the 1996 elections, in which the party lost almost half of its seats in the lower house and half of the seats in the Senate, led to divisions within the party and to a change in leadership that eventually led to the party's demise. Gheorghe Funar was replaced by a less charismatic leader, causing a sharp decline in support for the PUNR. Funar left the party to join the PRM. The PUNR has never been able to pass the electoral threshold again and was eventually absorbed into the PC (Conservative Party, former Romanian Humanist Party, PUR).

The PSM (Socialist Labor Party) was created in late 1990 by high-ranking officials in the former PCR (Romanian Communist Party) and is seen as a direct continuator of the PCR. Its leader, Ilie Verdeţ, was a prime minister under Nicolae Ceauşescu. It has been the only post-1989 party to claim a direct connection to the defunct PCR. In the 1992 elections the party barely passed the 3 percent electoral threshold, winning 13 seats in the lower chamber and 5 seats in the Senate. The party did not hold cabinet positions but supported the PDSR-led government. Ever since, the PSM has not been able to pass the electoral threshold, and in 2003 it was absorbed into the PSD. Together with the PUNR, the PRM, and the PSD, it formed the so-called *Red Quadrilateral*, the coalition that supported the government during 1992–1995 when the PSM and the PRM left the coalition.

The most successful of the three nationalist parties has been the PRM (Great Romania Party), largely due to the charisma of its leader, Corneliu Vadim Tudor. The party was established in 1991 and was able to maintain a constant presence in Romanian political life. From 1992 to 1995 it supported the PDSR government. Using the party's newspaper, *Romania Mare* (*Great Romania*), to pay tribute to Corneliu Vadim Tudor and denigrate his opponents, PRM has been a virulent attacker of ethnic minorities, intellectuals, leaders of the historical political parties, civil society, and the independent media. The party is also xenophobic and promotes the idea of reconstituting a greater Romania—hence the name of the party—by reclaiming territories from neighboring states that were part of the pre–World War II Romania (Ciobanu 2007). The PRM progressively increased its number of seats in the lower house from 16 in 1992 to 19 in 1996 to a spectacular 84 in 2000 when the party came in second after the PSD, winning close to a quarter of the seats, while its candidate Corneliu Vadim Tudor came in second in the presidential race (Project on Political Transformation and the Electoral Process in Postcommunist Europe 2002). After 2000, the PRM started to decline, winning 48 seats in the lower house and 21 seats in the Senate in the 2004 legislative elections, and in the 2008 elections it did not gain seats in any of the houses (Biroul Electoral Central 2004 and 2008).

In the 2000 electoral campaign, the PRM's discourse blamed the Hungarians and the Jews for the country's problems and proposed to cease submitting to the requests of a foreign oligarchy represented by the IMF and the World Bank and govern with an iron fist (Popescu 2003). Analyzed with the hindsight of PRM's electoral defeat in the subsequent 2008 elections, the party's ephemeral victory suggests a protest vote by an electorate whose expectations had been frustrated by both the left and the right, and who resented what it perceived as an unjust rejection by the West—Romania's recent rejection by NATO in 1997. Despite PRM's astonishing success, PSD chose instead to rely on the parliamentary support of the Hungarian UDMR. In the 2008 elections, PRM suffered a major electoral defeat and did not win seats in any of the houses, largely due to the change in the electoral system from proportional representation to a single ballot mixed system (Feşnic and Armeanu 2009). The party returned in 2009 when it won 8.65 percent of the votes in the elections for the European Parliament, winning three seats in the European Parliament. Previously the PRM had a noticeable presence on the European scene when in 2007 the five PRM members in the European Parliament helped establish the short-lived nationalist Identity, Tradition, Sovereignty group.

Role of Political Parties and Coalitions in Pension Reform

Three successive governments faced the need to reform the Romanian pension system (Table 4.1). The center-left PDSR government under premier Văcăroiu (1992–1996), supported by a coalition of nationalist parties, avoided any decisive steps toward reform. Reform came on the government agenda and was supported by the World Bank and the IMF, but it encountered great domestic opposition. Some of the strongest opponents of reform were the trade unions, who wanted to be included in the reform process (Chiriţoiu 2001). Prime Minister Văcăroiu preferred instead short-term measures to address the crisis, such as the erosion of existing benefits through inflation and increasing the contribution rate. As a result of these policies, inflation rate reached values above 250 percent a year in 1993 (World Economic Outlook 1999). The PDSR government enjoyed a solid majority of 53.66 percent seats in the lower house and faced a weak and divided opposition. The center-right parties accounted for only around 33

percent of the seats, including the Hungarian UDMR (Project on
Political Transformation and the Electoral Process in Postcommunist
Europe 2002). Pension reform was avoided altogether.

A major attempt at pension reform took place under the subsequent center-right government that came into power following the
1996 elections. This government gravitated around the coalition of
the Democratic Convention and the Democratic Party, which were
joined by the ethnic Democratic Alliance of Hungarian in Romania
(Uniunea Democrată a Maghiarilor din România, UDMR). The
coalition of the CDR, PD and UDMR prepared the project for pension reform under Prime Minister Victor Ciorbea. The bill for the
reform of the public PAYG pension system reached the parliament in
September 1998, under the succeeding Prime Minister Radu Vasile,
and was adopted on 7 March 2000 as Law 19/2000 on the public
pension system and other social insurance benefits[30] (De Menil and
Sheshinski 2001). The first pillar reform achieved a moderate reform
of the public system: it increased the retirement age to 65 for men
and 62 for women, which will take place gradually over a period of
15 years. The law has embedded occupational privileges for certain
categories of workers, such as those in the mining industry, in the
form of higher benefits and early retirement. Subsequently, Vasile's
government also submitted to the parliament the bill for the creation
of a mandatory, fully funded pension scheme (second pillar), with a
proposed 30 percent of the total pension contribution to be directed
toward the funded pillar.

Political conflict within the governing coalition and the opposition to the second pillar bill by the trade unions led to delays
that prevented the parliament from passing the second pillar reform by the end of its term (Chirițoiu 2001; Early Warning Report
2002: 26). The government decided instead to promulgate the
second pillar bill as an emergency ordinance (O.G. 230/2000),
which had to be approved by the subsequent legislature elected in
the December 2000 elections. Quite the opposite happened: the
new center-left government formed by the PSD (Social Democratic
Party, formerly PDSR) under the premier Adrian Năstase cancelled
the emergency ordinance and put the reform process on hold for
almost four years. The important achievement of the CDR-PD-
UDMR coalition was ultimately the passage of the public system
bill and bringing pension privatization into the public debate. Law
19/2000 subsequently suffered approximately 40 alterations but
still defines the legal framework for the organization of the public
pension system.

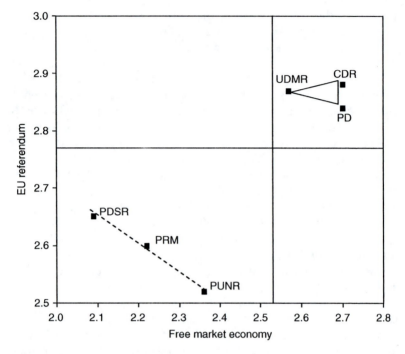

Figure 4.3 Romania, 1997. Party constituencies and attitudes toward a free market economy and international institutions

CDR = Democratic Convention of Romania, alliance of Christian democrats (PNȚCD), liberals, and environmentalists (35.57%); PDSR = Romanian Party of Social Democracy (26.53%); PD=Democratic Party (12.53%); UDMR = Democratic Alliance of Hungarians in Romania (7.29%); PRM=Great Romania Party (5.54%); PUNR = Romanian National Unity Party (5.25%); PSM=Socialist Labor Party (0%).

----- The coalition of PDSR, PRM, PSM, and PUNR avoided pension reform, although reform was on the agenda (1992–1996).

——— The coalition of CDR, PD, and UDMR passed first and second pillars reforms (1996–2000).

Reform suffered a major reversal and numerous alterations by subsequent governments. Numbers in parentheses represent the percentage of seats in the 1996 elections. Scale on each axis range from 1 = strongest opposition to 3 = strongest support.

Source of public opinion data is the *Central and Eastern Eurobarometer 8: Public Opinion and the European Union, October–November 1997* and source of election data is *Project on Political Transformation and the Electoral Process in Postcommunist Europe*, http://www.essex.ac.uk/elections/

Figure 4.3 illustrates parties' constituencies during the CDR-PD-UDMR coalition's term in office, during which pension reform was first adopted (1996–2000).[31] The data comes from the *Central and Eastern Eurobarometer 8: Public Opinion and the European Union, October–November 1997*, for which the public opinion survey took

place in 1997 (details about the particular questions asked are provided in Appendix D). According to the spatial distribution depicted
in Figure 4.3, there is only one likely pro-reform coalition, the center-
right coalition of the CDR (Democratic Convention of Romania),
the PD (Democratic Party), and the UDMR (Democratic Alliance
of Hungarians), while all the other parties are natural enemies of
reform. Romania was in a weaker position than both Hungary and
Poland because, as Figure 4.3 shows, the two main political cleavages
reinforce each other, leading to a deep divide between a right cosmopolitan camp and a left nationalist camp. Because of the strength of
the unreformed communist party PDSR/PSD, the pro-reform right
did not gain access to power for the first seven years after the onset of
the transition, explaining the delay of reform in Romania compared
to both Hungary and Poland.

The center-left PSD government under Prime Minister Năstase
(2004–2008) confronted a deepening pension crisis coupled with a
need to coordinate the system of social protection with European
Union policies in preparation for Romania's access to the European
Union in 2007 (Lambru and Chirițoiu 2002). After spending four
years in opposition during the previous term in office, PSD showed a
moderation of its earlier hard-line stance regarding economic and social reforms and rejected an alliance with the nationalists, forming instead a minority government relying on the support of the Hungarian
UDMR, and eventually put forward the laws creating mandatory private pension funds (second pillar) and occupational pensions.

Law 411/2004 on private pension funds[32] passed on 18 October
2004, just a few weeks before the general elections scheduled for
November 2004, by the coalition of the PSD, PUR/PC (Romanian
Humanist Party, renamed the Conservative Party in 2005), and the
UDMR. This highly controversial and long-delayed bill was rushed
through the parliament at remarkable speed. Privatization of the pension system had been in the public debate for nearly a decade as one
of the most contentious topics of postcommunist reforms. Its incon-
spicuous and nearly consensual adoption contrasts profoundly with
its previous notoriety. This piece of legislation generated little parliamentary debate and few amendments were made to the government's
project (most of the amendments took place in the committees). In
the Chamber of Deputies session of 28 September 2004, the final
vote on this important piece of pension reform was almost forgot-
ten and took place just before the meeting was adjourned. Says Valer
Dorneanu, leader of the Chamber: "I am reminded by the staff that I
skipped point #22 on today's agenda, the law regarding the creation

of private pension funds [...]. With 220 votes in favor, 1 vote against, and 19 abstentions this law is adopted."[33] This law was subsequently amended three times in a market-oriented direction by the center-right government in power during the 2004–2008 term.

Law 204/2006 on voluntary pensions[34] established the third pillar of the pension system and was adopted on 26 April 2006 by the center-right coalition of the PNL (National Liberal Party), the PD-L/PD (Democratic Party), the PUR/PC, and the Hungarian UDMR. The opposition parties PSD and PRM (Great Romania Party) also voted for the bill.[35] The law was amended once in 2008 by the same center-right coalition that adopted the bill. This law replaces the previous law on occupational pensions, which proved to be impracticable because the incentive structure provided little benefits to participants and the legislative framework was burdensome to providers (Diaconu 2008).

Main Features of the Romanian Pension Reform

The legislative framework for the public pension system (first pillar) remains Law 19/2000, which in the meantime has suffered numerous alterations. The public system is a PAYG scheme using a point system to calculate the benefits. For each contributor, the number of points is determined by the relative size of the contributor's wage to the average wage. Benefits are calculated at retirement based on the total number of points accumulated throughout the entire work career, as opposed to the previous system, which only included the best five years in the calculation of benefits. Retirement age will increase gradually for both sexes from 62 to 65 for men and from 57 to 60 for women until 2015. To receive a full pension, men need to work 30 years and women 25 years, and those periods will increase by 2015 to 35 and 30 years, respectively. The minimum contributory period to qualify for benefits is 15 years (Holzmann and Guven 2009). The new system more closely ties the contributions with the benefits and attempts to reduce the high redistributive element of the old pension system. Contributions are tax-free, while benefits are taxed. Contributions are collected and administered by the National House of Pensions, which functions under the supervision of the Ministry of Labor, Family and Social Protection. Law 19/2000 has embedded in the public pension system a series of occupational privileges in the form of a more favorable calculation of benefits for certain categories of work under "special conditions," such as mining. The law allows these categories of workers to draw higher benefits relative to their contributions and the other categories of workers, and to benefit from early retirement. The reform of the public pension system has also left in place a series of separate pension systems for special categories of employees that function in parallel with the public pension system, such as those for military personnel, policemen, and lawyers.

Law 411/2004 (modified through Law 23/2007) establishes the legislative framework for the second mandatory private pillar. Contributions for the second pillar began in May 2008. Participation in the second pillar is mandatory for contributors to the public pension system under 35 years of age and voluntary for contributors between 36 and 45 years of age. The second pillar initially started on a small scale, with only 2 percent of the total pension contributions being directed toward the private pillar. This value will increase to 6 percent of the total contribution over a period of eight years. Contributions and investment income are tax-free, while the benefits are taxed.

The number of participants in the second pillar reached close to 5 million in September 2009. At the end of 2009 there were 14 companies administering the private pension funds in Romania. The market is dominated by international companies such as the Dutch ING (market share 32 percent in 2010), the German Allianz (known in Romania under the name Allianz-Țiriac or AZT, market share 25 percent), and the Italian Generali Group (known in Romania under the name ARIPI, market share 10 percent), but some Romanian banks, such as the BCR and the BRD, are also present on a smaller scale. The total value of the assets in the private pension funds was €146 million in 2010 or the equivalent of US$197 million (Ministerul Muncii, Familiei și Protecției Sociale 2009 and 2010).

The third pillar is regulated by the new law on voluntary pensions (Law 204/2006), which replaces the previous law on occupational pensions, and went into effect in July 2007. Under the new law, employees may contribute to a pension fund independent of the decision of employers or unions. Pension funds are administered by pension companies, asset management companies, or insurance companies. Contributions are limited to 15 percent of the gross wage and there is a cap of €200 on the amount that is tax deductible. The benefits are subject to taxation, and the investment income and capital gains of the pension fund are tax deferred. The law sets limits on the investments that the funds can make in different markets within and outside Romania and the European Union. For example, investment in bonds issued by the government of Romania and other European Union countries is capped at 30 percent, investment in bonds issued by countries other than those within the European Union is limited at

10 percent, and investment in private bonds is limited to a maximum of 5 percent (Ministerul Muncii, Familiei şi Protecţiei Sociale 2008).

The law provides a minimum return guarantee: if the return of a given fund falls below the minimum rate of return of all funds for more than a year, the authorization of the fund will be withdrawn. The administrative fees cannot be higher than 5 percent of contributions. Contributors can receive a pension when they reach the age of 60 if they contributed for at least 7.5 years. In the case of the death of a contributor before reaching the retirement age, the value of the contributions in the account is paid to the inheritors (Ministerul Muncii, Familiei şi Protecţiei Sociale 2008).

The Aftermath of the Reform

The Boc government that came into power following the 2008 elections, supported by a cross-spectrum coalition of the PD-L and PSD, has attempted to attack the widespread occupational privileges, some of which are outside of the public pension system, under a series of separate laws for certain categories of public employees, while other privileges have been embedded in the public pension system (first pillar) through Law 19/2000.

The occupational privileges embedded in the public pension system have been one of the most contentious issues since the beginning of the reforms in 2000, with enormous opposition from the miners, trade unions, and the left to any reduction in the benefits. In 2007 the PSD even proposed to increase the benefits for the miners and to once again create a special occupational pension system for miners, but the bill was rejected by the lower house.[36]

To avoid the small pensions in the public pension system, several privileged categories, such as judges, public attorneys, members of the parliament, diplomats, and members of the uniformed forces, have received pensions under a series of separate pension laws adopted by both the center-left government of the PSD and the following center-right government of PNL-PD. The pensions received under these special laws are not calculated based on the point system used in the first pillar, but as a percentage of the wage, and generously amount to 60, 80, and sometimes 100 percent of the previous wage (Moise 2009). It is estimated that around 250,000 people or approximately 5 percent of retired individuals benefit of special pensions (Moise 2009; Noghiu 2009).

Several bills regarding elimination of special pension laws have reached the parliament but they have been rejected. The members of the PD-L-UDMR governing coalition who supported the Boc government have also voted against the bills, despite the stated campaign by the government to eliminate the special pensions. In February 2010 Boc government introduced to the Parliament the bill on a unified system of public pensions,[37] with the goal to improve the financial sustainability of the pension system. The bill proposes to eliminate special pensions, increase retirement age to 63 for women and 65 for men,[38] limit early retirement, and tighten eligibility criteria for invalidity pensions. Under the new bill, workers working in special conditions, such as underground, with radioactive material, and in national security, still benefit from early retirement and higher pensions than the rest of the workers. However, their pensions will be incorporated into the general public system, the benefits will be tied to their lifelong contributions, and the additional benefits that they receive will be covered by their employers and not from the general budget. Mihai Şeitan, the minister of labor, family, and social protection, estimates that the elimination of special pensions will save the state budget around RON300 million a month, which amounts to approximately €840 million a year or the equivalent of US$1 billion a year (Mediafax 2010).

The deep divisions that characterized pension politics in Romania seemed to have been bridged to a large extent, at least with respect to the basic framework of a three pillar pension system. Once the stalemate that prevented the adoption of the private pension funds was overcome by a shift in the position of the main center-left party (the PSD, which has come to accept the need for reform), the three pillar structure has begun to operate, and it is not likely to be fundamentally altered in the future because all the main right and left political parties contributed to its adoption. However, the fact that political life in Romania continues to be plagued by government instability, corruption and political scandals, major ideological shifts in the main political parties, and a disconnect between the political parties and their constituents, it is likely that subsequent alterations of the three pillars will be seen for a while. The one important area that has lagged behind is that of occupational privileges, but given the fierce controversies surrounding it, it is too early to tell how future coalitions will tackle it.

SLOVAKIA: LEFT NATIONALISM AND THE STRUGGLE FOR REFORM

Similar to Romania, Slovakia has also been a late reformer. No major pension reforms were seriously considered in the first decade of postcommunist transition, during which the political landscape was dominated by a coalition of left-nationalist and populist political parties that opposed any major departure from the existing pension system. The electoral defeat of the nationalists put an end to the stalemate. Pension reform in Slovakia was eventually adopted in the early part of the second decade of transition and came into force in the mid-2000s. The overall pattern is characterized by a major lack of consensus between the main left and right political actors for the first 15 years of transition until the reforms were implemented, followed by some degree of acceptance of the reforms by the left since 2006. The persisting disagreements have led to marginal adjustments by the left government in power during the 2006–2010 term, but the basic framework of the pension reform has remained unaltered.

Slovakia, like Poland, Hungary, and Romania, adopted the World Bank three-pillar pension system (World Bank 1994). The reform was completed by a center-right coalition of the SDKU (Slovak Democratic and Christian Union, Slovenská demokratická a kresťanská únia), KDH (Christian Democratic Movement, Kresťanskodemokratické hnutie), ANO (Alliance of a New Citizen, Aliancia Nového Občana), and the SMK (Hungarian Coalition, Strana maďarskej koalície–Magyar Koalíció Pártja) under premier Dzurinda during the 2002–2006 legislative term. The Social Insurance Act (No. 461/2003)[39] is the public pension system reform bill (first pillar), the Old-Age Pension Savings Act (No. 43/2004)[40] establishes mandatory private pension funds (second pillar), and the Supplementary Old-Age Pension Savings Act (No. 650/2004)[41] reforms the voluntary private funds (third pillar). The public pension system and second pillar bills have subsequently been amended by the left government in power during the 2006–2010 term, with the intent of reducing the scope of the private pillar.

Like most other postcommunist countries, Slovakia had confronted a pension crisis since the beginning of the transition. In the early 1990s the demographic structure of Slovakia was comparable to that of its neighbors, with the population aged 60 and over representing about 22 percent of the total population and about 28 percent of the working-age population (Palacios and Pallarès-Mirales 2000). Long-term projections showed that the population aged 60 and over would rise to 62 percent of the working-age population by 2040 (Palacios and Pallarès-Mirales 2000). The system dependency ratio, representing the number of pensioners divided by the number of contributors to the pension system, rose steadily from 40 pensioners for every 100 workers in 1990 to almost 57 pensioners for every 100 workers in the mid-1990s (Palacios and Pallarès-Mirales 2000).

The adverse demographic trends were compounded by the negative effects of economic transition, such as an increase in the unemployment rate from 2.4 percent in 1991 to 15.2 percent in 1995 and an increase in the informality of the labor market, and as a result contributions to the pension system declined while expenditures remained at a constant level, which led to a deficit in the pension system in the late 1990s. The deficit was expected to rise to 3 percent of GDP in the medium term and to 11 percent of GDP in the long term, which was not acceptable given Slovakia's intention to join the European Union (World Bank 2004).

All of Slovakia's post-independence governments had pension reform on their agendas, but like Iliescu in Romania, Mečiar's government was not ready to tackle a politically controversial and unpopular reform. Mečiar's international isolation placed him in a unique position to deflect the pressures from the World Bank and the IMF. Pension reform was eventually adopted in 2003–2004 and has since encountered relatively minor challenges compared to Romania.

The Party System

Similar to Romania and unlike Hungary and Poland, Slovakia's political configuration prevented pension reform from being seriously considered until the end of the 1990s, despite the fact that the country experienced one of the largest pension deficits in the region. The political dominance by Mečiar's Movement for a Democratic Slovakia (Hnutie za demokratické Slovensko, HZDS), which was strongly anti-reform, prevented any serious attempt at reform until 1998. Slovakia bears some resemblance to Romania in that the dominance of a large anti-reform party prevented reform from being considered for most of the first decade of postcommunism, but also some marked differences. In Romania the main opposition came from the unreformed communist party and relied on a leftist discourse, while in Slovakia HZDS is a nationalist-populist party and its nationalist-authoritarian political discourse preempted any meaningful debate on economic and social issues.

Slovakia is a singular case among the four countries examined because of its late formation as an independent state in 1993 when the Czechoslovak federation dissolved. Its "stateness" problem related to its consolidation as an independent state coupled with the difficulties of the economic transition that were common across the region created fertile terrain on which nationalism flourished. HZDS started as a splinter of Public Against Violence, which was the Slovak opposition movement to the communist regime and the counterpart of the Czech Civic Forum. HZDS soon grew into a large nationalist-populist party led by the charismatic Vladimír Mečiar. Mečiar embraced an authoritarian style both within the party and in policy making, which transformed the party into a one-man party (Tudoroiu, Horváth, and Hrušovský 2009). Mečiar's dominance caused much tension within the party and, as a result, many of its members left to form new parties or join existing ones. Mečiar adopted a nationalist-populist and authoritarian discourse that was targeted at the Hungarian minority, which represented about 10 percent of the population, as well as the Czech Republic and the West (Tudoroiu, Horváth, and Hrušovský 2009). His favorite themes were nation building and preserving the Slovak identity, which he claimed was threatened by foreign influences. He intimidated and controlled the media to exclude his critics from the public discourse to create a cult of personality.

> The prime minister became the focus of an aggressive personality cult. State and HZDS-controlled mass media systematically presented him as the "father of the nation." While picturing himself as the savior of the country, Mečiar deliberately polarized Slovak society. Ethnic, class, and urban/rural differences were used to divide the people and weaken the opposition. (Tudoroiu, Horváth, and Hrušovský 2009)

In economic and social policy making he did not have a clear program, evidenced by his declaration that he favored an economic system that was "neither socialist, nor capitalist," and instead he opted for populist and short-term solutions to the economic crisis (Elster, Offe and Preuss 1998). Although the party claimed to support a free market and privatization, in practice it used privatization as a source of patronage, and instead of building market relations it established patron-client exchanges based on political loyalty (Fish 1999; Tudoroiu, Horváth, and Hrušovský 2009). Mečiar's nationalism and authoritarian style had cost Slovakia a significant delay in its integration efforts into the Western structures. Together with Romania, Slovakia was excluded from the first wave of NATO expansion that took place in 1999 and it joined NATO in the second wave of 2004. Slovakia was also initially excluded from the first wave of European Union eastern enlargement, being singled out as the only candidate that did not fulfill the democratic conditions for accession (European Commission 1997; Vachudova 2008). Slovakia eventually joined the European Union in the first wave of 2004 after the country's democratic performance improved following Mečiar's electoral defeat. One of the legacies of Mečiar's era that had long-lasting consequences for Slovakia's political landscape was a shift in political discourse toward nationalist themes and away from economic debates, which preempted the development of the other political parties. The latter could not attack Mečiar's nationalist claims, for fear of being perceived as anti-Slovak, and could not differentiate one from the others on economic issues, which were for the most part absent from the political debate.

One of the parties that suffered the most from Mečiar's rhetoric was the former communist party, which was transformed into the Party of the Democratic Left (Strana demokratickej ľavice, SDL). The more radical communists had left to form the Communist Party of Slovakia (Komunistická strana Slovenska, KSS), which allowed SDL to reform into a social democratic moderate party. However, SDL did not attain the prominent role of its Hungarian and Polish counterparts, because it had little room to maneuver between the HZDS on the one hand and Christian democrats and liberals on the other. SDL decisively parted with its communist past and, at its core, favored a free-market economy, Slovakia's integration into the European Union and NATO, and a moderate welfare state, which under standard politics would have offered a viable center-left alternative. Mečiar's presence, however, created a division between "standard" democratic parties and "non-standard" parties (nationalist-populist and authoritarian). SDL did not find a niche in this political spectrum and switched back and forth between moderate nationalism, a pro-Western attitude, support for a free-market economy, and support for the welfare state (Bugajski 2002; Grzymała-Busse 2002). In the early post-independence period, the popular perception of SDL was that it was the party most likely to lessen the economic burden and to increase pensions and other benefits (Grzymała-Busse 2002). After the 1998 elections that marked Mečiar's marginalization and the advent of democratic politics, SDL joined the center-right coalition under premier Dzurinda. Due to internal splits, the party did not pass the 5 percent threshold in the 2002 and 2006 elections and has almost disappeared from the political scene.

Several small parties of different ideological orientations comprise the center-right of the Slovak party system. The dominant force has been former premier Dzurinda's Slovak Democratic and Christian Union (SDKU), which in the first Dzurinda government created after the 2002 elections was joined by the Christian Democratic Movement (Kresťanskodemokratické hnutie, KDH), the Party of the Hungarian Coalition (Strana maďarskej koalície, SMK or MK), and the Alliance of a New Citizen (ANO). The center-right pole has been characterized by internal fragmentation and extreme volatility. Some of the parties participating in the second Dzurinda government were newly created such as ANO, which was established only few months before the 2002 elections. Other parties that were prominent during the previous terms disappeared or were reduced to insignificance, such as the Democratic Union (Demokratická únia, DU); the Democratic Party (Demokratická strana, DS), which merged into the SDKU; and the populist Party of Civic Understanding (Strana občianskeho porozumenia, SOP), which fell apart. ANO, too, was reduced to insignificance after the 2006 elections when it gained only 1.42 percent of the votes and did not pass the electoral threshold (Statistical Office of the Slovak Republic 2006).

Role of Political Parties and Coalitions in Pension Reform

Reform came first on the agenda of Mečiar's government (1994–1998; Table 4.1). During the electoral campaign of 1994, Mečiar promised fundamental reform to the pension system to address the adverse demographic trends. Once in power, he drastically reconsidered his approach. While still maintaining some of the reformist rhetoric, in practice his administration delayed all major reforms. Mečiar's approach to pension reform was called the "Social Security Transformation Programme of the Slovak Republic" and stressed the need to reform the existing defined benefit system into a defined contribution system and to unify the old-age, disability, and survivor schemes into a single pension system (Bednárik 2004). However, little was done to reform the public system. The 1994 act on the Social Insurance Agency (Act 274/1994) was mainly concerned with issues of implementation and did not alter the benefit calculation or the scope of benefits (Bednárik 2004). Mečiar guaranteed instead to maintain the current retirement age, to allow early retirement for certain categories of workers, and to establish a separate pension scheme for workers in high-risk workplaces (Woleková 1997). The only progress achieved was the establishment in 1996 of a privately managed defined benefit pension system (third pillar) that supplemented on a small scale the public PAYG system (Goliaš 2005:3; Národná banka Slovenska n.d.). Mečiar's government was supported by a coalition of left nationalist parties: the HZDS (Movement for a Democratic Slovakia), the SNS (Slovak National Party, Slovenská národná strana), and the ZRS (Association of Workers of Slovakia, Združenie robotníkov Slovenska). The HZDS-led coalition enjoyed a solid majority of 55.33 percent of the seats in the National Council and faced a weak and fragmented opposition (Project on Political

Transformation and the Electoral Process in Postcommunist Europe 2002). As a result pension reform was not seriously considered until the 1998 elections, which brought into power a center-right coalition of democratic and pro-reform parties.

Figure 4.4 illustrates party constituencies during Mečiar's last term in office (1994–1998).[42] The data comes from the *Central*

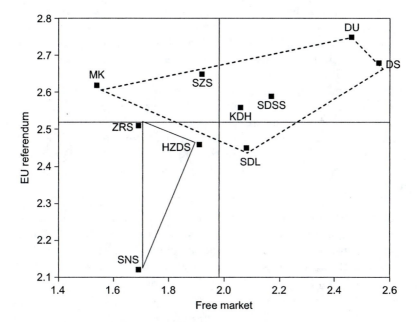

Figure 4.4 Slovakia, 1995. Party constituencies and attitudes toward a free market economy and international institutions

HZDS = Movement for a Democratic Slovakia (40.66%); SV = Common Choice (12%), alliance of SDL (Party of the Democratic Left), SDSS (Slovak Social Democratic Party), and SZS (Green Party of Slovakia) in 1994 elections; KDH = Christian Democratic Movement (11.33%); MK (or SMK) = Party of the Hungarian Coalition (11.33%); DU = Democratic Union (10%); ZRS = Association of Workers of Slovakia (8.67%); SNS = Slovak National Party (6%); DS = Democratic Party (0%).

―――― The coalition of HZDS, ZRS, and SNS avoided pension reform, although reform was on the agenda (1994–1998).

------ All the other parties supported the government of premier Dzurinda, which began the pension reform process during the subsequent term (1998–2002) and completed it during the 2002–2006 term.

Numbers in parentheses represent the percentage of seats won by each party in 1994 elections. Scale on each axis range from 1 = strongest opposition to 3 = strongest support.

Source of public opinion data is the *Central and Eastern Eurobarometer 6: Economic and Political Trends, October-November 1995* and source of election data is *Project on Political Transformation and the Electoral Process in Postcommunist Europe*, http://www.essex.ac.uk/elections/

and Eastern Eurobarometer 6: Economic and Political Trends, October–November 1995 and were gathered in October–November 1995 (details about the particular questions asked are provided in Appendix D). The spatial distribution of party constituencies shows that the coalition supporting the government led by Vladimír Mečiar, formed by the HZDS (Movement for a Democratic Slovakia), the SNS (Slovak National Party), and the ZRS (Association of Workers of Slovakia), was the least likely to attempt a major pension reform because it was based in constituencies that were both left and nationalist. These parties' constituencies were not likely to favor a market solution to the existing problems of the pension system or give up their secure benefits provided by the public PAYG system. The fact that pension reform was promoted by the World Bank and the IMF and involved opening up the Slovak pension market to foreign banks and insurance companies was fueling their fears of change and provided the nationalist parties ammunition to fight any significant departure from the old pension system. Therefore, the lack of any major reform during the HZDS-led coalition comes as no surprise.

The plot in Figure 4.4 also implies that the most likely reformers were the liberal DU (Democratic Union), the DS (Democratic Party), the KDH (Christian Democratic Movement), and the SDSS (Slovak Social Democratic Party, Sociálnodemokratická strana Slovenska), with or without the support of the socialists (Party of the Democratic Left, SDL) and the greens (Green Party of Slovakia, Strana zelených na Slovensku, SZS). The constituencies of these parties were located in a center-right position, thus favoring a market approach to pension provision. They also occupy (with the exception of the SDL) a pro-Western position that is supportive of integrating Slovakia economically and politically within the West. Subsequent developments showed this to be the case.

The spatial distribution of party constituencies reflected in Figure 4.4 also illustrates a high fragmentation and ideological diversity among the pro-democratic parties, which predicted great difficulties in achieving a consensus and low efficiency in policy making. The greater ideological coherence of the nationalist-populists and their strong anti-reform stance raises questions about the prospects for reform sustainability. Chances are good for sustainable reform only if nationalist parties cannot gather a strong enough anti-reform coalition in the medium term until the reform creates new groups of beneficiaries and gathers some measure of public acceptance, thus making it more difficult to overturn.

During the following term under premier Dzurinda (1998–2002), the center-right coalition of the Slovak Democratic Coalition (SDK, Slovenská demokratická koalícia) (comprising the DU, the DS, the KDH, the SZS, and the SDSS), the socialist SDL, the Hungarian SMK, and the new populist SOP (Party of Civic Understanding) began the reform effort. The government of premier Mikuláš Dzurinda was in a relatively weak position, being a very broad coalition of several small parties that were brought together by a desire to put an end to Mečiar's regime rather than by a common ideology. The ideologies of the eight parties forming the coalition ranged from liberal to Christian democrat to social democrat and populist. The government affirmed its pro-market and pro-Western orientation and embarked on an ambitious reform program, which included a radical pension reform. In 1999, the government launched the "Draft Concept of Social Insurance Reform" and opened it to public discussion (Bednárik 2004). Public opinion surveys conducted at the time showed the rather inconsistent views regarding the provision of old-age benefits held by the Slovaks: although people were supportive of a defined contribution pension system that would closely tie contributions and benefits, hoping for higher returns, they did not want to give up the existing system and they opposed raising the retirement age (Bednárik 2004). As luck would have it, the new pension system reflected these contradictions, without fully addressing the demographic problem.

Due to the diversity of views within the coalition, which comprised eight small and ideologically diverse parties, and to the numerous tasks that it had to face, its achievements in social security reform were rather modest. The government completed only a moderate reform of the public PAYG system, put to vote on 29 May 2002 (the New Social Insurance Act), which never came into force (Bednárik 2004). Among the provisions was an increase in the retirement age for women at 60, equalizing it with that for men, and marginal changes in the benefit calculation method. This act, however, represented a stepping stone that facilitated subsequent reforms. Until the September 2002 elections, the government did not have time to put forward the second pillar legislation, which was finalized during the second government of premier Dzurinda.

The new government that emerged after the 2002 elections was also a center-right government headed by premier Dzurinda, although the configuration of parties that supported it had changed. The four-party coalition was somewhat more coherent internally and included two Christian democratic parties, the SDKU (Slovak Democratic and Christian Union) and KDH (Christian Democratic Movement), a new liberal party ANO (Alliance of a New Citizen), and the SMK (Hungarian Coalition) (see Figures 5.8 and 5.9 in chapter 5). The government continued the reform process and on 24 September 2003 the parliament passed[43] the Social Insurance Act (No. 461/2003),[44] which represented a major reform of the public pension system, and on 16 December 2003[45] it passed the Old-Age Pension Savings Act (No. 43/2004)[46] for the establishment of mandatory private funds (second pillar) (International Organisation of Pension Supervisors 2008d). The bills passed with the exclusive support of the governing coalition and were opposed by the HZDS, the KSS (Communist Party of Slovakia), and Direction (Smer). As part of the same package, the Supplementary Old-Age Pension Savings Act (No. 650/2004),[47] which reformed the legislative framework for the voluntary private funds (third pillar), was passed. With the adoption of the three bills, Slovakia caught up with Hungary and Poland in the pension reform process after almost seven years of delay.

Pension reform was very popular in Slovakia and extremely well received by the public. An opinion poll published by the Labour Ministry at the end of 2004 showed that almost 60 percent of the respondents approved of it and believed it to be the most valuable of the reforms introduced in Slovakia, and 53 percent of those interviewed planned to join the second pillar (Slovak Spectator 2004). Pension reform had been accompanied by a 10-month-long advertising campaign by the government, financed by a World Bank €1 million (approximately US$1.25 million) loan.

Main Features of the Slovak 2003–2004 Pension Reform

The new pension system adopted in Slovakia through the reforms of 2003–2004 follows, as do those of Hungary, Poland, and Romania the World Bank blueprint of a three-pillar system. The system is universal and covers all working-age citizens, with the exception of the members of the armed forces, police, Intelligence Service, customs officers, and prison guards, with the expectation that these categories of workers will be incorporated in the general system later in the future (Goliaš 2005: 4; International Social Security Association 2008; Sociálna poisťovňa; World Bank 2004: 12). The first pillar introduced through Social Insurance Act 461/2003 is a public PAYG pension system administered by the state-owned institution the Social Insurance Agency (Sociálna poisťovňa) and is supervised by the Ministry of Labour. It covers all members of the workforce and is financed by a 14 percent contribution by the employer and a 4 percent contribution by the employee. For those who join the second pillar, 5 percent of the employer's contribution and all of the employee's contribution (a total of 9 percent) are directed toward the second pillar. The system has been transformed from a defined benefit system into a point system in order to more closely relate contributions and benefits. The retirement age is 62 for men and will gradually increase to 62 for women until 2023 (Sociálna poisťovňa n.d.).

Retirement age prior to reform was 60 years for men and 53–57 for women, depending on the number of children they had raised. Although other countries in the region, such as Poland, opted for a higher retirement age for men (65), which was also proposed in Slovakia by the ILO (International Labour Organization 2007), the low life expectancy of Slovak males and strong public opposition to increasing the retirement age prompted the government to take a cautious approach in this respect. The reform has also brought under one roof the old-age, invalidity, survivor's, widower's, and orphan's pensions, which are now all part of the first pillar system. Unlike many of its neighbors, Slovakia does not have a minimum pension that is provided from the first pillar (World Bank 2004: 10). Instead, those whose income in old age falls below the subsistence level, which is set by the government to the level of the minimum wage, will receive social assistance benefits financed from the general state budget. Pensions from the first pillar are completely non-taxable, whereas they were taxable in Slovakia before reform, which is a very generous provision that few countries in the postcommunist region, such as Lithuania, have chosen (World Bank 2004: 8).

The second pillar of the pension system established by Old-Age Pension Savings Act 43/2004 is the largest in the region and is financed by a 9 percent contribution, 5 percent of which is paid by the employer and 4 percent by the employee. The Social Insurance Agency continues to collect all contributions, but for those who join the second pillar, half of the overall 18 percent retirement contribution is directed to the pension asset management company (PAMC) of their choice. The second pillar is a mandatory defined contribution (DC) pension system that automatically enrolls all new entrants in the labor market. Workers who were already in the workforce prior to 1 January 2005 when the new system began operating had, for a limited period of time, the option of joining the second pillar (Goliaš 2005: 12; World Bank 2004: 13).

The pension market is dominated by international banks and insurance companies. There are currently six PAMCs operating in Slovakia under the supervision of the National Bank of Slovakia: Allianz (market share[48] 31 percent at the end of 2008), AXA (28 percent), VUB Generali (15 percent), ING (11 percent), AEGON (10 percent), ČSOB (6 percent) (International Organisation of Pension Supervisors 2008d; Národná banka Slovenska 2009: 136; Pénzeš 2007). During the first year and a half after the creation of the second pillar, approximately 1.5 million people had joined the second pillar and the number has remained relatively consistant ever since (ILO 2007; Národná banka Slovenska 2009: 136). In 2009, the total value of the assets in the second pillar was around €2.32 billion (approximately US$3.36 billion) (Slovak Spectator 2009). The PAMCs are required to invest a minimum of 30 percent of the assets in the Slovak economy (World Bank 2004). PAMCs may charge a fee of up to 0.065 percent of monthly assets for every pension fund and an additional 1 percent of monthly contributions for each personal account they administer (International Organisation of Pension Supervisors 2008d). An individual qualifies for the payment of a life annuity from the second pillar if he or she contributes for at least 10 years and reaches the retirement age. The contributions can be inherited only in the case in which the insured dies before converting the lump sum into a life annuity (ILO 2007). The contributions, the pension benefits, and the investment income are all tax-free (Goliaš 2005: 12; International Organisation of Pension Supervisors 2008d).

The third pillar was established during Mečiar's administration in 1996 as a privately managed defined benefit pension system (Goliaš 2005: 3; Národná banka Slovenska n.d.). During the reforms of 2003–2004, the Supplementary Old-Age Pension Savings Act (No. 650/2004) transformed the third pillar into a private, voluntary, fully funded defined contribution (DC) system. The third pillar operates similarly to the second pillar and is open to anyone over the age of 18. Both employers and employees can make contributions to voluntary savings accounts, but the employers have mainly been making these contributions under collective agreements (International Organisation of Pension Supervisors 2008d). To receive a pension, an individual is required to contribute for at least 10 years and to reach the retirement age. The funds are managed by Supplementary Pension Asset Management Companies (SPAMCs), which are licensed and supervised by the National Bank of Slovakia. There are five SPAMCs licensed to operate in the third pillar: ING Tatry-Sympatia (market share[49] 40 percent at the end of 2008), Tatra Banky (market share 28 percent), Stabilita (19 percent), AXA (13 percent), and AEGON (0 percent) (International Organisation of Pension Supervisors 2008d; Národná banka Slovenska 2009: 137; Pénzeš 2007). Unlike the revenues in the second pillar, which are protected against fraud and underperformance of the investments, there are no guarantees on returns in the third pillar. The SPAMCs may charge up to 3 percent of the yearly value of the assets in the fund (International Organisation of Pension Supervisors 2008d). Each individual is allowed to contribute to several SPAMCs, without a contribution limit. The total value of the funds in the third pillar was higher than SKK 25 billion (approximately US$1.25 billion) and the number of participants was close to 850,000 at the end of 2008 (Národná banka Slovenska 2009: 137). Both employee and employer contributions enjoy tax exemptions up to a ceiling (International Organisation of Pension Supervisors 2008d).

The Aftermath of the Reform

The large size of the second pillar (9 percent), which takes away half of the overall employer and employee pension contributions, compounded by the unexpectedly large number of people who joined the second pillar led to a large financial deficit in the public first pillar. The government planned to cover this deficit with revenues from the privatization of large state-owned companies. For example, the sale of the state gas and electricity companies provided around SKK 60 to 70 billion (approximately US$3–$3.5 billion), but that was only enough to cover the short-term deficit (ILO 2007).

The new government of Robert Fico that came in power after the June 2006 elections was supported by a left-nationalist coalition that opposed pension reform and attempted to reverse it, using as a pretext the large deficit in the first pillar and the global economic crisis (Slovak Spectator 2009a). Fico's party, Smer, is a new party on the Slovak political scene and was formed as a splinter from the SDL (Party of the Democratic Left) in 1999. Smer[50] is a left-populist party that has rapidly grown in popularity and has become the major party on the left, overshadowing both the SDL and the former ruling party HZDS. Fico had several options for the formation of the governing coalition following the 2006 parliamentary elections, but he chose the nationalist SNS (Slovak National Party) and Mečiar's HZDS, whose nationalist-authoritarian and populist rule had cost Slovakia years of international isolation. As a result of this alliance, Smer was excluded from the Party of European Socialists (Palata 2009). Fico has relied on a populist discourse, using virulent verbal attacks against the opposition, the media, and the Hungarian minority (Palata 2009). His policies showed attempts at restraining judicial independence and reducing active government involvement in fighting corruption, and led to a rise in tensions with the Hungarian minority due to an aggressive rhetoric, especially by the SNS and its leader Jan Slota (Pridham 2008).

The Fico government asked an ILO mission to come to Bratislava to propose solutions to undo the pension reform of his predecessor, knowing that the ILO takes a more cautious approach to pension privatization than the World Bank. Indeed, the ILO criticized the large size of the second pillar, which creates a large deficit in the first pillar, and suggested instead a series of reforms within the first pillar to address the demographic problem, such as an increase in the retirement age to 65, an increase in the contributions, and a reduction of benefits. For example, the ILO proposed to eliminate the right to work for those who retire early (ILO 2007). The ILO also suggested to reduce the size of the second pillar, allow people who joined the second pillar to return to the public pillar, and introduce a guaranteed minimum pension in both the first and second pillars (ILO 2007). Furthermore, the ILO decried the lack of consultation with the trade unions during the adoption of the 2003–2004 reforms. In particular, the KOZ SR (Trade Unions Confederation of the Slovak Republic, Konfederácia odborových zväzov Slovenskej republiky) was involved in the early stages of pension reform, but was left out later on during the actual adoption of the reform (Svoreňová 2006).

Of the ILO package, the Fico government hand-picked those reforms that were favored by the parties in the governing coalition. As did its predecessor, the government left out the unpopular reforms of the first pillar, which represented the core of the ILO solution. Between the World Bank market solution adopted by the Dzurinda government and the ILO proposal for a comprehensive public pillar reform, the Fico government chose the populist solution of undoing the second pillar without addressing in any other way the demographic problem. On 30 October 2007 the parliament adopted an amendment to the Social Insurance Act that allowed people who had joined the second private pillar to return to the public first pillar. The second pillar was opened up between January and June 2008 and then again between November 2008 and June 2009. During the first opening more than 100,000 people left the second pillar and over 20,000 joined it (Slovak Spectator 2009a). During the second opening, about 65,000 people left the second pillar and about 14,000 entered it, according to the Social Insurance Agency (Slovak Spectator 2009b).

The parliament also adopted an amendment to the Old-Age Pension Savings law on 11 March 2009, which became effective 1 July 2009, that reduced the administration fee of the second pillar from 0.065 percent to 0.025 percent of the monthly value of the assets in the fund and introduced a guarantee in the second pillar so that the individual accounts will not drop below the principal sums that were invested in them (Slovak Spectator 2009a). The National Bank of Slovakia argued that the proposed level of 0.025 percent will not cover the pension fund management companies' administrative costs, but was ignored by the Parliament. For the third pillar, the administrative fee was reduced to 0.165 percent of the monthly value of assets in the contribution fund (Slovak Spectator 2010). These changes produced widespread dissatisfaction among the managers of the private pension fund companies and the opposition parties. They saw the changes as an attempt by the Fico government to attract media attention that will do little to protect the interests of the savers. Economic analysts cautioned against the perverse incentives that these changes created for pension fund managers, who would look for low-risk investments that will generate only low returns. Pension fund managers said they need a longer time horizon to function and that the government interventions have adversely affected their operations by reducing the number of participants, forcing them to choose short-term invest-ments, reducing the services they provided to clients, and reducing the returns on investments (Slovak Spectator 2009b).

The lack of consensus between the major political parties is likely to lead to further changes in the Slovak pension system, such as addi-tional readjustments of the administrative fees. The system is also likely to see in the future a broader reform of the public first pillar in order to complement the private pillars in addressing in a comprehen-sive way the financial pressures arising due to adverse demographic trends. However, the basic structure of the three pillar system will continue to define the pension system, even if its initial adoption was not consensual. Once the second and the third pillars have started to operate, one with 1.5 million people, the other with about 850,000 participants, it will be nearly impossible for any future coalition of parties to eliminate the private pillars and return to an exclusively state-provided alternative. It is also unlikely that a reduction in the size of the second pillar will occur, as the ILO proposed: the left-nationalist Fico government, which came into power in the midst of the global economic crisis and soon after the public system started to accumulate deficits, was in a strong position to reduce the second pillar. The fact that it did not shows the beginning of a minimal con-sensus among the major Slovak parties regarding the need to move away from the old pension system.

PATTERNS OF PENSION REFORM IN CENTRAL AND EASTERN EUROPEAN COUNTRIES

The countries analyzed in this chapter cover a broad range of party systems and coalitions and provide a variety of outcomes. Table 4.1 summarizes the findings and also includes additional information about other Central and Eastern European countries not discussed in this chapter. Hungary had the best prospects for reform of all four countries and it achieved an early comprehensive pension reform. The early transformation of the former communist party into a modern social democratic party placed the social democrats in an influential position with respect to pension reform, which allowed them to pursue fundamental reform without alienating the trade unions and the left constituents that were co-opted in the reform process. At the same time, the existence of a weak left-right divide allowed the formation of a socialist-liberal coalition in which both parties shared a commitment to major pension reform. The Hungarian government was in the strongest position relative to the pro-reform governments of the other three countries. The coalition was internally cohesive with respect to pension reform and enjoyed a large majority of 72 percent of the seats in the legislature, allowing it to pass both first and second pillar reforms in one shot. This very strength, however, caused the government to pursue reform without securing the consent of the opposition, which later put the reform at risk of reversal. The amendments made by the subsequent center-right government were not major and did not fundamentally alter the structure of the new pension system, but they do suggest the dangers that come from a lack of initial consensus about the basic framework of reform.

Poland had good prospects for reform as well, but not as great as Hungary because the persistence of a strong postcommunist/anti-communist cleavage precluded the formation of coalitions based on policy affinities. Therefore, the social democrats in Poland did not have the choice to ally with the liberals with whom they shared many interests, and instead formed a coalition with the anti-reform Polish People's Party (PSL). The price paid for PSL's participation in the coalition was the adoption of only the least controversial part of reform by the socialist-peasant coalition and a limitation of the scope of reform, resulting in the sheltering of the farmers' pension system from reform. The subsequent center-right coalition was in a stronger position and passed the more difficult reform of the public pension system. Because of the strong connections of both left and right parties with the trade unions, the system of pension privileges has been extremely resilient in Poland and has remained largely unaltered. The attempts by subsequent governments to expand existing pension privileges suggest the perils associated with incomplete reforms in this area.

Romania was in the worst situation of the four countries and experienced the most protracted and thorny reform process. The existence of a strong unreformed communist party that relied on the support of nationalists put reform on hold for several years. The chances of a pro-reform coalition coming to power were low in the first years of transition, and when such a coalition finally gained power, it faced numerous other tasks. The pro-reform government was in a weaker position than both its Hungarian and Polish counterparts, being a loose alliance of eight parties that held only 58 percent of the seats in the legislature. Due to its internal weakness, this coalition was able to adopt only a moderate reform of the public pillar and passed the second pillar bill as an emergency ordinance. The cancellation of the emergency ordinance by the subsequent PSD center-left government shows the deep controversies still plaguing Romanian political life at the end of 2000 and the lack of a basic agreement between the left and the right regarding the structure of the pension system. The legislation of the second pillar was eventually adopted consensually under the PSD government, and the law for the third pillar also passed consensually under the subsequent center-right government. As in Poland, pension privileges, which have been defended mainly by the left, have been the most resilient to reform, because all governments irrespective of their political color have avoided dealing decisively with them . Romania's experience shows how a late transformation of the ex-communist party played a key role in blocking major pension reform. It is also suggestive of how a weak and divided right encounters enormous difficulties in advancing its political agenda.

Slovakia is an intermediate case, with a party system configuration closer to that of Romania rather than Hungary or Poland. Its difficulties in adopting reform stem from a combination of factors. On the one hand, like Romania, the dominance by the nationalist HZDS during the early period after independence delayed any attempt at reform. On the other, when the opposition to Mečiar's HZDS finally came to power, it was a loose alliance of many small parties that were unable to effectively pursue reform within their term limit. Slovakia was able to achieve reform during the subsequent term because a new center-right coalition that had a close composition to the first one and under the same premier followed in power and continued the reform process. Similar to Hungary and Romania, where reform (or part of it) was also adopted unilaterally and then reversed by a new government, in Slovakia pension reform was amended by a subsequent coalition. However, the changes in Slovakia were not major, particularly considering the initial large political divide existent in Slovakia between the nationalist left and the cosmopolitan right. The relatively small scope of these changes suggests the stickiness of the policies adopted, who create new constituencies of support.

All four cases made various attempts at reform reversal by subsequent governing coalitions; therefore, it is important to compare conditions for reform sustainability across the four countries. Poland had the best chance for reform to endure because reform was more consensual than in any of the other countries examined, and all four major parties participated at different stages in its elaboration and adoption. The socialist-peasant coalition in power from 2001 to 2005 had little incentive to reverse it because it had contributed to its adoption. In 2005 it intervened to expand pension privileges for the miners, but it left the main framework untouched. The subsequent Law and Justice minority government was more concerned about its own survival than attempting a major reversal and had to call for early elections. The following center-right coalition of Civic Platform and Polish People's Party supported the initial reform on ideological grounds and made some amendments with the intent to follow up and deepen the reforms adopted, such as limiting the scope for early retirement. Overall, pension reform in Poland proved to be sustainable and no major attempts at reversal took place. The only issue that is likely to resurface is that of pension privileges.

At the other extreme is Romania, which experienced a major reversal of the second pillar legislation. The reform process in Romania was also the most difficult and prolonged and experienced the most numerous alterations of the reforms adopted. In recent years we have seen more consensus emerging in Romania as well, with the involvement of the center-left in the reform process and the near consensual passage of the second and third pillar legislations. This suggests that the part of reform concerning the second and third pillars is likely to endure. In contrast, the fact that the first pillar was adopted without the opposition's consensus is likely to generate controversies in the future. An indication of this is the numerous amendments to the public pension system bill. A second contentious issue in Romania, as in Poland, remains the system of special pensions, which have been for a long time excluded from reform and only recently has been considered seriously in the Parliament. Special pensions are likely to keep coming back until the issue is fully addressed.

Hungary falls in between Poland and Romania. The lack of consultation with the opposition made reform less likely to endure in Hungary than in Poland. On the other hand, the main opposition party was a right nationalist party, which ideologically was less averse to reform than the left nationalists in Slovakia and the unreformed left in Romania. Moreover, the costs of reversal are high for such a party, which cannot credibly pose as a defender of the welfare state.

In Slovakia, the chances for reversal were high because a left government supported by the nationalists came to power and the left parties were not consulted and did not agree to the reform. Unexpectedly, the Smer government made marginal alterations to the reform, such as allowing people to leave the second pillar and return to the public pillar, but it left the basic three-pillar structure unchanged. This suggests that Slovakia also has good prospects for sustainability because of the absence of a major party to challenge the new pension system.

How do the theoretical propositions advanced in this chapter square with the evidence brought by the four-country comparison? Although four cases represent a sample too small for rigorous testing, they bring some support or raise questions about the theoretical argument.

Proposition 1. Coalitions dominated by parties that oppose both diffuse and concentrated redistributive consequences of reform will make only marginal changes to the existing pension system.

For the first seven years of transition Romania had a large unreformed communist party and for the first five years Slovakia had a large nationalist party that opposed reform, and these countries had the greatest difficulties in adopting reform. Romania did not adopt any significant reform during the period in which the unreformed communist party was in power. Slovakia adopted reform only after the nationalist party lost its dominance. In contrast, Poland and Hungary did not have any large party opposing reform and accomplished major reforms earlier and easier. The evidence thus strongly supports this proposition.

Proposition 2. Parties that accept both diffuse and concentrated redistributive consequences of reform will support all pro-reform coalitions because any move away from the status quo brings the outcome closer to their ideal.

Liberal parties, which accept both types of reform costs, participated in pro-reform coalitions in all four cases with no exception, therefore bringing strong support to this proposition. It is important to mention, though, that in all four countries liberal parties are small and they always need to build coalitions with either the social democrats or the Christian democrats in order to pass reform.

> *Proposition 3. Parties that accept one type of consequence but not the other do not always significantly benefit from a move away from the status quo. They will support a reform proposal provided that it is closer to their ideal point than the status quo and provided that the costs associated with reform do not exceed the benefits.*

Social democrats eventually supported reform or parts of it in all four countries. Of these cases, social democrats supported reform unconditionally only in Hungary where they are very ideologically close to the liberals. In Poland, after the initial support, they turned against the more controversial parts of reform, hoping to gain popularity. In Slovakia, the social democrats only participated in the first round of very moderate reforms, after which they did not win any more seats in the legislature, and thus it is not clear whether they would support more radical reforms. In Romania, the social democrats (the PSD) supported the second and third pillars, but only after the party suffered an ideological transformation in the sense of parting with its previous hard-line stance.

Christian democrats supported reform in Poland, Slovakia, and Romania, but not in Hungary. In Romania and Slovakia, they supported reform unconditionally, most likely because it was a test of their commitment to democracy, a free market, and integration into international organizations and not because they fully agreed with it. In Poland, where the pro-democratic and pro-Western orientation of the major parties was not questioned, the Christian democrats accepted only part of the reform and forced their liberal partners into a compromise. In Hungary, the Christian democrats were not consulted in the reform process, and when they got their chance they amended the reform without endangering the overall project. The evidence suggests that both social democrats and Christian democrats in the four countries have been generally supportive of the reform, but every now and then they acted opportunistically by either avoiding or turning against the most contentious aspects of reform, bringing support to proposition 3.

> *Proposition 4. The equilibrium outcome of a coalition government formed by two parties lies on the line connecting their ideal points and it is close to the median voter on a single dimension. When multiple parties*

participate in the coalition, the outcome is close to the median voter on both dimensions.

In Hungary, Slovakia, and the public reform in Romania the governing coalitions adopted reform without reaching toward the opposition. The outcome in their cases was a more radical reform closer to their ideal. In Poland, where three main parties crossing the ideological line contributed to the design of the reform, the outcome was more consensual. The private pillars in Romania were also adopted with the involvement of several parties and the outcome was consensual.

Proposition 5. *When a party system contains a large party that opposes both diffuse and concentrated consequences of pension reform, there is a high risk of reform reversal.*

The case of Romania shows that a large party (the unreformed communists) that opposes reform was capable of reversing it. In Hungary and Slovakia a nationalist-conservative party and a left-populist party, respectively, opposed reform, but only altered it marginally. In Poland, no large party opposed it and reform endured. The evidence is mixed and suggests that a large party averse to reform may reverse it, but may not necessarily chose to do so.

Proposition 6. *Sustainability of reform in the medium term is more likely when reform is a consensual solution among multiple parties than when it is adopted by a two-party coalition at its ideal point.*

Of the four cases, Poland adopted the most consensual reform and also has the best chance for long-term sustainability. Romania lacked consensus with the opposition and experienced a major reversal. Hungary and Slovakia also lacked consensus and experienced a setback, but not a major one.

To sum up, the four-case comparison allows the formulation of several general statements about the pension reform in Central and Eastern Europe. First, countries that have a strong party that opposes reform, such as the unreformed communists or nationalists, have the worst chances of accomplishing reform and the highest risk of reversal, as the cases of Romania and Slovakia show. Second, countries that have a viable social democratic alternative, such as Poland and Hungary, are the most likely to accomplish and sustain reform. Third, reform is more likely to endure in countries in which the outcome is more consensual than radical.

Table 4.1 The governing coalition's characteristics and role in pension reform in Central and Eastern Europe, 1992–2010

Country	Left-right position	Favors radical reform	Role in pension reform[a]	Prime minister	Parliamentary support[b]
Bulgaria	Center-right	Yes	Passed all three pillars	Kostov (1997–2001)	ODS (57.08%)
Croatia	Right	Yes	Passed all three pillars	Mateša (1995–2000)	HDZ (59.05%)
Czech Republic	Center-right	No	Passed third pillar and very limited reform of the public pillar	Klaus (1993–1997)	ODS/KDS (38%), KDU-CSL (7.5%), ODA (7%)
	Center-left	No	Debate over second pillar	Zeman (1998–2002)	CSSD (37%)
	Broad	No	Alternative proposals for reform	Paroubek (2005–2006)	CSSD (35%), KDU-CSL (11%), US-DEU (4.5%)
Hungary	Socialist-liberal	Yes	Passed radical pension reform	Horn (1994–1998)	MSzP (54.15%), SzDSz (17.88%)
	Center-right	No	Partly reversed reform at the implementation stage	Orbán (1998–2002)	FIDESz-MPP (38.34%), FKgP (12.43%), MDF (4.4%)
Latvia	Center-right	Yes	Passed the first two readings of the law on public pillar	Gailis (1994–1995)	LC (36%)
	Broad	Yes	Passed the last reading of the law on public pillar and third pillar	Šķēle (1995–1997)	DPS (18%), TB (14%), LC (8%), LNNK (8%), LVP (17%), LZS (8%)
	Broad	Yes	Passed second pillar	Šķēle (1999–2000)	LC (21%), TP (24%), TB/LNNK (17%), JP (8%)
Poland	Center-left	Yes	Passed second and third pillars	Cimoszewicz (1996–1997)	SLD (37.17%), PSL (28.69%)
	Center-right	Yes	Passed public pillar reform but left pension privileges in place	Buzek (1997–2001)	AWS (43.69%), UW (13.04%)
	Center-left	No	Expanded pension privileges	Belka (2004–2005)	SLD-UP (46.95%)
	Center-right	Yes	Reduced pension privileges	Tusk (2007–present)	PO (45.43%), PSL (6.73%)
Romania	Center-left	No	No major piece of legislation Short-term measures to address the crisis	Văcăroiu (1992–1996)	FDSN/PDSR (35.67%), PUNR (9.15%), PRM (4.88%), PSM (3.96%)

Country	Orientation	Reform	Description	Prime Minister (term)	Coalition parties
	Center-right	Yes	Passed public pillar reform Passed second pillar reform as an emergency ordinance	Ciorbea (1996–1998) Vasile (1998–1999)	PNTCD (24.19%), PNL (7.28%), PD (12.53%), UDMR (7.29%), PSDR (2.91%)
	Center-left	No/Yes	Cancelled the emergency ordinance for second pillar reform Later passed second pillar reform	Isărescu (1999–2000) Năstase (2001–2004)	PDSR/PSD (44.93%)
	Center-right	Yes	Modified second pillar law	Tăriceanu (2004–2008)	PNL (19.27%), PD (14.45%), UDMR (6.6%), PUR (5.7%)
	Conservative-socialist	Yes	Passed third pillar reform Proposal to eliminate special pension systems	Boc (2008–2009) Boc (2009–present)	PD-L (34.43%), PSD (32.93%) PD-L (34.43%), UDMR (6.58%)
Slovakia	Left-nationalist	No	Reform on the agenda, but government never intended to adopt it Third pillar reform adopted under pressure from trade unions	Mečiar (1994–1998)	HZDS (40.5%), SNS (6%), ZRS (8.67%)
	Broad	Yes	Moderate reform of public pillar	Dzurinda (1998–2002)	SDK (28%), SDL (15.33%), SMK (10%), SOP (8.67%)
	Center-right	Yes	Passed all three pillars	Dzurinda (2002–2006)	SDKU (18.67%), SMK (13.33%), KDH (10%), ANO (10%)
	Left-nationalist	No	Reduced the scope of second pillar, allowing subscribers to return to public first pillar	Fico (2006–2010)	Smer (33.33%), SNS (13.33%), LS-HZDS (10%)
Slovenia	Center-left	No	Moderate reform of public pillar Second pillar legislation rejected	Drnovšek (1997–2000)	LDS (27.77%), SLS (21.11%), DeSUS (5.55%)
	Center-right	No	No major piece of legislation	Bajuk (May–November 2000)	[SLS+SKD+NSi] (32.22%), SDS (17.77%)
	Center-left	No	No major piece of legislation	Drnovšek (2000–2002)	LDS (37.77%), ZLSD (12.22%), [SLS+SKD] (10%), DeSUS (4.44%)

Continued

Notes: Party names' abbreviations are as follows:

Bulgaria: ODS (Alliance of Democratic Forces)

Croatia: HDZ (Croatian Democratic Union)

Czech Republic: CSSD (Social Democratic Party), KDU-CSL (Christian Democratic Union-People's Party), ODA (Civic Democratic Party/Christian Democratic Party), US-DEU (Union of Freedom—Democratic Union)

Hungary: FIDESz-MPP (Alliance of Young Democrats—Civic Party), FKgP (Independent Smallholders Party), MDF (Hungarian Democratic Forum), MSzP (Hungarian Socialist Party), SzDSz (Free Democrats)

Latvia: DPS (Democratic Party "Saimnieks"), JP (New Party), LC (Latvia's Way), LNNK (National Independence Movement), LVP (Unity Party), LZS (Farmers' Union), TB (Fatherland and Freedom), TP (People's Party)

Poland: AWS (Solidarity Electoral Action), PO (Civic Platform), PSL (Polish People's Party), SLD (Democratic Left Alliance), UP (Labour Union), UW (Freedom Union)

Romania: FDSN/PDSR/PSD (Democratic National Salvation Front/Party of Social Democracy in Romania/Social Democratic Party), PD-L (Democratic Party/Democratic-Liberal Party), PNL (National Liberal Party), PNȚCD (National Peasant Christian Democratic Party), PRM (Great Romania Party), PSDR (Romanian Social Democratic Party), PSM (Socialist Labour Party), PUNR (Party of Romanian National Unity), PUR (Humanist Party of Romania), UDMR (Democratic Alliance of Hungarian in Romania)

Slovakia: ANO (Alliance of a New Citizen), HZDS/LS-HZDS (Movement for a Democratic Slovakia/People's Party—Movement for a Democratic Slovakia), KDH (Christian Democratic Movement), SDK (Slovak Democratic Coalition), SDKU (Democratic and Christian Union), SDL (Party of the Democratic Left), SMK (Party of the Hungarian Coalition), Smer (Direction), SNS (Slovak National Party), SOP (Party of Civic Understanding), ZRS (Association of Workers of Slovakia)

Slovenia: DeSUS (Democratic Party of Pensioners of Slovenia), LDS (Liberal Democracy of Slovenia), NSi (New Slovenia—Christian People's Party), SKD (Christian Democratic Party), SLS (Slovenian People's Party), ZLSD (United List of Social Democrats)

[a] Most pension reform proposals envision three pillars for the new pension system. The first pillar represents the reformed public pay-as-you-go system. The second pillar administers private mandatory savings, while the third pillar comprises voluntary private pension savings.

[b] Numbers in parentheses represent the percentage of seats for a party/coalition supporting the executive.

Source: Main sources for pension legislation are The World Bank, Pensions, available at www.worldbank.org/pensions, accessed 27 December 2009; and International Labour Organization, Pensions, available at http://www.ilo.org/public/english/protection/secsoc/areas/policy/pensions.htm, accessed 27 December 2009.

Main sources of election data are Project on Political Transformation and the Electoral Process in Post-Communist Europe, http://www.essex.ac.uk/elections/, accessed 28 December 2009, and Inter-Parliamentary Union, available at http://www.ipu.org/parline-e/parlinesearch.asp, accessed 7 January 2010.

Reproduced with permission from Europe-Asia Studies. © Copyright 2010 Taylor & Francis.

Tables 4.1 also reveals broader patterns of pension reform across Central and Eastern Europe. It is apparent from the data that pro-reform coalitions are more often center-right or broad spectrum then center-left: there were eight center-right as opposed to four broad spectrum and three center-left. The numbers are reversed for anti-reform coalitions, where three coalitions were center-right as opposed to one broad spectrum and eight center-left. This accounts for the tendency to explain pension reform as being promoted by the right and opposed by the left. However, the exceptions are numerous and warrant a closer examination of the role that political parties and coalitions play in pension reform. An examination of center-left and broad spectrum pro-reform coalitions reveals a socialist-peasant coalition in Poland, a socialist-liberal coalition in Hungary, a center-left and a conservative-socialist coalition in Romania, a broad spectrum coalition with the participation of socialists in Slovakia, and two broad spectrum coalitions with the participation of left parties in Latvia. Not only did the left parties dominate the coalitions in Poland, Hungary, and Romania, but they also had a strong presence in the other cases. There are some remarkable center-right anti-reform coalitions as well, such as those supporting the Klaus government in the Czech Republic, the Orbán government in Hungary, and the Bajuk government in Slovenia. The data in Table 4.1 also show several attempts at reform reversal by subsequent governing coalitions, as illustrated by Romania and Slovakia and, to a lesser extent, Hungary and Poland, suggesting that reform sustainability cannot be taken for granted.

CHAPTER 5

Mapping Parties' Spatial Positions with Roll Call Analyses and Expert Surveys in Poland, Hungary, Romania, and Slovakia

In this chapter, the focus shifts from the identification of general patterns of pension reform in Central and Eastern Europe (CEE) to a more direct test of the relationship between the configuration of the party system and the coalition formation process, on the one hand, and the outcome and sustainability of pension reform on the other. The analysis in this chapter also makes cross-national comparisons. However, unlike chapter 4, whose main goal is to provide a general overview of the pension reform process in Central and Eastern Europe and detailed case study data to inform subsequent chapters, the objective of this chapter is to offer accurate representations of the party system configurations and relate them to specific reform outcomes. Therefore, this chapter provides a more direct test of the hypotheses outlined in chapter 3.

Given that the actual configuration of the party system is not directly observable and that the various ways to estimate it are subject to controversy, I use two alternative ways to delineate it: roll call analyses of voting in legislatures and expert surveys of party positions. The cases covered include Poland, Hungary, Slovakia, and Romania. The roll call analyses of voting in the Polish, Slovak, Romanian, and Hungarian legislatures correspond to the terms under which one or more of the pension bills were adopted. Roll call analyses identify the major divisions of the political space and estimate parties' positions and legislators' ideal points with respect to these divisions. For each country, the results of roll call analyses are compared to party spatial positions obtained by surveying country experts. The cases are analyzed in turn and the chapter concludes with a discussion of the main findings.

DATA AND METHOD

The roll call analysis of voting comes from the rational choice tradition and reflects a strand in rational choice institutionalism preoccupied with the effects of institutions, in this case political parties and legislatures, on policy choice. The focus is on the proximate causes of pension reform outcome, which are represented by the strategic interactions among parties in legislature. This approach provides the micro-foundations for the macro-level phenomena uncovered in the previous chapter by creating links to the individual behavior of legislators (Weingast 1996).

The main goal of this analysis is to provide a spatial representation of political parties and legislators using scaling techniques. Based on individual voting choices over a multitude of issues during a legislative term, the roll call analysis estimates ideal points for each legislator with respect to a few underlying dimensions of the political space. I use W-NOMINATE, a statistical scaling program developed by Poole and Rosenthal (Poole 2005; Poole and Rosenthal 1997), to analyze the roll call data (more details about the method are provided in Appendix B).

For each case, I begin by evaluating the dimensionality of the political space, taking into account the contribution that each additional dimension brings to the total variance explained by the model. I then map legislators' ideal points in a two-dimensional space for the term when the pension bill was debated in the legislature. In order to identify the content of each of the two dimensions, I isolate the roll calls that benefit the most from the addition of a second dimension, based on the differences in the proportionate reduction in error (PRE) between the two-dimensional and the one-dimensional model estimation (Poole and Rosenthal 1997: 48–51). For a particular roll call, the higher the reduction in error brought by the addition of a second dimension, the higher the explanatory power of the second dimension.

I use my own roll call data sets, which I created using the voting records available on the Web sites of the Polish, Slovak, Hungarian, and Romanian parliaments. At the moment, there are few roll call data sets readily available for the Central and Eastern European countries, many of which do not even record roll calls. For Poland, I look at the roll calls from the third term (1997–2001) of the Polish Sejm, during which the reform of the public pension system was adopted. For Slovakia, I examine the roll calls from the first half (2002–2004) of the 2002–2006 term of the National Council of the Slovak Republic, during which the National Council adopted both the reform of the public system and the creation of the second pillar of mandatory private pension funds. For

Hungary, I do a roll call analysis of voting in the Hungarian National Assembly during the 1994–1998 term, when both the first and second pillar reforms passed, and for Romania I analyze the roll calls for the period of 2006–2008 of the 2004–2008 term of the Romanian Chamber of Deputies, during which the third pillar law was adopted and the second pillar law was amended. Prior to 2006 Romania used a secret vote; therefore, there are no roll calls available for the terms when the first and second pillar laws were adopted.

In order to validate the spatial maps obtained with the roll call analysis, I compare them with party spatial positions given by an expert survey. The data come from Benoit and Laver (2006) and were gathered in 2003–2004. Country experts were required to rank party positions on various policy dimensions on a scale of 1 to 20. The policy issues covered and the exact wording of the questions are presented in Appendix C.

Poland: A Roll Call Analysis of Voting in the Sejm (1997–2001)

Poland has accomplished one of the most comprehensive pension reforms within the Central and Eastern European region (see Table 4.1), consisting of both the rationalization of the public PAYG system (first pillar) and the creation of privately funded systems (second and third pillars). Reform in Poland passed in two steps. In the second term of the Polish Sejm (1993–1997), a center-left coalition of the Democratic Left Alliance (SLD) and Polish People's Party (PSL) adopted the bills that established the private pension funds. In the following term (1997–2001), a center-right coalition of Solidarity Electoral Action (AWS) and Freedom Union (UW) passed the reform of the public system. A superficial look might tempt one to say that the case of Poland supports the view according to which the left and right converge in pension politics. However, as the evidence in this chapter will show, the convergence is only fragmentary and the left and right maintain distinct positions. The reason for their apparent convergence is the existence of internal splits within the two major parties, AWS and SLD, and the resulting inconsistent behavior.

The governing SLD launched the pension reform process with the informal support and expertise of specialists from the Freedom Union, then in opposition. PSL, the junior coalition partner, initially opposed the project, but was convinced to support it after the farmers' pension system was sheltered from reform. The parliament passed the least controversial parts of the reform, i.e., the creation of the second and third pillars of the pension system, in the summer of

1997 before the general elections scheduled for September 1997. The bills were adopted almost unanimously with support from both the governing coalition and the opposition. After the elections, a center-right coalition of AWS and UW adopted the public system reform bill against the opposition of SLD and PSL.

Dimensions of Political Space and Legislators' Ideal Points

The Sejm is the lower and more powerful chamber of the Polish bicameral legislature. The upper chamber, the Senate, can only propose amendments to the bills approved by the Sejm, but the lower chamber can turn them down through a majority of votes. The Sejm has 460 legislators and since the introduction of an electronic system of voting in early 1990s, all bills are voted by roll call. I use a representative random sample of 76 final bills of the 621 (approximately 12 percent) passed during the third term of the Sejm (31 October 1997–19 October 2001). The roll call analysis brings evidence for the dimensionality of the political space, legislators' ideal points, party spatial positions, the degree of party discipline, and the coalition formation process.

One can estimate the dimensionality of the political space by analyzing the eigenvalues and the corresponding variation explained by the addition of subsequent dimensions (Poole 2005: 145–147). The pattern of the eigenvalues demonstrates that a substantial gain may be achieved by adding a second dimension to the political space, which increases the correct classification of the legislators by more than 6 percent, a value that is double compared to the threshold suggested by Poole and Rosenthal, and that there is little to be gained from the addition of three or more dimensions (Poole 2005: 145–147; Poole and Rosenthal 1997: 28). The overall pattern, however, suggests rather chaotic voting, in which the total variation explained by the two main dimensions is only 35 percent. This is especially evident when it is compared to the U.S. legislature, in which two dimensions often account for more than 80 percent and sometimes even 90 percent of the variation explained (Poole and Rosenthal 1997: 54).

The plot in Figure 5.1 presents legislators' coordinates in a two-dimensional space. W-NOMINATE constrains legislators situated at the extremes to lie on the unit circle, accounting for the circular shape of the image. The left-right dimension represents the major divide between the governing coalition of AWS and UW and the opposition, represented by the SLD and PSL. The second dimension mainly differentiates the parties within each coalition and the members within each party. Each of these two dimensions collapses multiple policy issues. There are four major groupings, roughly corresponding to the

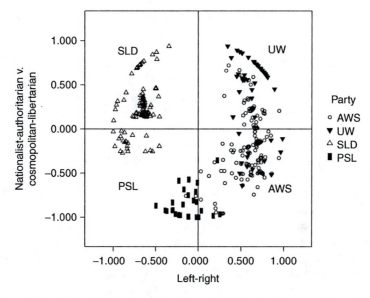

Figure 5.1 Poland, 1997–2001. Legislators' ideal points in a two-dimensional political space (W-NOMINATE coordinates)

AWS=Solidarity Electoral Action (43.69%), SLD=Democratic Left Alliance (35.65%), UW=Freedom Union (13.1%), PSL=Polish People's Party (5.86%). AWS and UW formed the governing coalition, and SLD and PSL were in opposition.

Numbers in parentheses represent the percentage of seats won by each party in 1997 elections.

The estimates of legislators' ideal points produced by W-NOMINATE lie within a circle with the radius of one, which explains the circular shape of the image and the values of the scales shown on the two axes.

Source of election data is *Project on Political Transformation and the Electoral Process in Postcommunist Europe*, http://www.essex.ac.uk/elections/

Reproduced with permission from Europe-Asia Studies. Copyright 2010 Taylor & Francis Group.

four largest parties. The group in the upper right quadrant encompasses most of the UW legislators and about one-third of the AWS legislators. The lower right quadrant is mainly occupied by the AWS legislators and by some UW and independent legislators. Social democrats (SLD) are mainly situated in the upper left quadrant. The fourth group includes PSL and some AWS legislators and is located in the lower left quadrant. The overall image is one of high party cohesion, especially among the social democrats and the Polish People's Party members. There is significant overlap between the AWS and the UW legislators, which could be explained, in part, by the unifying effect of the governing coalition, which acts as a binder. A lower degree of overlap exists between the PSL members and some AWS members.

The main dimension identified corresponds to the division between the government and the opposition and generally reflects the left-right divide, as the plot in Figure 5.1 shows. The comparison of the differences in the proportionate reduction in error between the two-dimensional versus the one-dimensional model estimation suggests that the roll calls that are strongly two dimensional in Poland mainly concern family issues, such as family code and alcoholism prevention. This is consistent with the authoritarian-particularist versus cosmopolitan-libertarian and the religious-authoritarian versus secular-libertarian dimensions identified by Kitschelt (1992) and Kitschelt et al. (1999), respectively. At one pole are the liberal UW, most of the social democrats, and some AWS members. Clustered at the other pole are the PSL members, who share a traditionalist view of family and social life inspired by the Catholic doctrine, and the more conservative members of the AWS.

The two-dimensional spatial map of legislators and parties suggests that voting coalitions during the third term mainly formed according to a left-right logic, with the social democrats presenting the strongest opposition to the governing coalition of the AWS and UW. The junior opposition party, Polish People's Party, had a more ambiguous position with its deputies frequently voting with the coalition government, which explains their spatial closeness, while the SLD is distinctly apart from both the PSL and the governing coalition. This pattern is consistent with the expectation that the persistence of a deep cleavage between the former communists, who were transformed into social democrats, and the former anti-communist Solidarity movement represented by the AWS prevents the formation of voting coalitions that crosscut the regime divide. The smaller PSL, although a former satellite of the communist party, is not identified as strongly with the communist regime as the SLD. The regime divide constrains to a lesser extent its participation in voting coalitions; however, it does prevent PSL from overt participation in governing coalitions with AWS and UW.

Voting on the Public System Pension Bill

Divisions between the AWS and UW on the one hand, as well as those within both the AWS and the opposition SLD, on the other, regarding the proposed bill of the first pillar pension reform were apparent during the parliamentary debates of the bill that was introduced in May 1998. AWS members held all the important government positions relevant to social security reform, including those of the minister who coordinated the social sector reforms, the plenipotentiary for social security reform, and the president of the pension insurance institute ZUS. AWS also wanted to head the Extraordinary Parliamentary Commission, which was created to discuss the public system pension bill (Orenstein 2000). At the same time, UW felt excluded from the decision-making process and insisted on leading the Commission. The controversies ended with a representative of the UW winning the presidency of the Commission, with the support of the UW and the opposition SLD (Orenstein 2000). This episode demonstrates the formation of voting coalitions that crosscut the government-opposition divide.

The votes on the amendments to the public system pension bill, held 26 November 1998, echo these divisions. Many votes on amendments did not align on the left-right divide and instead reflect a variety of voting coalitions that crosscut not only party lines, but also coalition lines. For example, on amendment 173 concerning the obligation of newly created pension fund administrators to inform potential beneficiaries that their benefits could decrease by switching from the public pension scheme to a private pension fund, most of the AWS deputies and the PSL formed a conservative coalition against the liberals in the SLD and the Freedom Union. This is an example of a coalition that cuts across the left-right divide and aligns on the second dimension of the political space.

The final bill[1] on the first pillar pension reform was passed on 26 November 1998 by the governing coalition of AWS and UW, with the opposition of the social democrats and the PSL.[2] The vote was strongly determined by the government versus opposition divide and showed a very high level of party discipline; overall, only four deputies voted against their own party or abstained. This vote was remarkable because of the large number of absentees: more than 30 percent of the 460 Sejm members did not participate in the vote. Given the importance of the bill and the strong party discipline showed by those present, the high absenteeism suggests disagreement with the party line. The pattern of absenteeism points in the same direction. The AWS absentees, for example, in large part belonged to the conservative faction of the AWS who opposed radical pension reform. For instance, among the absentees were Marian Krzaklewski, then chairman of the AWS and leader of the Solidarity trade union; a group of AWS members who in 2001 joined the newly formed conservative Law and Justice party (Prawo i Sprawiedliwość, PiS) and several AWS members who later joined the nationalist League of Polish Families (Liga Polskich Rodzin, LPR). The nearly unanimous vote disguised differences within the AWS that had not been settled.

The final vote also obscured important differences among the legislators that were evident during the parliamentary debates and in the votes on amendments to the bill. Two main factors concurred to generate this voting pattern, despite the existence of divisions within the parties and SLD's role in launching the reform during the previous term. On the one hand, the existence of a deep regime divide in Poland between the postcommunist SLD and PSL on one side and the Solidarity-based AWS and UW on the other precludes not only the formation of governing coalitions across the divide, but also the formation of voting coalitions on controversial bills, such as pension reform, that crosscut the regime line. The restrictions on the formation of voting coalitions are less stringent when it comes to minor votes, such as the votes on amendments, in which differences within each party become apparent and voting coalitions crosscut party and coalition lines.

On the other hand, the unpopularity of the first pillar pension bill, coupled with the fact that the ruling coalition had sufficient votes to pass it, led even the opposition legislators who favored the reform to vote against it. During the previous term, SLD supported the creation of the second and third private pension pillars, which were very popular and did not affect existing benefits under the public PAYG system. When the unpopular public system reform came up for vote, however, SLD turned against it. This shift is consistent with the party's social democratic orientation, which creates the opportunity to attract dissatisfied voters from the AWS-UW coalition. A second reason for the shift might have to do with the dynamics of coalition government. When in government, SLD had to promote its own reform program, while in opposition the party could afford to adopt a more populist stance, given that the AWS-UW coalition had enough votes on its own to pass the bill.

In contrast, PSL's opposition to reform comes as no surprise. The spatial position of the Peasant Party, which is situated both to the left and toward the nationalist-authoritarian pole, makes it a natural enemy of reform. PSL mainly represents rural voters, who are negatively affected by reform. The only reason for PSL to have supported SLD's *Security through Diversity* program during the previous term was that the program protected peasants' separate pension system, KRUS, against reform as a side-payment to PSL (Golinowska 1999). PSL's constituency was therefore secure when the first pillar bill reached the floor during the third term, and PSL had no reasons to support the reform proposed by the AWS-UW coalition.

Expert Evaluations of Party Spatial Positions

For comparison, the plot in Figure 5.2 illustrates party positions provided by an expert survey (Benoit and Laver 2006). The reference

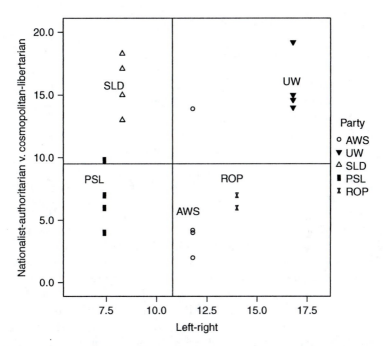

Figure 5.2 Poland, 2003–2004. Party positions according to expert evaluations

SLD-UP=Democratic Left Alliance-Labour Union (46.96%), PSL=Polish People's Party (9.13%), AWS=Solidarity Electoral Action (0%), UW=Freedom Union (0%), ROP=Movement for the Reconstruction of Poland (0%).

SLD-UP and PSL formed the governing coalition; AWS and UW did not win any seats.

Numbers in parentheses represent the percentage of seats won by each party in 2001 elections.

Party scores on nationalist-authoritarian vs. cosmopolitan-libertarian dimension from highest to lowest:

AWS: joining EU; religion; nationalism; social. UW: joining EU; nationalism; religion; social
SLD: joining EU; religion; social; nationalism. PSL: joining EU; religion; social; nationalism
ROP: nationalism; joining EU

Source of expert survey data is Benoit and Laver 2006. Source of election data is *Project on Political Transformation and the Electoral Process in Postcommunist Europe*, http://www.essex. ac.uk/elections/

lines are drawn at the mean of all party positions considered (for a complete list of parties, see Appendix C). The horizontal dimension reflects the traditional left-right economic dimension, in which the left pole promotes maximum state ownership of business and industry and the right pole opposes any state ownership of business and industry. On the vertical axis, the plot presents party positions with respect to four distinct policy questions:

1. **Joining EU**: 1 = opposes; 20 = favors
2. **Nationalism**: 1 = strongly nationalist; 20 = strongly cosmo-politan[3]
3. **Religion**: 1 = promotes Christian principles in politics; 20 = promotes secular principles
4. **Social**: 1 = opposes liberal policies on abortion, homosexuality, and euthanasia; 20 = favors such policies

The overall pattern obtained in Figure 5.2 is strikingly similar to that obtained by roll call analysis (Figure 5.1), and the same four main poles are visible in the corresponding quadrants. The dispersion of party positions on the vertical dimension is relatively similar to the dispersion of legislators' ideal points obtained by the roll call analysis. Party positions on the four policy issues are relatively close for each of the five parties depicted in Figure 5.2, suggesting that the four issue areas can be subsumed under a single dimension that ranges between a nationalist-authoritarian pole and a cosmopolitan-libertarian pole.

Each party occupies the same quadrant as shown by the roll call analysis, and AWS espouses the highest dispersion of all parties, scoring low on religious and social values and high on its attitude toward the European Union. There are, however, some noteworthy differences regarding the relative closeness of parties within each coalition. AWS is closer to the center on the left-right dimension and farther away from UW, which could be explained by the fact that the data for the roll call analysis reflect these parties' positions when AWS and UW formed the governing coalition, while the expert survey took place during the following term when AWS and UW were both in opposition. Similarly, SLD and PSL are closer in the expert survey (undertaken while they governed jointly in coalition) than they were in the roll call analysis (covering a period in which neither was in government). Despite these differences, the overall party positions given by the roll call analysis and the expert survey are very similar, which is reassuring as a check on validity.

The dispersion of parties on the horizontal axis is very similar to their positions provided by the roll call analysis, with some differences. The UW appears as the most right party, while the AWS is just right of center in the expert survey. This largely corresponds to the roll call analysis results, but in the roll call analysis we see that the distance between the legislators of the AWS and UW on the left-right axis is almost negligible. A significant difference appears with respect to the relative positions of the SLD and PSL, which appears switched: the roll call analysis shows the SLD as the most left party, while the PSL occupies a center-left position; in the expert survey the PSL is located to the left of the SLD. These discrepancies are likely due to the fact that the data were collected in different terms, during which the relative positions of the parties shifted due to their participation in the governing coalition or in the opposition. For example, during the 1997–2001 term for which the roll call analysis was performed, the SLD represented the main opposition to the governing coalition of AWS-UW and not the smaller PSL, which could afford to adopt a more centrist position. SLD's opposition is reflected in Figure 5.1 by the large white space separating SLD from the AWS-UW governing coalition. SLD, however, has favored privatization to a larger degree than PSL, which is reflected in the ranking by the country experts.

Summary of Findings

The results of the roll call analysis of voting in the Polish Sejm support the theoretical expectations in a number of ways. First, they show that the strongest opposition to reform comes from the nationalist-conservative pole represented by the Polish People's Party, which has both a left orientation and is strongly connected with privileged occupational groups. However, given the relatively small size of the party and its well-delimited constituency, it could easily be bought off. The exclusion of the highly subsidized farmers' pension system from reform induced PSL to support SLD's reform project during the socialist-peasant government of the second term.

Second, the existence of a strong, modern social democratic left tremendously helped the reform process because SLD was the engine of reform, which it designed with the informal support of the liberal UW. It also ensures good chances for reform sustainability because three of the four main parties—SLD, UW, and AWS—participated at different stages in the reform process, and as a result the outcome of reform was relatively consensual.

Finally, the divisions within the right between a liberal camp represented by the UW and a small faction of AWS on the one hand and a nationalist-conservative camp including most of the AWS members on the other (Figure 5.1) altered the outcome of reform. Although the reform led to a profound restructuring of the public pension system and to privatization, which were supported by both the AWS and UW, it could not shatter occupational privileges, which were defended by the conservatives in the AWS, therefore leading to an incomplete reform.

HUNGARY: A ROLL CALL ANALYSIS OF VOTING IN THE HUNGARIAN NATIONAL ASSEMBLY (1994–1998)

Hungary carried out one of the earliest pension reforms of the cases examined in this study, including both a major restructuring of the public system (first pillar) and the creation of mandatory private pension funds (second pillar). A socialist-liberal coalition of the MSzP (Hungarian Socialist Party) and SzDSz (Alliance of Free Democrats) passed the reform with opposition from the Hungarian Democratic Forum (MDF), Independent Smallholders Party (FKgP), Christian Democratic People's Party (KdNP), and Alliance of Young Democrats (Fidesz). During the following term, a center-right coalition of Fidesz, FKgP, and MDF partially reversed the reform by reducing the scale of the private pillar. As with Poland, Hungary seems to be a case where the left and right converge in pension politics. However, as the evidence in this chapter shows, political space in Hungary is two dimensional and the alleged convergence takes place on one dimension, but not on the other, thus keeping the left and right distinct.

Dimensions of Political Space and Legislators' Ideal Points

The National Assembly is the unique chamber of the Hungarian legislature and has 386 legislators. Since the early 1990s, the Assembly has passed all final bills by roll call. I use a representative random sample of 121 of the 511 roll calls on the final passage of the bills recorded during the 1994–1998 term of the Assembly. The pattern of the eigenvalues shows, as in Poland that the addition of a second dimension increases the overall explanatory power by more than 3 percent, whereas the benefit from adding more than two dimensions is negligible. The voting pattern in Hungary is similar to that of Poland, with a total variation explained less than 40 percent.

The plot in Figure 5.3 illustrates legislators' coordinates in a two-dimensional space. In contrast to Poland, where the main axis separating the government and the opposition corresponds to the left-right divide (horizontal), in Hungary governments form along the vertical dimension of the political space. The coalition government occupies the upper quadrants, while the opposition is situated in the lower quadrants. The party system in Hungary has three main poles. The main social democratic pole occupies the upper left quadrant and corresponds to the Hungarian Socialists (former communist party). The second is a liberal pole located in the upper right quadrant, represented by the Free Democrats, and the third is a nationalist-conservative pole situated in the lower quadrants. This pole is fragmented by several parties, of which the MDF, the KdNP, and the Fidesz are to the right, while the FKgP is to the left. In the upper quadrants there is some degree of overlap between the MSzP and the SzDSz, in part due to the coalition effect. Even more overlap occurs among the opposition parties MDF, KdNP, and the Fidesz, which are hard to distinguish from one another.

Based on the comparison between the one-dimensional and the two-dimensional model estimation, one can isolate the roll calls that

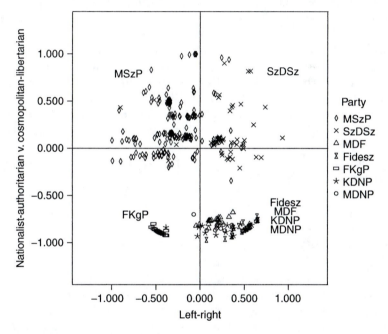

Figure 5.3 Hungary, 1994–1998. Legislators' ideal points in a two-dimensional political space (W-NOMINATE coordinates)

MSzP=Hungarian Socialist Party (54.15%); SzDSz=Alliance of Free Democrats (17.88%); MDF=Hungarian Democratic Forum (9.84%); FKgP=Independent Smallholders Party (6.74%); KdNP=Christian Democratic People's Party (5.7%); Fidesz=Alliance of Young Democrats (5.18%); MDNP=Hungarian Democratic People's Party (formed after the 1994 elections). MSzP and SzDSz formed the governing coalition, while MDF, FKgP, KdNP, Fidesz, and MDNP were in opposition.

Numbers in parentheses represent the percentage of seats won by each party in 1994 elections.

The estimates of legislators' ideal points produced by W-NOMINATE lie within a circle with the radius of one, which explains the circular shape of the image and the values of the scales shown on the two axes.

Source of election data is *Project on Political Transformation and the Electoral Process in Postcommunist Europe*, http://www.essex.ac.uk/elections/

are predominantly one dimensional from those that benefit the most from the addition of a second dimension. This comparison suggests that the main vertical axis separates a nationalist, authoritarian, and traditionalist view of family on one side and a libertarian-cosmopolitan attitude on the other, whereas the secondary horizontal axis reflects left-right distinctions between parties.

This configuration of the Hungarian party system is consistent with previous analyses. For instance, Kitschelt et al. (1999) note that in Hungary economic issues tend to weakly structure party alternatives and politicians and voters associate the meaning of left and right less with economic policy than with socio-cultural issues. According to these authors, all parties gravitate toward centrist economic positions, and the more pronounced divisions among political elites are over questions of national autonomy, traditional moral values, and religion. In the same vein, Cook, Orenstein, and Rueschemeyer (1999) observe that, because center-right parties in Hungary avoided liberal economic policies, the left was under greater pressure to pursue them to stay on the road to Europe. Given such a configuration of the party system, the coalition of socialists and liberals is not as unnatural as it may seem from the perspective of other countries' experiences.

Voting on Pension Bills

The Socialists held a majority during the 1994–1998 term, which alone would have been sufficient to pass the pension bills. In coalition with the liberals, they overpowered the opposition by being more than twice its size. They encountered few obstacles to their reform project and took little interest in bringing the opposition on board. The opposition criticized the reform during the parliamentary debates, accusing the government of importing a radical Chilean-style pension reform that would hurt the population in exchange for doubtful benefits, but its protest had no consequence.

The coalition government passed the reform package, which contained both the reform of the public system and the introduction of mandatory private funds, on 15 July 1997. An overwhelming majority of the governing coalition deputies voted for the package, while the opposition voted against it or abstained. The government's failure to secure a consensus with the opposition backfired during the following term, when the coalition of the Fidesz, the FKgP, and the MDF reduced the projected size of the private pillar from 8 percent to 6 percent of the payroll.

Expert Evaluations of Parties' Spatial Positions

The plot in Figure 5.4 presents for comparison party spatial positions based on the results of an expert survey conducted in 2002 (Benoit and Laver 2006). The survey is based on the opinions of country experts who ranked party positions on various policy issues on a scale of 1 to 20. The reference lines are drawn at the mean of all party positions included in the survey (for a complete list of parties,

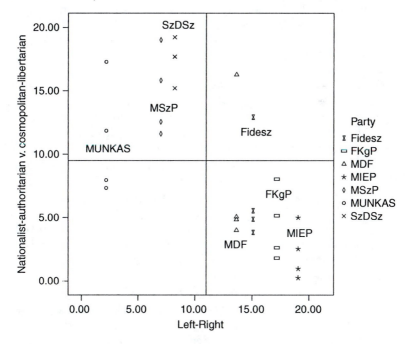

Figure 5.4 Hungary, 2003–2004. Party positions according to expert evaluations

Fidesz=Alliance of Young Democrats (48.7%); MSzP=Hungarian Socialist Party+MDF=Hungarian Democratic Forum (46.11%); SzDSz=Alliance of Free Democrats (5.18%); FKgP=Independent Smallholders Party (0%); MIÉP=Hungarian Justice and Life Party (0%); MUNKÁS=Workers' Party (0%).

Numbers in parentheses represent the percentage of seats in the 2002 elections.

Party scores on nationalist-authoritarian vs. cosmopolitan-libertarian dimension from highest to lowest:

MSzP, Fidesz, and FKgP: joining EU; religion; social; nationalism

SzDSz and MDF: joining EU; social; religion; nationalism

MUNKÁS: religion, nationalism; social; joining EU

MIÉP: religion; joining EU; social; nationalism

Source of expert survey data is Benoit and Laver 2006. Source of election data is *Project on Political Transformation and the Electoral Process in Postcommunist Europe*, http://www.essex. ac.uk/elections/

see Appendix C). The horizontal dimension reflects a general left-right perception of parties' positions. On the vertical dimension, the plot presents party positions with respect to four policy dimensions, cumulated in a single nationalist-authoritarian versus cosmopolitan-libertarian dimension:

1. **Joining EU**: 1 = opposes; 20 = favors
2. **Nationalism**: 1 = strongly nationalist; 20 = strongly cosmopolitan[4]
3. **Religion**: 1 = promotes Christian principles in politics, 20 = promotes secular principles
4. **Social**: 1 = opposes liberal policies on abortion, homosexuality, and euthanasia; 20 = favors such policies

Each party's positions on these four policy issues are relatively close, with the exception of the Fidesz and the MDF, which score high on joining the European Union and low on nationalism, religion, and social dimensions. On the nationalist-authoritarian versus cosmopolitan-libertarian axis (vertical), party positions roughly correspond to those resulting from the roll call analysis. The MSzP is in the upper left quadrant, whereas the MDF and the Fidesz are located in the lower right quadrants. Two parties appear to have shifted position relative to the roll call analysis: the SzDSz occupies the center-left, relatively close to the MSzP, which is probably due to SzDSz participation in a coalition with the socialists, while the FKgP is perceived as a right party, although on the roll call analysis its legislators are positioned on the left. The difference between the perception of a party as being on the left or right and the party's position obtained through roll call analysis is generated, as in the case of Poland, by the ambiguity in the terms "left" and "right." The FKgP is considered to be a right party because of its nationalist and conservative ideology, whereas SzDSz is seen as being on the left due to its long-standing alliance with the socialist party, with which it shared power for 14 years.

Summary of Findings

Hungary presents a useful contrast with Poland because the Hungarian party system is structured more along the nationalist-authoritarian versus cosmopolitan-libertarian axis than along the classic left-right axis. Hungary clearly demonstrates the relevance of the nationalist-conservative pole for pension reform outcome and sustainability. The major obstacle to reform adoption, implementation, and sustainability came from the nationalist-conservatives and not from the social democrats. The latter were the engine of reform, which they orchestrated in conjunction with the liberal SzDSz. This position should come as no surprise, given that the Hungarian Socialists parted with their communist past and have become a modern social democratic party committed to a market economy and to Hungary's integration into the European Union. The Hungarian case also shows the impact that a right divided between a liberal and a conservative camp has on the pension reform process.

Chances for long-term sustainability of pension reform in Hungary have been threatened by the access to power of the nationalist-conservative coalition, which was not consulted on the project and opposed it. However, despite important alterations to the project in its implementation phase, the Fidesz-MDF-FKgP coalition did not reverse the reform, which has already been in place for several years. The chances for long-term sustainability are good because there is no major party that would challenge it.

Romania: A Roll Call Analysis of Voting in the Chamber of Deputies (2006–2008)

Romania has had the most protracted pension reform process of the four cases analyzed. Unlike in any of the other three countries, in Romania reform was adopted in three stages each by a different governing coalition over a period of more than a decade, beginning when reform first appeared on the political agenda in early 1990s. The first pillar passed under a center-right coalition of the CDR, the PD, and the Hungarian UDMR at the end of the 1996–2000 legislative term. The second pillar was initially cancelled by a center-left PSD-led coalition and then was adopted by the same coalition at the end of the 2000–2004 term. The third pillar passed under a new center-right coalition of the PNL, the PD-L, the PC, and the UDMR during the 2004–2008 term.

Pension reform in Romania stands out in several respects. The stalemate of almost a decade, caused by the opposition of the former communist party, was unusually long relative to the other cases analyzed. Then, unexpectedly, the former communist party became involved in the reform process and supported the second and third pillars of reform. Finally, when the center-right came back into power, it amended the first pillar law that was adopted by a previous center-right coalition so many times that the population and the administrators of the system alike became confused. Spatially mapping the relative party positions and examining their evolution over time helps make sense of these rather unusual patterns.

Dimensions of Political Space and Legislators' Ideal Points

The Chamber of Deputies is the lower and more powerful chamber of the Romanian bicameral legislature. The Chamber of Deputies has decisional power regarding all bills with the exception of those pertaining to treaties and other international agreements, in which case the Senate has the power of decision. For bills not concerning international treaties, after a bill is discussed and amended by the Senate the fate of the bill lies with the Chamber of Deputies. The number of deputies and senators varies slightly from one term to another, relative to the country's population. For the 2004–2008 term, the number of deputies was 332, including 18 seats reserved for ethnic minorities, and the number of senators was 137. Until 2006, Romania did not use roll calls. Voting took place either by raising hands or, for some sensitive bills, by a secret vote using white and black balls. The vote by raising hands is still used, mostly for passing amendments, and every now and then even the secret vote with balls is used, but only rarely. Since January 2006 most bills have been voted by roll call. I use a random sample of 105 final bills of the 1793 (approximately 5.85 percent) bills passed during the period 2006–2008 of the 2004–2008 term of the Chamber of Deputies.

The pattern of the eigenvalues suggests a substantial gain from adding a second dimension to the political space, which increases the correct classification of the legislators by more than 5 percent, a value that is considerably higher than the threshold suggested by Poole and Rosenthal (Poole 2005: 145–147; Poole and Rosenthal 1997: 28). The overall pattern of voting is less structured in Romania compared to the other cases analyzed, with a total variation explained by the two main dimensions of only 21 percent, compared to Poland at 35 percent, Hungary at 37 percent, and Slovakia at 62 percent.

The plot in Figure 5.5 presents legislators' positions in a two-dimensional space. The pattern obtained may appear to be unexpected, given Romania's political configurations during the previous terms (Figure 5.7), and resembles that of Hungary more than any of the other three cases examined in this book. The party competition seems structured by the vertical dimension rather than the typical left-right horizontal dimension, which previously has not been the case in Romania. The vertical dimension differentiates between two main groups of parties. The group of parties that had supported the executive for most of the period covered by the analysis—PNL, UDMR, PC, and PSD—are closely clustered together mainly in the upper left quadrant. The two parties that had been in opposition during that time, the PD-L and PRM, occupy the lower quadrants. The

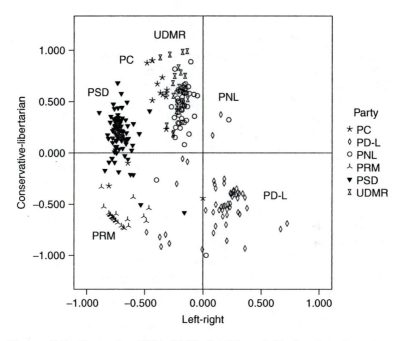

Figure 5.5 Romania, 2006–2008. Legislators' ideal points in a two-dimensional political space (W-NOMINATE coordinates)

PSD=Social Democratic Party (34.03%); PNL=National Liberal Party (19.27%); PD-L=Democratic Liberal Party (14.45%); PRM=Great Romania Party (14.45%); UDMR=Democratic Alliance of Hungarians in Romania (6.62%); PC=Conservative Party (5.72%)

Numbers in parentheses represent the percentage of seats won by each party in 2004 elections.

The estimates of legislators' ideal points produced by W-NOMINATE lie within a circle with the radius of one, which explains the circular shape of the image and the values of the scales shown on the two axes.

Source of election data is *Biroul Electoral Central*, http://www.bec2004.ro/rezultate.htm

left-right horizontal dimension shows divisions within each group. Each of these two dimensions collapses multiple policy issues. One can identify four major groups of legislators corresponding to the four largest parties. The largest and most clearly visible group is represented by the social democrats (PSD) mainly situated in the upper left quadrant, and fewer of them in the lower left quadrant. Another clearly identifiable but smaller group is located in the lower left quadrant and includes the PRM legislators. PD-L also forms a distinct group located predominantly in the lower right quadrant, which is the least compact of all: PD-L legislators spread out, merging into the adjoining groups of PRM to the left and PNL upward. The PNL, UDMR, and the PC occupy a central-left position in the upper left quadrant just to the right of the PSD and overlapping to a large degree. The overall pattern is one of high party cohesion, with the exception of the PD-L. The significant overlap between the PNL, the UDMR, and the PC legislators could be explained by the unifying effect of the governing coalition. To some extent these party positions resemble those found in Hungary, with the important difference that in Hungary the Alliance of Free Democrats, corresponding to the Romanian PNL, was located to the right of center (Figure 5.3).

Less intuitive is the location of the PD-L, which has migrated from the upper right to the lower right quadrant relative to the previous legislative terms (Figure 5.7). Two main explanations may account for this change. On the one hand, over time PD-L has suffered an ideological transformation from being the reformist wing of the ex-communist party to being a center and later center-right party. During the term 1996–2000, PD-L (under its previous name Democratic Party, PD) was a coalition partner of the Democratic Convention of Romania (CDR). After the disintegration of the CDR and the decline of the PNŢCD, the main Christian democratic party, PNL and PD-L remained the main contenders for the votes of the right. In order to differentiate itself from the PNL, PD-L shifted toward a more conservative position on social issues (depicted on the vertical axis in Figures 5.5 and 5.7). PD-L has quit the Socialist International and is currently a member of the European People's Party. The party describes itself as popular and both liberal and Christian democrat. The closeness of some PD-L legislators and the PRM is not accidental. In 2005–2006 a group of 10 PRM legislators defected and joined the PD-L. A big rift has taken place between the PNL and PD-L while in government, which ended with the expulsion of the PD-L ministers from the cabinet in April 2007. PNL and UDMR formed a minority government supported by the PSD. The split between the PNL and the PD-L may account, in part, for the great distance observed between the legislators of the two parties. An examination of the voting patterns shows that the PD-L, after the split, attempted to block any government bill that passed with the support of the PSD and often the PRM. This explains the isolation of the PD-L in the image, while the rest of the parties lie more closely together.

In order to identify the policy issues that correspond to each dimension, one can compare the results of the two-dimensional estimation with that of an estimate constrained to be unidimensional. Comparison of the differences in the proportionate reduction in error between the two-dimensional versus the one-dimensional model estimation suggests that the roll calls that are two dimensional in Romania (in this case corresponding to the horizontal dimension) are mostly left-right divisions between the parties, such as reform of the educational system, fighting corruption, restitution of the properties nationalized during the communist regime, and compensation rights to those persecuted during the communist regime. The roll calls that are strongly unidimensional and correspond in this case to the vertical dimension concern a broad range of issues, such as the reorganization of the government departments and other public institutions and offices, honoring the memory of the martyrs of the 1989 Romanian Revolution, providing compensation to the victims of forced collectivization, and building housing for the victims of natural disasters. Voting on these issues suggests that PRM and PD-L formed a conservative-populist pole in opposition to the libertarian pole represent by the parties supporting the executive. This is consistent with the authoritarian-particularist versus cosmopolitan-libertarian dimensions and the religious-authoritarian versus secular-libertarian dimensions identified by Kitschelt (1992) and Kitschelt et al. (1999), respectively. However, the content as well as the wide range of these issues seem to indicate not only ideological but also personal divisions between the members of the PNL and the PD-L.

The two-dimensional spatial map of legislators and parties suggests that voting coalitions during the second part of the 2004–2008 term formed mainly based on the vertical dimension of the political space, which separates the PNL, the UDMR, the PC, and PSD on one side from the PD-L and the PRM on the other. The horizontal axis is secondary in this case and reflects left-right distinctions between parties: the PSD and the PRM are located to the left, the PNL is at the center, the PC and UDMR are center-left, and the PD-L occupies a right position. This configuration resembles the one in Hungary and was not typical of Romania during the previous terms. The PD-L presents the strongest opposition to the coalition of the PNL, the UDMR, and the PSD. It is evident from this image that the PSD, although not formally a part of the governing coalition, was supportive of it.

Voting on Pension Bills

The three main pension bills were passed by three successive coalitions over a period of six years. The public pension system bill passed on 16 March 1999 with much support from the governing parties and the opposition. The bill, however, suffered modifications in the Senate, was debated in the mediation committee, and reached the Chamber again. The Supreme Court then turned it down for being unconstitutional on the grounds that under the new bill the judges and public prosecutors did not enjoy the same pension benefits as the military and other privileged categories of state employees. The chamber modified the bill accordingly, and the bill eventually left the chamber on 7 March 2000. The passage of this bill shows that, at the time, pension privileges were the most contentious issue of pension politics in Romania, and the bill left them untouched.

The bill on the second mandatory private pillar was eventually adopted on 18 October 2004 by the PSD-led coalition with broad consensus of all political parties. This consensus is in sharp contrast to the previous PSD position toward the bill only four years earlier when the PSD cancelled the emergency ordinance establishing the second pillar. The third pillar was created through Law 204/2006 adopted on 26 April 2006 by the center-right coalition of PNL, PD-L, UDMR, and PC, with broad support by the opposition.

The near consensual adoption of the three bills that define the three pillars of the new pension system profoundly contrasts with the 10-year stalemate preceding the reforms, with the numerous amendments to the bills since they were adopted, and with the ongoing controversies regarding pension privileges, which suggests that the consensus was only superficial and not all the details of the new system have been worked out between the main political parties.

Expert Evaluations of Parties' Spatial Positions

The plot in Figure 5.6 illustrates party positions provided by the expert survey conducted by Benoit and Laver (2006) in 2003–2004. The reference lines are drawn at the mean of parliamentary parties' positions for each dimension (see Appendix C). The horizontal dimension reflects parties' attitudes toward privatization, in which the left promotes maximum state ownership of business and industry and the right opposes any state ownership of business and industry.

On the vertical dimension, the plot presents party positions with respect to four distinct policy questions:

1. **Joining EU**: 1 = opposes; 20 = favors
2. **Nationalism**: 1 = strongly nationalist; 20 = strongly cosmopolitan[5]
3. **Religion**: 1 = promotes Christian principles in politics; 20 = promotes secular principles
4. **Social**: 1 = opposes liberal policies on abortion, homosexuality, and euthanasia; 20 = favors such policies

Positions on these four policy questions have been subsumed under a single dimension that ranges between a nationalist-authoritarian pole and a cosmopolitan-libertarian pole. On the vertical axis, there is a large dispersion of party positions, with all parties scoring highest on their attitude toward the European Union. As expected, center-right parties such as the PNL, the PD, and the ethnic UDMR are clustered in the upper right quadrant, while the nationalist PRM is located in the lower left quadrant. The PSD is divided between the upper and lower left quadrants, having pro–European Union and secular positions but being socially conservative and nationalist. The newer party PUR/

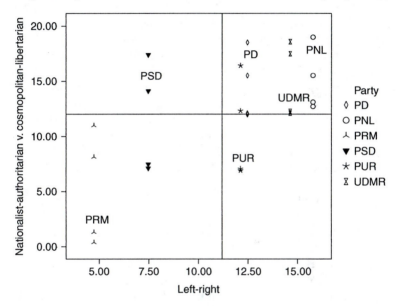

Figure 5.6 Romania, 2003–2004. Party positions according to expert evaluations

PSD=Social Democratic Party+PUR=Humanist Party of Romania (44.93%), PRM=Great Romania Party (24.35%), PD=Democratic Party (8.99%), PNL=National Liberal Party (8.7%), UDMR=Democratic Union of Hungarians in Romania (7.83%).

Numbers in parentheses represent the percentage of seats won by each party/alliance in the 2000 elections.

Party scores on nationalist-authoritarian vs. cosmopolitan-libertarian dimension from highest to lowest:

PD: joining EU; religion; nationalism; social

PNL: joining EU; social; religion; nationalism

PRM: joining EU; religion; social; nationalism

PSD: joining EU; religion; social; nationalism

PUR/PC: joining EU; religion; nationalism, social

UDMR: joining EU; nationalism; social; religion

Source of expert survey data is Benoit and Laver 2006. Source of election data is *Project on Political Transformation and the Electoral Process in Postcommunist Europe*, http://www.essex.ac.uk/elections/

PC (Humanist Party of Romania/Conservative Party) is also similarly split. In fact, the PSD and the PUR, which formed an electoral alliance in the 2000, 2004, and 2008 elections, appear almost identical on the social axis, but differ to a large extent on economic policy, in which the PUR is almost undistinguishable from the center-right PD.

On the horizontal axis, PRM is located most to the left and PSD occupies a center-left position. The rest of the parties are to the right, with PUR/PC and PD to the center-right, followed by UDMR and PNL which are most to the right. To some extent the overall pattern is similar to that obtained with the roll call analysis, with some notable differences. The positions of the PSD, PRM, and PUR/PC are consistent with those obtained by the roll call analysis: PSD is located in the upper left quadrant, PRM in lower left quadrant, and PUR/PC occupies a position close to the center. The major differences are in respect to the center-right parties. PNL and the ethnic UDMR appear more to the left in the roll call analysis than in the expert survey, which could be explained by the coalition effect with the PSD during the period covered by the roll call analysis. The important difference appears with respect to the PD/PD-L, which occupies a central upper position in the expert survey for the period 2003–2004 and appears to have migrated toward a right conservative position according to the roll call analysis during 2006–2008. As discussed above, this shift reflects both an ideological transition for the party between the two time periods covered and a sharp rift with the main coalition partner PNL, causing the PD-L to go into opposition in 2007.

Using different methods for spatially mapping party positions, Figure 5.7 presents the evolution of the Romanian party system over time. Figure 5.7A maps party constituencies during the 1996–2000 term using the data from the *Central and Eastern Eurobarometer 8: Public Opinion and the European Union, October–November 1997* (see Appendix D). Figure 5.7B maps parties' constituencies during the 2000–2004 legislative term. The data come from the *Public Opinion Barometer October 2003*, realized by the Soros Foundation Romania[6] (see Appendix D). Figure 5.7C maps party positions during the 2000–2004 term using the expert survey data by Benoit and Laver discussed above (see Appendix C). Comparison of the three spatial maps shows an important transformation of the party system that took place between 1997 and 2004 in Romania, which is difficult to discern at the level of the electorate alone.

We see that PUNR, one of the nationalist allies of PSD, has disappeared from the political scene. Instead, we note the emergence of a new centrist party, the conservative PUR/PC. To the right,

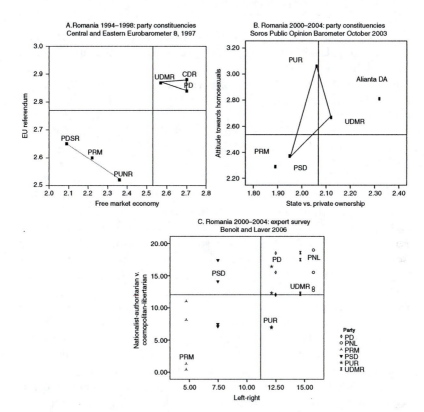

Figure 5.7 Romania, 1994–2004. Comparison of party spatial positions over time

Panel A: CDR=Democratic Convention of Romania (35.57%); PDSR=Romanian Party of Social Democracy (26.53%); PD=Democratic Party (12.53%); UDMR=Democratic Alliance of Hungarians in Romania (7.29%); PRM=Great Romania Party (5.54%); PUNR=Romanian National Unity Party (5.25%). Numbers in parentheses represent the percentage of seats in the 1996 elections. Scale on each axis range from 1=strongest opposition to 3=strongest support.

Panel B: PSD=Social Democratic Party+PUR=Humanist Party of Romania (44.93%); PRM=Great Romania Party (24.35%); Alianța DA=Truth and Justice Alliance (17.69%); UDMR=Democratic Alliance of Hungarians in Romania (7.83%). Numbers in parentheses represent the percentage of seats won by each party/alliance in the 2000 elections. Scale on the horizontal axis ranges from 1=a majority of firms to be in state ownership to 3=a majority of firms to be in private property. Scale on the vertical dimension ranges from 1=total disagreement toward accepting homosexuals in our society to 5=total agreement toward accepting homosexuals.

Panel C: PSD=Social Democratic Party+PUR=Humanist Party of Romania (44.93%); PRM=Great Romania Party (24.35%); PD=Democratic Party (8.99%); PNL=National Liberal Party (8.7%); UDMR=Democratic Alliance of Hungarians in Romania (7.83%). Numbers in parentheses represent the percentage of seats won by each party/alliance in the 2000 elections. Party scores on nationalist-authoritarian vs. cosmopolitan-libertarian dimension from highest to lowest: PD: joining EU; religion; nationalism; social. PNL: joining EU; social; religion; nationalism. PRM: joining EU; religion; social; nationalism. PSD: joining EU; religion; social; nationalism. PUR: joining EU; religion; nationalism; social. UDMR: joining EU; nationalism; social; religion.

Alianţa DA, the alliance of PNL and PD, has replaced the Democratic Convention, CDR. The electorates of PDSR/PSD and ethnic UDMR have remained largely unchanged. However, we observe in Figure 5.7C that in fact PSD has migrated from a strong nationalist, authoritarian, and socially conservative position toward a pro-European position and has become more open toward economic reform.

A confirmation of this shift in PSD's ideology is visible in Figure 5.7B in which we see that, despite the positioning of its constituency in the lower left quadrant and the possibility of forming a more natural alliance with PRM, PSD has chosen instead to form a pre-electoral alliance with the centrist PUR/PC and a governing coalition with PUR/PC and the ethnic UDMR, located in a center-right position in the upper right quadrant. The governing coalition PSD-PUR/PC-UDMR is a cross-spectrum coalition, which opens new policy avenues that were not accessible to the previous PDSR-PRM-PSM-PUNR coalition during the 1992–1996 legislative term.

The change noted in Figure 5.7 is no doubt complex, and no single factor may be solely responsible for it. It has also taken place over a long period and several factors, both domestic and external, are involved with different intensities at various times. Losing the 1996 parliamentary elections as well as the presidency for the first time since the collapse of communism was certainly a critical moment for PDSR/PSD that led the successor communist party to begin to search for a new identity. In the first stage domestic factors, represented by electoral defeat, played the dominant role. The timing coincides with the year in which the European Union committed itself to eastward enlargement, but Romania was not the first group to join. Hence there is no reason to believe that external considerations might have acted as a strong motivator on the PDSR/PSD at the time.

Later, in 2000, PDSR/PSD came back into power at a time when Romania was negotiating accession to the European Union and NATO. In this second stage, external factors helped deepen the transformation that had begun earlier. It is particularly telling that during the 2000–2004 term the PDSR/PSD avoided a coalition with the PRM (Great Romania Party), its previous coalition partner, because in Europe appearing arm in arm with the party of Corneliu Vadim Tudor was not a good idea. Instead, PDSR/PSD allied itself with the Conservative Party and the Hungarians' Party UDMR. The party has also cleaned up its credentials through several mergers with smaller parties, the most significant of which occurred in 2001 with the Social Democratic Party of Romania, PSDR, resulting in the change of name to PSD and the joining of the Socialist International in 2003 and the Party of European Socialists in 2005. The new vision embraced by the party is espoused in the 2002 party document, "Toward Normality—A Modern Social-Democratic Vision for the Future of Romania."[7] According to this document, PDSR/PSD is "a modern social-democratic party, future-oriented [. . .] open toward modernity and social development, a strong promoter of democracy and reform [. . .] mainly economic reform."[8] This was not just a cosmetic alteration; PDSR/PSD pursued the reforms necessary to bring Romania into NATO and the European Union.

After the 2004 elections, PSD found itself for a second time in opposition as a result of the Conservative Party switching sides to join the PNL and PD. In response to the electoral loss, PSD revised its programmatic appeal and made leadership changes.[9] By no coincidence, a generational replacement took place within the top party leadership, most notably the retirement of top party leader Ion Iliescu, who officially left the position to become president of Romania in 2000–2004 and afterward assumed an honorific role in PSD. Other high-ranking leaders retired from the PSD after the party's electoral defeat, such as Oliviu Gherman, former PSD president; Octav Cozmâncă,[10] former executive president; Miron Mitrea,[11] former general secretary, who had been investigated for corruption by the National Anticorruption Division;[12] and Răzvan Theodorescu,[13] former director of Romanian National Television (1990–1992) and former minister of culture in Năstase's cabinet (2000–2004). Mircea Geoană, former Ambassador in the U.S. and former minister of foreign affairs in Năstase's government (2000–2004), became the new president of the party. This third stage of transformation, caused mainly by internal factors, completes the PDSR/PSD transition to social democratization by severing the personnel continuity between the old and the new party. According to Pop-Elecheş (2008), there are three types of continuity between the former communist party and the successor communist party: institutional continuity, personnel continuity, and ideological continuity. PDSR/PSD has already cut the ideological continuity through the 2002 programmatic change. It has been less successful in severing institutional continuity, which it tried to dilute through the many mergers and name changes. Despite the name washing, in the literature it is still considered as the principal inheritor of the former communist party. PSD's contribution to pension reform suggests that the party has also severed its ties with the hard-line past in the policy arena by showing that its new social democratic outlook extends beyond the discourse level.

Summary of Findings

The analysis of party spatial positions using roll call analysis and expert surveys shows a transformation of the Romanian party system, during which the successor communist party has significantly changed its location over time, which explains the protracted and cumbersome process of pension reform in Romania. Pension reform was blocked for a decade because of the existence of a strong unreformed successor communist party. When this party modernized and transformed into a social-democratic party, it changed its location in the party system, moving closer to the center-right parties and supporting reform. In contrast to Hungary and Poland, where the ex-communist party undertook an early and rapid modernization, the late and slow modernization of the Romanian former communist party accounts for the timing and the long duration of the reforms.

Although the chances for reform sustainability were low during the first decade of transition because the unreformed communist party was opposing it, they considerably improved after the transformation of this party into a moderate social democratic party. Currently there is no large anti-reform party in Romania that would challenge the reforms.

SLOVAKIA: A ROLL CALL ANALYSIS OF VOTING IN THE NATIONAL COUNCIL OF THE SLOVAK REPUBLIC (2002–2004)

Like Romania, Slovakia has been a laggard in pension reform among the four countries analyzed. It approached reform several years after Hungary and Poland and hesitated for two terms until it finally took major steps. The delay was mainly due to its recent emergence as an independent state and the major economic, social, and political problems that followed. Nationalist concerns over its relationship with the Czech Republic led to a domination of the political life by Vladimír Mečiar's nationalist-populist Movement for a Democratic Slovakia (HZDS), which embraced a leftist agenda on economic and social issues.

Pension reform began to be seriously debated only after 1998 when a broad alliance of several small pro-democratic and anti-Mečiar parties came together and defeated the HZDS. The first post-Mečiar government of premier Dzurinda brought pension reform to the agenda, but the governing coalition was too heterogeneous and too overwhelmed with long-awaited reforms in other major domains to be able to decisively attack pension reform. Only in Dzurinda's subsequent term did a new coalition begin a major restructuring of the pension system. At the end of 2003 the parliament adopted the New Social Insurance

Law, which represented a major reform of the public pension system, and the law for the establishment of the mandatory private system (second pillar). The bills passed with the support of a center-right coalition of the Slovak Democratic and Christian Union (SDKU), the Christian Democratic Movement (KDH), the Alliance of a New Citizen (ANO), and the Hungarian SMK. The HZDS, the Communist Party of Slovakia (KSS), and Smer opposed the legislation.

Dimensions of Political Space and Legislators' Ideal Points

The unicameral National Council has 150 members. The Council has used roll calls since the first term of premier Dzurinda (1998–2002); however, only the roll calls recorded from 2002 forward are publicly available. The analysis in this study uses a representative random sample of 150 of the 331 roll calls on final bills recorded during the first half of the term (October 2002–October 2004).

The pattern of the eigenvalues suggests that the second dimension is less salient in Slovakia than it is Poland and Romania. Although the contribution of the second dimension to the overall variance explained is much lower compared to the first dimension, it is still considerable according to the criteria laid out by Poole and Rosenthal and increases the correct classification of the legislators by close to 3 percent (1997: 28). As in the case of the other three countries, the addition of more than two dimensions does not substantially increase the total explanatory power. However, unlike them, the overall variance explained is much higher at 62 percent, suggesting much more structured voting along the two main dimensions, compared to the rather chaotic voting in Poland, Hungary, and Romania.

The plot in Figure 5.8 outlines legislators' ideal points in a two-dimensional space. As in the case of Poland, the horizontal dimension separates the governing coalition of SDKU, KDH, ANO, and SMK, from the opposition being represented by the HZDS, KSS, and Smer. The vertical dimension distinguishes parties within each coalition. As in Poland, each party tends to mainly occupy one particular quadrant. However, the configuration of the party system is more fragmented relative to that of Poland, with five distinguishable groups.

Liberal parties, such as ANO and the Hungarian SMK, predominantly occupy the upper right quadrant. Christian democrats, such as SDKU and KDH, are situated close to the center in the right quadrants. HZDS is located in the lower left quadrant, while KSS forms a distinct left pole, which is close to the center on the vertical dimension. Finally, the fifth group in the upper left quadrant includes Smer and the independent faction KNP, representing a splinter of HZDS.

As in Poland, the overall image is one of high party cohesion with few overlaps between the parties. Parties in the governing coalition represent the exception to this pattern, which could be the result of the binding effect of governing together.

As in Poland, the main dimension (horizontal) corresponds to the left-right divide, as the plot in Figure 5.8 shows. The issue areas that generate a second-dimension vote reflect both nationalist and authoritarian concerns and correspond, as in Poland, to Kitschelt's authoritarian-particularist versus cosmopolitan-libertarian dimension. At one pole are the liberals and Smer; at the opposite pole is HZDS. The general voting pattern suggests that coalitions formed mainly based on the left-right divide and that the strongest opposition came from the HZDS, which is the farthest from the governing coalition, and the weakest opposition from the independent faction KNP.

Voting on Pension Bills

The deep divide between the government and the opposition evident in Figure 5.8 was also manifest in the debates over the pension reform. Opposition parties accused the government of undertaking a project that would impoverish the population and lose people's money. The government passed the public system reform bill on 24 September 2003. Although president Rudolf Schuster vetoed the bill on 22 October 2003, the parliament overrode his veto on 30 October 2003. The president argued that the proposed reform would make life harder for old people with low income. The bill passed each time with the support of the governing coalition of SDKU, KDH, ANO, and SMK, and was opposed by the HZDS, KSS, Smer, and KNP, a faction of independents.

For the second passage, a majority of all deputies was required to override the president's veto, i.e., 76 of 150. Although the government had lost its majority through defections from premier Dzurinda's SDKU, the required majority was achieved with all 75 of the governing coalition deputies being present and voting in favor of the bill and three additional in-favor votes being cast by independents. No opposition deputies voted in favor of the bill at either passage. The adoption of the bill was aided each time by the massive absence of the independents' faction and the opposition HZDS deputies. The very sharp divide between government and opposition suggests how controversial and unpopular the bill was.

The bill that established the mandatory private funds (second pillar of the new pension system) passed soon thereafter on 16 December

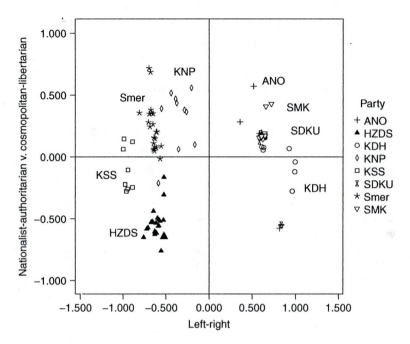

Figure 5.8 Slovakia, 2002–2004. Legislators' ideal points in a two-dimensional political space (W-NOMINATE coordinates)

HZDS=Movement for a Democratic Slovakia (24%); SDKU=Slovak Democratic and Christian Union (18.67%); Smer=Direction (16.67%); SMK=Party of the Hungarian Coalition (13.33%); KDH=Christian Democratic Movement (10%); ANO=Alliance of a New Citizen (10%); KSS=Communist Party of Slovakia (7.33%); KNP=independents' faction (formed after the 2002 elections mostly by defections from HZDS). SDKU, SMK, KDH, and ANO formed the governing coalition, while HZDS, Smer, and KSS were in opposition.

Numbers in parentheses represent the percentage of seats won by each party in 2002 elections.

The estimates of legislators' ideal points produced by W-NOMINATE lie within a circle with the radius of one, which explains the circular shape of the image and the values of the scales shown on the two axes.

Source of election data is *Project on Political Transformation and the Electoral Process in Postcommunist Europe*, http://www.essex.ac.uk/elections/

2003. Overall, the voting pattern resembles the votes on public system reform, showing a clear demarcation between the government and the opposition. The vote on the second pillar was characterized by an even larger number of abstentions and absentees among opposition deputies (all HZDS and Smer deputies and most of the KSS and KNP deputies were either absent or abstained from voting), which suggests that privatization was less controversial than the reform of the public system, which most opposition deputies voted against. The second vote on mandatory private funds, which overrode the presidential veto, took place on 20 January 2004 and showed a relatively similar pattern, with the main difference that there were few absentees among the opposition deputies, and those present were about equally split between "no" votes and abstentions.

Expert Evaluations of Parties' Spatial Positions

The plot in Figure 5.9 shows party positions with respect to various policy dimensions based on an expert survey of country experts (Benoit and Laver 2006). The reference lines are drawn at the mean of all party positions included in the survey (for a complete list of parties, see Appendix C). The horizontal dimension reflects the left-right dimension, in which the left pole promotes maximum state ownership of business and industry and the right pole opposes any state ownership of business and industry. On the vertical axis, the plot presents party positions with respect to four distinct policy questions:

1. **Joining EU**: 1 = opposes; 20 = favors
2. **Nationalism**: 1 = strongly nationalist; 20 = strongly cosmopolitan[14]
3. **Religion**: 1 = promotes Christian principles in politics; 20 = promotes secular principles
4. **Social**: 1 = opposes liberal policies on abortion, homosexuality, and euthanasia; 20 = favors such policies

In general, parties occupy positions similar to those obtained through the roll call analysis. ANO is at the core of the liberal pole in the upper right quadrant, while KDH and SDKU form a Christian democratic pole in the lower right quadrant. The Hungarian SMK is split between nationalist issues on the one hand, on which it embraces a pro–European Union and cosmopolitan outlook, and social and religious issues on the other, in which it is close to the traditionalists KDH and SDKU. Smer is located in the upper left quadrant, with the exception of a strong nationalism, on which it scores close to HZDS.

KSS forms a distinctly left pole situated toward the center of the nationalist-authoritarian versus cosmopolitan-libertarian dimension. It scores higher on social and religious issues, on which it adopts a libertarian attitude, and lower on nationalism, being anti–European

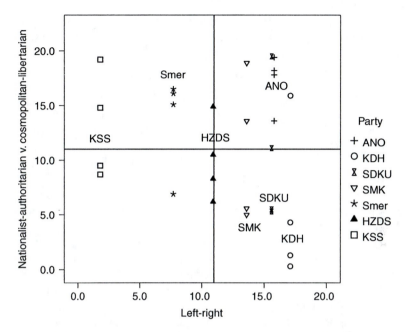

Figure 5.9 Slovakia, 2002–2004. Party positions according to expert evaluations

HZDS=Movement for a Democratic Slovakia (24%); SDKU=Slovak Democratic and Christian Union (18.67%); Smer=Direction (16.67%); SMK=Party of the Hungarian Coalition (13.33%); KDH=Christian Democratic Movement (10%); ANO=Alliance of a New Citizen (10%); KSS=Communist Party of Slovakia (7.33%); KNP=independents' faction (formed after the 2002 elections mostly by defections from HZDS). SDKU, SMK, KDH, and ANO formed the governing coalition, while HZDS, Smer, and KSS were in opposition.

Numbers in parentheses represent the percentage of seats won by each party in 2002 elections.

Party scores on nationalist-authoritarian vs. cosmopolitan-libertarian dimension from highest to lowest:

ANO and HZDS: joining EU; social; religion; nationalism

KDH and SMK: joining EU; nationalism; religion; social

SDKU: joining EU; nationalism; social; religion

Smer: religion, joining EU; social; nationalism

KSS: religion; social; joining EU; nationalism

Source of expert survey data is Benoit and Laver 2006. Source of election data is *Project on Political Transformation and the Electoral Process in Postcommunist Europe*, http://www.essex. ac.uk/elections/

Union and nationalist. Of all parties, HZDS's position differs the most from that of the roll call analysis. The expert survey shows HZDS being situated at the center and distinct from both the right and the left parties, while the roll call analysis places it clearly to the left. On the vertical dimension, HZDS is nationalist and socially conservative but supports joining the EU.

Summary of Findings

The evidence from Slovakia supports several of the theoretical propositions developed in this study. First, it shows that the existence of a strong nationalist-populist party, Mečiar's HZDS, hindered reform for as long as the party was in power. This party embraced left policies while in government and also developed into a clientelistic party; therefore, both its ideological orientation and its connections with privileged groups concurred to produce its anti-reform stance. Second, the lack of a powerful modern social democratic left posed a challenge to the process of reform, which was adopted with a very narrow margin, and threatened its long-term sustainability. Smer, which claimed to be playing this role, adopted a nationalist-populist rhetoric and to a large extent is a one-man party, which precluded it from offering a viable center-left alternative. Finally, the fragmentation of the right among several relatively small parties delayed the reform until the second term of a center-right coalition under premier Dzurinda, and therefore risked the fate of the reform in a party system in which the right has tremendous difficulties in gathering and maintaining a majority.

The structure of the party system predicts moderate chances for reform sustainability in Slovakia because of the risk of reversal by a subsequent left-nationalist coalition. However, given that the coalition of Smer, HZDS, and SNS did not accomplish a major reversal of reform during the 2006–2010 term, but only a reduction in the scope of the second pillar, further chances for sustainability have considerably improved.

DISCUSSION

This chapter presented two alternative ways of mapping party spatial positions: roll call analyses of voting in legislatures and surveys of country experts. The two estimating procedures produced reasonably consistent results, which suggests that both offer accurate estimates of party spatial positions. However, rather than substituting for each other, to a large extent the two methods are complementary. Roll call analyses make available a finer level of analysis by estimating legislators' ideal points, and they prove extremely useful when party discipline is low and when there are splits within the parties. They also make a multi-dimensional political space more manageable by collapsing the multitude of policy issues into a few underlying dimensions. They are less precise, however, about the substantive significance of each dimension and require additional knowledge about the main political divisions and parties' positions, such as that offered by expert opinions or in-depth knowledge of the cases.

The expert survey, on the other hand, provides good estimates of party positions on as many dimensions as the investigator considers useful, at the same time making it more difficult to work with a multidimensional space. A second drawback of the expert survey comes from different understandings of terms such as left and right, which sometimes leads to inconsistency in results produced by alternative questions. The need to use the two methods in conjunction is even greater in the Central and Eastern European context, in which many countries do not record roll call data and expert surveys do not cover all countries and time periods.

The results obtained through alternative estimation means provide support to the theoretical argument developed in this study, which unambiguously shows that the configuration of the party system and the coalition formation process shape pension reform outcome and its long-term sustainability in decisive and identifiable ways. This chapter provides evidence that pension politics cannot be reduced to a single left-right dimension and that a two-dimensional estimation of party configuration is necessary. It also shows the complex role in pension reform played by the major poles of the party system—left, right, and nationalist—as well as the critical influence of their internal divisions and the alliances between them.

A central finding of this chapter is that two dimensions of the political space are relevant for the process of pension reform. The four cases discussed in this chapter showed the importance of the nationalist-conservative pole of the party system, in addition to the left and right poles. The nationalists hold a distinct position regarding pension reform, which has influenced the outcome of pension reform in all four countries, irrespective of their party system configurations. For instance, in three of the four cases, Hungary, Romania, and Slovakia, the nationalist-conservatives presented the strongest opposition to reform and they also have threatened reform sustainability. Although the nationalists are less powerful in Poland, they managed to limit the scope of reform.

The evidence discussed in this chapter also showed the essential role that the left plays in pension reform. In three of the four cases the social-democratic left was instrumental in passing the major pension reform legislation. In Poland and Hungary, the ex-communist party transformed early into a viable social democratic alternative that is committed to a market economy and European integration; these parties forged coalitions with the pro-reform liberals and became the architects of pension reform. In Romania, reform was blocked for more than a decade by the unreformed ex-communist party; when this party modernized, it became the promoter of reform. In contrast, Slovakia lacked such a center-left alternative, which delayed the reform process for several years.

The strenght of the right was also important for the fate of reform in all cases. They all started with a weak and fragmented right that had difficulties advancing its political agenda. Slovakia presented the highest fragmentation of all four cases, with a right coalition composed of numerous small and ideological diverse parties. Romania is an intermediate case, in which the right started fragmented and later consolidated in two stronger parties. Poland and Hungary, on the other hand, despite overcoming relatively early the initial fragmentation, present a right that is split between a liberal and a conservative camp. The divisions within the right raised important difficulties either in adopting pension reform or created opposition that led to limitatios or reversals of the reforms adopted. In Hungary, the conservatives reduced the size of the private pillar, while in Poland they contributed to maintaining previous occupational privileges.

The four cases examined present a variety of coalition formation processes that determined the fate of reform. Pro-reform coalitions did not necessarily follow a left-right logic. Hungary provides a noteworthy example of a pro-reform coalition structured by a value dimension rather than the classic economic dimension. Slovakia is at the other extreme with pro-reform coalitions that are strictly formed along the left-right divide. Poland falls in between, offering an example of a center-left, a center-right, and a socialist-liberal pro-reform coalition that participated at different stages in the reform process, each leaving a distinct mark on the outcome. Coalitions in Romania resemble those in Poland: a center-right, a center-left, and again a center-right coalition participated successively in pension reform.

The evidence presented in this chapter also shows the impact of the outcome of reform on its long-term sustainability. Hungary and Slovakia, where reform was designed and adopted without consultation with the opposition, experienced a partial reversal. A similar fate was suffered by the initial second pillar reform in Romania, which was adopted against the oppositions' will and was completely reversed. In contrast, in Poland, which adopted a more limited and more consensual reform, all major parties accepted the outcome and the reform has endured without major changes.

Ideology, Interest Group Politics, and Pension Reform

In this chapter, I provide a different kind of empirical test to the theoretical argument regarding the role of the party system and the coalition formation in the outcome and sustainability of pension reform. In chapters 4 and 5, I tested the argument in comparative cross-national analyses and showed that the variation in the configuration of the party system adequately explains the variation in pension reform outcomes. Chapter 6 shifts the analysis to a lower level of aggregation and looks within a single case, Poland, at the mechanism underlying the pattern that we observe at the aggregate level. It directly tests the hypothesized relationship between parties' ideological orientations and their connections with privileged groups, on the one hand, and the outcome of pension reform, on the other, by examining in detail the legislative process surrounding the passage of the public system pension reform bill.

Empirical evidence comes from a roll call analysis of voting in the Polish Sejm, but this time I focus on amendments to the pension bill rather than on final bills, as I did in the previous chapter. The roll call analysis in chapter 5 estimated the overall political space during the third term of the Sejm, whereas the analysis in this chapter delineates the "pension political space," i.e., it identifies the main lines of conflict among parties and legislators regarding the specific provisions of the public system pension bill and shows the formation of pro-reform and anti-reform coalitions on individual pension issues. It thus provides direct evidence that ideological differences and connections with privileged groups are the two major divisions regarding pension reform.

Poland represents an interesting case for at least two important reasons. First, pension reform in Poland passed in two steps under two different coalition governments, which allows for comparison of the impact of various coalitions on the outcome of reform within the same setting, the equivalent of a "most similar systems" design. Second, Polish pension reform raises a number of puzzles that are not well accounted for by existing theories. This section thus serves a twofold purpose: it provides empirical evidence to test the argument of this paper and it sheds light on Polish pension reform using the theoretical framework developed above. In the next section, I outline the role that the major parties and the center-left and center-right coalitions played in the reform process in Poland and highlight the puzzles that the Polish case raises. I then present the results of the roll call analysis on pension bill amendments and show how they explain these puzzles. Finally, I compare the results with those obtained from the previous analysis of final bills performed in chapter 5 and conclude the chapter with a summary of the findings.

LEFT, RIGHT, AND PENSION REFORM IN POLAND

As chapters 4 and 5 emphasized, Poland is a case in which different coalitions participated at various stages of the reform process, which challenges the conventional view about the role of the left and the right in pension reform. The main promoter of pension reform in Poland was the ex-communist Democratic Left Alliance (SLD). An informal coalition of the SLD with the liberal Freedom Union (UW) devised the reform proposal, which passed in two steps. The center-left governing coalition of the SLD and Polish People's Party (PSL) adopted the first and more popular part of reform, consisting of the creation of private pension funds (second and third pillars of the new pension system), which also received the legislative support of the opposition. During the following term, the center-right coalition of the AWS and UW passed the more controversial reform of the public pension system, which the SLD and PSL opposed.

Pension reform in Poland raises several puzzles that existing theoretical approaches cannot adequately explain. First, why was the SLD, a transformed communist party, the driving force of pension reform? Second, why was reform designed by a coalition of SLD with the liberal UW, which crosscut the left-right divide and coalition lines, and not by the governing coalition of the SLD and PSL? Third, why did the SLD, when in opposition during the 1997–2001 term, turned against the reform? And finally, why did the AWS almost unanimously passed the controversial public system reform, despite the presence of a strong trade union component within its ranks?

Voting on Pension Reform in Poland: Results of Roll Call Analysis

In order to address these questions, I examine in detail the legis-lative process in the Sejm (the lower and more powerful chamber of the Polish bicameral legislature) surrounding the passage of the controversial public pension system bill during the third term (1997–2001). I use the 92 roll calls on amendments to the bill,[1] voted on 26 November 1998. The idea of scaling a subset of roll calls concerning a particular issue area is not new and has been used in the literature (e.g., Bailey 2001), and it serves two main goals: first, to identify the basic dimensions underlying voting on the pension bill, and second, to position parties with respect to these basic dimensions.

The variance in voting on amendments to the public pension bill explained by the addition of subsequent dimensions, using the criteria laid out by Poole and Rosenthal (Poole 2005: 145–146; Poole and Rosenthal 1997: 28), suggests the presence of two main dimensions of the political space, as hypothesized, which together explain over 76 percent of the total variation. There is little more to be gained from the addition of three or more dimensions. In fact, after the third dimension the explanatory power of each subsequent dimension drops to a level close to zero. The first dimension has, as expected, the highest explanatory power because it tends to echo the main division between the AWS-UW government and the SLD-PSL opposition, being a marker of the degree of party discipline and the divisive-ness of the issues. The explanatory power of the second dimension is predictably lower, especially in high-profile issues such as pension reform, because it mainly mirrors disagreements within each coali-tion. Nonetheless, the second dimension increases the correct classifi-cation of the legislators by more than 8 percent, a value that is almost three times higher compared to the threshold suggested by Poole and Rosenthal, and therefore it makes a considerable contribution the total variation explained (Poole and Rosenthal 1997: 28). The plot in Figure 6.1A presents legislators' ideal points with respect to the two main dimensions identified, each of which collapses multiple policy issues related to the public pension system bill. The spread of the leg-islators' ideal points on the second dimension (vertical) is almost as large as that on the first one (horizontal), providing further support to the divisiveness of the second dimension issues. In order to identify which pension issues correspond to each dimension, I compared the results of the two-dimensional model depicted in Figure 6.1A with those of a similar model constrained to be one dimensional. One can isolate the roll calls that benefit the most from the addition of a second dimension based on the differences in the proportionate reduction in error (PRE) between the two-dimensional versus the one-dimensional estimation (Poole and Rosenthal 1997: 48–51). For a particular set of votes, the higher the reduction in error brought by the addition of a second dimension, the higher the explanatory power of the second dimension.

The results suggest that the issue areas that are mainly one dimensional concern, among others:

- The maximum value of the contribution base, representing a ceiling on the reference wage used in the calculation of benefits. SLD and PSL wanted a higher contribution base compared to AWS and UW (roll call 115, rejected).
- The calculation of benefits for workers with short or interrupted contributory periods (less than 10 years). SLD and PSL proposed a more favorable calculation for these categories, while AWS and UW opposed (roll calls 116 and 117, rejected).
- Benefit indexation. SLD and PSL proposed increasing pension annuities with a quota corresponding to economic growth, while AWS and UW opposed (roll call 131, rejected).
- Inclusion in the calculation of benefits of certain non-contributory periods. AWS and UW were in favor, SLD was against, and PSL was split (roll call 111, accepted).
- Social assistance to persons who have children in their care. SLD and PSL favored maintaining the existing system of benefits, while AWS and UW voted for its replacement with a system of social annuities (roll call 149, accepted).

Among the issue areas that are strongly two dimensional, one can find the following:

- For members of trade unions that functioned illegally under the communist regime, such as Solidarity, recognition of the years of illegality as part of the contributory period used in the calculation of pension benefits. SLD was split on this vote, while most others favored it (roll call 112, accepted).
- The right of certain occupational categories, such as military and civil servants who have separate pension schemes, to receive pensions from the public system if they do not fulfill the conditions for pension under their special scheme, even in the absence of any contribution. A majority of SLD deputies favored it, while the other parties opposed it (roll call 108, rejected).

- Maintaining special pension indexation provisions for military, police, intelligence, border guards, firemen, prison guards, and their families. SLD favored a generous pension indexation, which would keep pace with wage indexation for the corresponding active categories, while the other parties opposed and opted instead for applying the general indexation rules to these categories (roll call 151, rejected).
- Entitlement to early retirement for certain categories of workers who work in particular conditions, such as miners, railroad employees, uniformed forces, and teachers, even if they did not fulfill the minimum required contributory period of 20 years for women and 25 for men. A majority in each party opposed (roll call 189, rejected).
- More favorable calculation of benefits for workers in the above-mentioned categories who are allowed to retire early. SLD and PSL were in favor, AWS and UW opposed (roll call 192, rejected).
- Allowing financial independence to the office supervising the pension funds by permitting it to generate its own revenues and increasing the fees that would finance the office. AWS and PSL favored it, while SLD and UW were split (roll calls 172 and 173, accepted).

These issues provide evidence that the first dimension (horizontal) mainly reflects the controversy over the diffuse costs of pension reform. This dimension corresponds to the left-right divide between the governing coalition of AWS and UW, which espouse a pro-market stance, and the opposition of SLD and PSL, which support more state involvement and income redistribution. In contrast, the second dimension (vertical) predominantly echoes the debate over the elimination of previous pension privileges, bringing support to the theoretical argument of this book. The second dimension sets apart the UW, about half of the SLD, and a small fraction of the AWS, who are in favor of withdrawing the privileges, from most of the AWS, PSL, and the other half of SLD, who favor maintaining them (Figure 6.1A).

To a lesser extent, the two-dimensional roll calls concern the novel privileges granted to a new range of occupational categories, such as, increasing the financial independence of the office supervising pension funds (roll calls 172 and 173). A component of this controversy involved funds specifically designed to sponsor bonuses for the

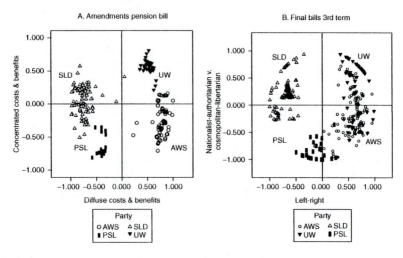

Figure 6.1 Poland, 1997–2001. Comparison of legislators' ideal points regarding amendments to the public pension system bill (26 November 1998) to their ideal points regarding final bills passed during the third term of the Polish Sejm (1997–2001) in a two-dimensional political space (W-NOMINATE coordinates)

AWS = Solidarity Electoral Action (43.9%), UW = Freedom Union (13.1%), SLD = Democratic Left Alliance (35.8%), PSL = Polish People's Party (5.9%). AWS and UW formed the governing coalition, and SLD and PSL were in opposition.

Numbers in parentheses represent the percentage of seats won by each party in 1997 elections. The estimates of legislators' ideal points produced by W-NOMINATE lie within a circle with the radius of one, which explains the circular shape of the image and the values of the scales shown on the two axes.

Source of election data is *Project on Political Transformation and the Electoral Process in Postcommunist Europe*, http://www.essex.ac.uk/elections/ Reproduced with permission from Europe-Asia Studies. © 2010 Taylor & Francis.

managerial team running the office, which was part of a larger effort to provide spoils to a new category of recipients in the form of positions in the administration of the restructured pension system.

Each major party predominantly occupies one particular quadrant; however, there are visible splits within the two major parties. AWS, the main governing party, has a cohesive position regarding the diffuse costs of reform, being situated to the right, but it is split regarding the elimination of privileges between a small liberal wing close to the UW and a large conservative faction. This is consistent with case study evidence, which reveals dissensions within the AWS between a group committed to radical reform and deputies linked to Solidarity unions that opposed elimination of special occupational pensions (Orenstein 2000). The Solidarity Miners' union was particularly vociferous, occupying the Ministry of Labour for two days. Above all, they felt hard hit by the proposed increase in retirement age, especially at a time when they were facing a restructuring of the mining industry and the subsequent loss of benefits for those who did not accumulate a long enough work history under their previous pension scheme (Orenstein 2000).

Figure 6.1A shows that SLD, the main opposition party, also has a coherent position against the diffuse costs of reform with all of the party's deputies being situated on the left with only one exception, but similar to AWS, it is split between two approximately equal factions, one favoring withdrawal of pension privileges and the other supporting them. This comes as no surprise, given that the SLD was an alliance of the SdRP (Social Democracy of the Republic of Poland), the communist successor party, and the post-communist OPZZ unions, which elected 42 deputies to the Sejm in 1997 (Mahr and Nagle 1995). Although the OPZZ trade unions opposed radical reform, SdRP contained a significant managerial faction that was close in outlook to the UW (Bugajski 2002; Orenstein 2000).

UW, the junior governing party, espouses a coherent position for a radical reform and accepts both the diffuse and concentrated costs involved, while the reverse is true for the PSL, the second largest opposition party, which opposes both. The Polish People's Party represents mainly rural voters who have a separate pension system, KRUS. The *Security through Diversity* program, developed by the experts from the SLD and UW during the previous term under an SLD-PSL coalition, protected KRUS against reform as a side payment to PSL in exchange for its support for the overall reform (Golinowska 1999). PSL's constituency was secure at the time the first pillar bill reached the floor during the third term; therefore, PSL's opposition is most likely accounted for through strategic considerations. Being in opposition, it was more productive to oppose unpopular aspects of reform.

The interpretation of these results in light of the theoretical framework discussed above provides answers to the aforementioned puzzles raised by pension reform in Poland. First, SLD, a transformed communist party, was the driving force of pension reform because of the existence of a strong managerial faction within SLD, which was situated in the upper left quadrant and far away from the status quo. The reformists within the SLD were linked to the Ministry of Finance and, after the new reformist prime minister Włodzimierz Cimoszewicz took office in 1996, the SLD reformists also got ties to the newly created Office of the Plenipotentiary for Social Security Reform; meanwhile the Ministry of Labour and Social Policy maintained a more conservative position (Chłoń et al. 1999; Guardiancich 2004; Müller 1999; Orenstein 2000). As Figure 6.1A shows, the reformists within SLD and the AWS were about equally distant from the status quo located in the lower left quadrant; thus, theoretically, they were both as likely to favor radical pension reform, although each supported a different variety. When the SLD entered the government for the first time in October 1993, Poland was experiencing economic and international pressures for reform and it was SLD's first chance to prove internationally that it had parted with its communist past. Moreover, SLD approached only the most popular aspects of reform, such as the creation of private pension funds, which did not create as much dissension within the party as public system reform did. Therefore, a whole array of factors might have motivated SLD to launch a major reform.

Second, reform was designed by a coalition of SLD with the liberal UW, which crosscut the left-right divide and coalition lines, and not by the governing coalition of SLD and PSL because UW has its ideal point situated farthest from the status quo and would participate in any coalition attempting a major effort for radical reform. PSL, on the other hand, is situated very close to the status quo and hence is a natural enemy of radical reform. In order to be induced to support SLD's plans for reform, the farmers' pension system had to be excluded from reform.

Third, there are several rationales, both substantive and strategic, for SLD to turn against the reform when in opposition. As Figure 6.1A illustrates, a powerful faction of the party opposes the elimination of pension privileges involved in the public system reform. The OPZZ unions opposed government proposals to eliminate occupational privileges and in the fall of 1998 called for a strike (Aleksandrowicz 2007; Orenstein 2000). Furthermore, a change in SLD leadership during the AWS-UW government brought former Labor Minister Leszek Miller, a strong opponent of radical reform, to the forefront again as leader of the SLD parliamentary caucus (Orenstein 2000), which shifted the party's overall position in favor of the anti-reform faction.

There are also strategic grounds for SLD's opposition to the public system reform. Being a center-left party, SLD could capitalize on the unpopularity of the public pension system reform and thus attract dissatisfied voters from the AWS and UW. The fact that the coalition of AWS and UW moved the proposed reform away from SLD's ideal point offered SLD the excuse to do precisely that. Although the move was not major, it allowed SLD to turn against reform without losing credibility. The AWS-UW coalition had a majority by itself; therefore, the lack of SLD's support did not endanger the passage of reform.

Finally, the AWS supported reform despite the opposition of the Solidarity trade union faction for several reasons. When AWS was created in 1996 as a heterogeneous coalition of over 30 parties and the Solidarity trade union, the unions were given the upper hand in the AWS governing bodies, including the chairman, who was the Solidarity unions' head (then Marian Krzaklewski). However, the elections shifted the balance of power within the AWS away from the trade unions. The elections created an independent center of power in the parliamentary representation of the AWS, in which the trade union faction was less dominant than the list-order at the elections because of the electorate's preferences for non-union candidates (Wenzel 1998). The 201 AWS deputies were divided into three roughly equal sized factions: the trade unionists, the nationalist-Catholics, and the moderates (Wenzel 1998). Moreover, the moderates in the AWS gained influence after the elections because they were in a better position to negotiate a coalition with the UW, and some of them also had governing experience from holding cabinet posts during the previous term (Wenzel 1998: 155).

Voting on Amendments Compared to the Final Vote on
the Public Pension System Bill
The final bill on the public pension system reform reflects the controversies and compromises reached among the four main parties. Although it represents a significant departure from the status quo regarding the diffuse consequences of reform (horizontal dimension), it is rather limited with respect to the elimination of pension privileges (vertical dimension). The most significant achievements are the introduction of a notional defined contribution scheme that ensures a tight link between contributions and benefits, an increase in the retirement age for both men and women, and the financing of the minimum guaranteed pension from the general state budget instead of the pension fund. All of them combined led to a dramatic elimination of redistribution within the public system, consistent with the center-right character of the AWS-UW coalition. However, because of Solidarity trade unions' opposition, some concessions were made regarding benefit indexation and equal retirement age for men and women (Aleksandrowicz 2007; Müller 1999; Orenstein 2000).

In contrast, the system of pension privileges was not fundamentally altered, reflecting a deep split within the AWS regarding the withdrawal of occupational privileges (Figure 6.1A). The pro-reform governing team faced strong opposition from the Solidarity trade unions, which culminated in public protests and the occupation of the Ministry of Labour by the miners' union in the fall of 1998 (Orenstein 2000: 55). A unified public system was not attained and numerous occupational categories, such as farmers, policemen, soldiers, and prison guards, continued to possess separate and highly subsidized pension schemes. Others, for instance, miners, railroad employees, teachers, and those whose work poses a health hazard, continued to benefit from their previous privileges within the public scheme. This outcome is not surprising given that AWS and UW, the governing parties, agreed on the diffuse consequences of reform but strongly disagreed regarding the withdrawal of occupational privileges (Figure 6.1A).

The final bill was passed on 26 November 1998 by the governing coalition of AWS and UW, with the opposition of SLD-PSL.[2] The vote was substantially divided along party and coalition lines and showed a very high party discipline. The comparison of this vote with the votes on amendments reveals three important characteristics of the pension bill: its salience, divisiveness, and unpopularity. The cohesiveness in voting on the final bill within each party and coalition is at odds with the important differences evident during the parliamentary debates and in the votes on amendments (in particular within the two major parties), showing the salience of the bill. The clear distinction in voting on the final bill between the government and the opposition suggests its divisiveness. Finally, the fact that a great number of opposition deputies who supported, at least in part, the government proposal voted against it demonstrates the unpopularity of the bill and reveals the opposition's strategic calculation to trade off its policy ideal for future votes.

Voting on Pension Reform Compared to the General Voting Pattern
The comparison of parties' and legislators' spatial positions regarding the amendments to the pension bill (Figure 6.1A) with their positions vis-à-vis all final bills passed by the Sejm during its third term (Figure 6.1B) offers further insights into the politics of pension reform, providing evidence of its divisiveness, unpopularity, and the importance of interest group politics. Although the patterns in the two plots depicted in Figure 6.1 are strikingly similar, there are some noteworthy differences.

First, although each party occupies the same quadrant, there is considerable overlap among the legislators of the AWS and UW with respect to the final bills, but no overlap regarding the amendments to the pension bill, which confirms the existence of important divisions within the ruling coalition relating to the pension bill that pull the AWS and UW farther apart compared to their relative positions on the rest of the bills passed during that term. Second, PSL is closer to and overlaps, to some extent, the conservative wing of the AWS with respect to all final bills, although the two parties were wide apart regarding the pension bill, which again suggests the divisiveness of the pension reform. Third, the opposition parties SLD and PSL are closer on the pension bill than they are in the overall political space, which could be the result of strategic calculations to trade off policy positions for future votes, given the unpopularity of the pension bill. Finally, the comparison of the two spatial maps also reveals that the factions within the two major parties—AWS and SLD—that defend the old pension privileges (lower quadrants in Figure 6.1A) are larger than their corresponding factions in the general political space (Figure 6.1B), which is an indication of the strength of groups with entrenched interests in the old pension system.

DISCUSSION

The evidence presented in this chapter, which is based on a roll call analysis of voting in the Polish Sejm, unambiguously demonstrates the existence of divisions within the party system regarding both the diffuse costs of pension reform and the elimination of occupational privileges, and the formation of pro-reform and anti-reform coalitions crosscutting the left-right divide. The controversy over the diffuse costs of pension reform reflects the classic left-right divide and distinguishes between the center-right coalition of AWS-UW and the center-left coalition of SLD-PSL. The second dimension of pension politics mirrors the disagreements regarding the elimination of inherited pension privileges and mainly separates the parties within each coalition and the factions within each party. The latter sets aside forward-looking political forces, such as the UW and the managerial wing of the SLD, which do not have ties with occupational groups that hold entitlements under the old pension system, from backward-looking parties that have strong ties with privileged occupational groups, such as the unionist wing of the SLD, PSL, and the conservative wing of the AWS. This analysis showed that the alleged convergence between the political left and right in pension politics in fact disguises a complex process of divergence among parties and factions within parties regarding the twofold costs of pension reform. The left and right continue to hold distinct positions, as Figure 6.1 shows, and their internal divisions create opportunities for left-right alliances on specific issues.

Based on the distinction between the diffuse and concentrated costs of pension reform, the chapter analyzed the implications of various formal and informal pro-reform and anti-reform coalitions for the reform outcome and sustainability. Poland successfully implemented a pension reform that represents a significant departure from the old pension system. Major reforms were possible in Poland because of the existence of a strong managerial faction within the SLD, which gained the upper hand over the unionist faction in the party and was able to form an informal alliance with the liberal UW. The process was aided by the fact that the parties/factions opposing both diffuse and concentrated costs of reform, such as the PSL and the unionist wing of the SLD, were too weak to dominate the coalition formation process. These parties, however, being supported by the conservative wing of the AWS, were strong enough to preserve some of the previous occupational privileges.

The chances of reform sustainability in Poland are good because reform was based on a consensus forged through the participation of multiple parties and coalitions in the process. This very consensus, however, led to the preservation of some of the pension privileges granted under the old regime, thus limiting the scale of reform. The politics of pension reform in Poland reveals some of the inherent trade-offs between achieving one's policy ideal and building a consensus; between policy and votes; and between the scope of reform and its long-term sustainability.

CHAPTER 7

Conclusion: Analyzing Pension Politics

The goal of this book is to contribute to a better understanding of the politics of unpopular policies in general and of pension reform in particular. The focus has been on Central and Eastern Europe, but the theoretical framework could prove useful in the study of other regions of the world. The theoretical perspective brings together two major approaches within the new institutionalism—historical and rational choice—which permits an exploration of both long-term processes of development and immediate causes of policy change. More specifically, the book is informed by and contributes to the theories of political parties and coalitional politics. Methodologically, it combines a four-case comparison of Hungary, Poland, Romania, and Slovakia with roll call analyses of voting in legislatures, which paves the way for the integration of developments in the study of American politics into the research of Central and Eastern European political systems.

This final chapter is organized as follows: in the next section, I summarize the research question and the main findings; I then review the theoretical and policy implications; finally, I suggest several directions for future research.

SUMMARY OF THE FINDINGS

This book is concerned with a broad problem in comparative politics and political economy and a set of more focused research questions. The broad problem regards the role of political factors and their interplay with economic and international forces in shaping the outcome of pension reform in Central and Eastern Europe. The more specific questions are: What accounts for the variation in the types of pro-reform coalitions across the region? How is the outcome of reform related to the characteristics of the coalition that adopts it? Why is reform sustainable in some countries but not in others?

The theoretical approach developed in this book represents a significant departure from the previous literature in several respects. First, unlike the literature on welfare retrenchment in the West and an important strand of the literature on pension reform in Central and Eastern European countries, which stress the demand-side factors such as pension crises and international pressures, this study focuses on the supply of reform represented by domestic politics. Given the pervasiveness of pension crises across the globe, the factors that contribute to the deterioration of a pension system cannot explain the large variation in the outcomes observed. These factors are no doubt useful in explaining what brings pension reform into the public debate, but they can account for neither the timing of reform nor the particular content of a reform package (Pierson and Weaver 1993). As some authors have observed, it is almost tautological to say that reform follows crisis (Müller 1999; Rodrik 1996).

International factors, on the other hand, are best at explaining the observed convergence in the content of reform among various countries. As mentioned above, the international financial institutions support the so-called new orthodoxy of pension reform, which represents a neo-liberal approach to reform based on the Washington Consensus. Countries that adopt reform tend, to a larger extent, to follow the neo-liberal blueprint prescribed by the World Bank and the IMF rather than competing proposals. All four cases examined have pursued the three-pillar pension model advocated by the World Bank. However, the convergence of the paths followed by different countries should not be overstated. Within the three-pillar framework, there is substantial variation across countries in the extent of public system reforms, the size of the second mandatory private pillar, and the elimination of occupational privileges. The pressures from the international financial institutions do not adequately explain why some countries engage in reforms while others do not, nor do they account for the degree of reform accomplished in a given country.

In contrast, this book finds evidence that in the specific context of Central and Eastern European countries, accession to the European Union served as an incentive for governments contemplating pension reform to pursue it. All four cases passed significant pension reforms in the eve of joining the European Union. It might be difficult to disentangle domestic from international factors in this case, since joining the European Union was itself the result of a long process of political transformation including the moderation of ex-communist and nationalist parties. Nevertheless, if the European Union's effect was not direct, it still created incentives for political moderation, helping to explain the passage of reform by the social democratic government in Romania and the lack of major reform reversal by the left-nationalist coalition in Slovakia.

Second, this study emphasizes different political factors than a large part of the existing literature does. Unlike the retrenchment literature, which stresses policy legacies and attributes a limited role to political institutions, here the balance shifts in favor of political institutions, in particular the party system and the processes of coalition formation, although it recognizes the important role of past legacies. The analysis also departs to some extent from the studies that highlight the role of power concentration and of veto points in enabling or hindering reform, and instead finds that consensual politics is more conducive to sustainable reform. Finally, this study reaches different conclusions from the "power resources theory" concerning the role of left parties in supporting the welfare state. I find that the role of the left in pension reform is complex and depends on both the historical evolution of the left, as well as on its coalitional potential with the liberal right or with the nationalist parties.

The results clearly show that the configuration of the party system and the coalition formation process shape pension reform outcome and its long-term sustainability in critical and identifiable ways. The study provides evidence that pension politics cannot be reduced to a single left-right dimension, and that a two-dimensional estimation of party configurations is necessary. It also shows the complex role of the major poles of the party system, left, right, and nationalist, in pension reform as well as the critical influence of their internal divisions and alliances.

All four cases examined show that, in addition to the left and right, there is a nationalist-conservative pole of the party system that holds a distinct position regarding pension reform. The four party systems examined differed in their configurations; however, the existence of a nationalist-conservative pole has been consequential for pension reform in all four cases, albeit in different ways. In Hungary and Slovakia, the main opposition to reform came from the nationalist-conservatives, who also constitute the main threat to the sustainability of reform. In Poland, where the nationalist-conservatives were comparatively weak, they were still able to limit the scope of reform, while in Romania they were instrumental in providing the necessary majority to block or overturn reforms.

The characteristics of the left also had a great impact on the reform process in all four countries. In Poland and Hungary, where the former communist parties modernized early and constitute a viable social democratic alternative that is committed to a market economy and European integration, such parties were the driving force of pension reform, which they accomplished by forging cross-spectrum coalitions with the liberals. In Romania, by contrast, the extended survival of a strong unreformed ex-communist party that relied on the support of the nationalists prevented reform for as long as the party was in power and threatened its sustainability. Slovakia constitutes an intermediate case, where the former communist party modernized early but failed to play a prominent role, which allowed the nationalists to seize the political scene and put off the reform process for several years.

The divisions within the right were also consequential for the fate of reform in all cases. In Poland and Hungary, the split of the right between a liberal and a conservative camp led to significant opposition from the conservatives, which altered the reform project in long-lasting ways. In Hungary, the conservatives scaled down the private pillar, while in Poland they narrowed the scope of reform by preserving previous occupational privileges. In Slovakia and Romania, internal divisions within the right posed a different challenge. The fragmentation of the right among multiple small parties created problems of coordination and efficiency and delayed the adoption of reform, threatening its viability and leading to a reversal in Romania.

In addition to the ideological distinctions between parties, the study also finds that parties' connections with occupational groups that held privileges under the previous regime are consequential for the outcome of reform. Not only will these parties oppose elimination of occupational privileges, but they are also likely to oppose the pension package as a whole. The parties that are more likely to have such connections are those originating in the previous regime, such as the former communist parties, both reformed and unreformed, and the nationalist and agrarian parties. There are instances, however, in which Christian democratic parties also have such connections, for example, the AWS in Poland. For the unreformed communists and the left nationalists, ideology and connections combine to establish a strong anti-reform position. In contrast, for the reformed communists and the Christian democrats, ideology and connections provide competing incentives, which can lead to splits within the parties and inconsistent positions toward reform, as the examples of the SLD and AWS in Poland suggest. Of the four cases covered, Poland and Romania have encountered the most difficulties in addressing occupational privileges, which have remained in place despite several attempts at reform.

The four cases examined also present a range of coalition formation processes that decisively shaped the fate of reform. Pro-reform coalitions do not necessarily follow a left-right logic. Hungary provides a noteworthy example of a pro-reform coalition structured by a social dimension rather than the classic economic dimension. Slovakia is at the other extreme, with pro-reform coalitions strictly forming along the left-right divide. Poland and Romania fall in between, offering examples in which both center-left and center-right coalitions participated at different stages in the reform process, each leaving a distinct mark on the outcome.

Which pro-reform coalitions are more likely to form in a country depends to a large extent on parties' previous history of cooperation and conflict and the strength of the divides between them. Romania in the 1990s is an extreme example due to its legacy of possessing the most repressive communist regime of all four cases, which left behind a strong resentment crystallized into a deep former-communist versus anti-communist divide. This divide was reinforced in the first decade of postcommunist transition by the presence of strong left versus right and nationalist-authoritarian versus cosmopolitan-libertarian divisions. These divisions were generated by the limited transformation of the former communist party that had adopted a left and nationalist stance, leading to an extreme polarization of the political system between "us" and "them." Poland resembles Romania in the strength of the former-communist versus anti-communist divide, which precluded the formation of governing coalitions across the divide. However, a mitigating factor in the Polish case was the early modernization of the former communist party, which positioned this party on numerous policy positions in the proximity of the liberals, and over time it led to the development of numerous personal ties and informal cooperation between the leadership of the two parties.

At the other extreme is Hungary, in which the mildness of "goulash" communism and a tradition of pluralism within the communist party and the attempts at economic reform during the last decade of the communist regime contributed to the waning of the former-communist versus anti-communist divide, which allowed the formation of governing coalitions based on similarity of policy positions. Slovakia resembles Hungary in that the absence of significant repression and a disproportionate targeting of resources toward Slovak as opposed to Czech territories in the post-1968 period led to a low salience of the former-communist versus anti-communist divide, which allowed for cooperation between the transformed communist party and parties of the right during post-communism. In contrast to Hungary, however, because of its late emergence as an independent state, Slovakia developed a strong nationalist division that separated between "standard" democratic parties and "non-standard" authoritarian and nationalist parties, precluding alliances between the two groups.

The evidence presented also shows that the outcome of reform has important consequences for long-term sustainability. Reforms in Hungary, Slovakia, and the early reforms in Romania, which were designed and adopted without consultation with the opposition, were subject to various degrees of reversals. In contrast, in Poland, where all major parties participated in the adoption process, the result was a consensual reform and chances for sustainability are good.

Despite the variety of experiences with pension reform of the four cases, some general patterns can be identified. First, countries that have a strong party that opposes reform, such as the unreformed communists or nationalists, have the lowest chance of accomplishing reform, as the cases of Romania and Slovakia during the 1990s show. In such instances, the chances of a pro-reform coalition of acceding and maintaining power are low. If the pro-reform coalition is also internally divided, the likelihood of reform is substantially diminished. Second, parties may oppose reform not only for ideological reasons, but also because of their connections with privileged occupational groups. If the two coincide, it leads to a strong anti-reform position, whereas if they create competing incentives, it may generate internal party splits and inconsistent positions toward reform, as the examples of social democrats and Christian democrats in Poland show.

Third, countries that have a viable social democratic alternative, such as Poland and Hungary, are the most likely to accomplish and sustain reform. Social democrats occupy a pivotal position with respect to pension reform because they can mediate between the liberals, who favor radical reform, and the trade unions and left constituencies, who demand more social protection. They are best suited to forge a consensus among diverging interests. Finally, reform is more likely to endure in countries where the outcome is more consensual than where it is more radical, as suggested by the contrasting experiences of Poland, on the one hand, and the other three countries, on the other.

Theoretical Implications

This study has three major implications for theories of the welfare state. First, it suggests a need to bring back the power resources theory before dismissing it as being irrelevant to the recent developments of the welfare state. This study finds that social democratic parties and organized labor are crucial actors in the process of pension reform, though not the only important actors. Unlike in the West, in which the position of social democrats toward pension reform has increasingly converged with that of the right (Bonoli 2000; Schludi 2003), social democrats in Central and Eastern Europe promote a distinct social-market approach regarding the transformation of the welfare state that attempts to maintain the social protection functions of the state and simultaneously pursue a free-market and pro-Western agenda. The ways in which social democrats are capable of translating their position into policy to a large extent depends on their ability to forge alliances with the liberal right or the nationalists. Where they formed coalitions with the liberals, they supported comprehensive reforms; where their coalition partners were the nationalists, the social democrats opposed radical transformation of the welfare system.

The second theoretical implication concerns an expansion of the past legacy theory of retrenchment in order to take into account not only the policy legacy, but also the historical developments that shape the current configuration of the political system. This analysis showed that the past shapes actors' identities and their interactions. Finally, there is a need to incorporate policy sustainability in the study of the welfare state. Neither theories of welfare state expansion nor those of retrenchment pay attention to the chances of a policy to endure. Pension reform in Central and Eastern Europe provides several instances of policy reversal, which is not well theorized yet. This study suggests that consensus with the main opposition actors is a sufficient but not a necessary condition for sustainability. Changing policy is costly, and even if major players in the political system do not like the policy outcome, the costs of change may outweigh the benefits.

Policy Implications

There are three main policy implications of this analysis. First, pension reform involves a number of trade-offs that political parties must be aware of: between achieving one's policy ideal and building a consensus, between policy and votes, and between the scope of reform and its long-term sustainability. Second, in party systems characterized by deep divisions and high polarization, securing the opposition's consent might not be an option. In such a situation, the governing coalition may try to raise the cost of policy reversal using several means. If cooperation with the opposition is not feasible, it might be possible instead to reach directly toward the societal actors concerned, such as trade unions and pensioners' associations, and engage them in the reform process, with the inevitable price of limiting the scope of reform. Once they participate and agree with the outcome, it is less likely that they will support a policy reversal. Alternatively, the pro-reform coalition may choose a more moderate reform in order to decrease the incentives of the opposition to reverse it. Finally, the governing coalition could provide side payments to key actors, such as trade unions, by offering them a stake in managing the new pension industry. In this way, opponents may turn into allies and the development of constituencies that benefit from the new policy may be fostered. Last but not least, an important policy implication of the study is the lesson that external pressures for reform should be applied cautiously, because under certain configurations of the party system they do not work; moreover, they may have the opposite effect of strengthening the anti-reform coalition by fueling the nationalist-populist parties.

DIRECTIONS FOR FUTURE RESEARCH

This approach opens the door to promising directions for future research. The study of pension reform could benefit from cross-regional analyses. Such analyses would identify the relevant dimensions of pension politics in other regions of the world and would test whether party competition in different settings provides similar results and predictions. Future research might also consider how parties' preferences translate into policy outcomes by expanding the range of independent variables to include cabinet efficiency, political actors, and policy design. This analysis could be taken further by examining how groups adversely affected by pension reform mobilize against it, how successful they are in influencing the end result, and the role of trade unions in mediating and articulating their demands.

Appendix A

Measures of the Independent Variables

Political Parties and Party Systems

→ **Ideological orientation**. Party positions on policy issues are estimated using three alternative methods: roll call analyses of voting in legislatures, expert surveys, and public opinion surveys for estimating the positions of party constituencies.

→ **Connections with privileged groups**. I estimate parties' connections with privileged occupational groups by using roll call analyses of voting in legislatures. I also examine connections with trade unions and occupational groups using secondary sources.

→ **Relative strength**. I measure the relative strength of a party or coalition by its share of seats in the legislature.

→ **Strategic interaction between parties**. I assess the likelihood of parties joining a coalition based on their previous history of cooperation or conflict and the strength of the divides between them, which I estimate using secondary sources.

Governing Coalitions

→ **Type**. Center-right, center-left, cross-spectrum, nationalist.

→ **Internal cohesion**. I measure internal cohesion by the number of parties in the coalition and their ideological diversity.

→ **Previous involvement in reform**. Support versus opposition to reform and direct participation in the development of the reform proposal.

→ **Relative cost of reversal**. I assume this to be higher for right than for left parties because pension reform is a pro-market reform that right parties are expected to endorse. By not doing so, their policy position enters into conflict with their ideology, which may be costly in electoral terms. There is no expectation that right parties may attract voters who are dissatisfied with the pro-market reforms adopted by the left; therefore, there is no likely gain for the right from the reversal of such reforms. On the contrary, the right may lose voters to the left if it is perceived as not committed enough to a free market. In contrast, the left anticipates electoral gains from reversing the pro-market reforms adopted by the right by attracting dissatisfied voters from the right.

I also consider the cost of reversal to be higher for parties that previously supported reform (the pro-reform coalition) than for parties that opposed it. For the former, there is a loss of credibility associated with inconsistent behavior, whereas for the latter an attempt at reversal only reinforces their prior position.

Measures of the Dependent Variables

Reform outcome. I estimate the outcome of reform by examining four dimensions of reform: (1) the degree of reform of the public system, (2) the establishment of a mandatory private pillar (second pillar), (3) the elimination of occupational privileges, and (4) the timing of reform adoption. In the literature on pension reform in Central and Eastern Europe there has been a tendency to characterize the degree of reform based largely on the presence or absence of the second pillar and to overlook first-tier reforms and occupational privileges. This tendency is largely due to the prevalence of the new pension orthodoxy in the study of pension reform in developing countries, whose promoters advocate the partial replacement of the public PAYG scheme with a funded mandatory private pension scheme (second pillar). In this view, radical reform entails the introduction of the second pillar, while reforms within the public pillar are labeled as "parametric reforms." This term is defined as an adjustment of the parameters that characterize the public system, such as the retirement age and the formula used to calculate the benefits, and is seen as a mere attempt at salvaging a system that is not sustainable over the long term and is not a radical reform.

This study has a different view regarding pension reforms. As some scholars have noted (Müller 1999), it is sometimes more difficult to implement public system reforms or to eliminate pension privileges than to introduce private pillars because the reduction of entitlements is more visible to the public in the first case. From a political economy perspective, the reform of the public system can be even more challenging than the introduction of the private pillars. Moreover, this study provides evidence that the elimination of occupational privileges may be the most challenging task for a pension reformer, without which reform can be considered neither radical nor comprehensive, even if the second pillar has been adopted. Although the creation of the second pillar may represent the most radical departure from the old pension system, it may not be the most difficult to adopt.

I evaluate the degree of reform of the public pillar based on the extent to which the link between contributions and benefits is tightened in order to remedy the financial imbalance of the system. The most important measures in this respect are the use of a non-redistributive pension formula and the raising of retirement age for both men and women. A non-redistributive formula eliminates redistribution from high to low wages and is expected to create incentives for workers to contribute more in order to receive a higher pension.

In addition to the three components of pension reform, I also consider the timing of adoption as an important dependent variable. By introducing this measure I do intend to suggest neither that all countries in a region should attempt pension reform at the same time, nor that they should all attempt to adopt pension reform eventually. However, in practice pension reform, as other reforms, has tended to occur in waves because countries in the same geographic area tend to share similarities that may create a need for such a reform. In Central and Eastern Europe, all countries have the demographic, economic, and international factors present that brought pension reform on the political agenda early during the postcommunist transition. From a political economy perspective, it is important to measure the timing between the moment when pension reform arrived on the agenda and the moment of adoption because there is wide variation among countries.

The overall degree of reform in a country is estimated based on the degree of public pillar reform, the presence of a mandatory private pillar, the elimination of occupational privileges, and the timing of adoption.

Reform sustainability. The second dependent variable is the long-term sustainability of pension reform. I measure it by looking at whether the first subsequent government that was supported by a different coalition of parties than the government that adopted reform attempted to halt the process, reverse it or alter it.

APPENDIX B

THE ROLL CALL ANALYSIS OF VOTING

The roll call analysis of voting in legislatures offers a way of mapping party positions in a multi-dimensional space. The analysis is based on scaling techniques and could be considered as an alternative to factor analysis. Its main goal is to graphically reproduce the distance among legislators with respect to policy issues. Based on each legislator's voting record on multiple issues during a legislative term, the roll call analysis estimates legislators' ideal points on a spatial map. The closer the voting records of two legislators are, the closer their ideal points are on the map. Scaling could be one dimensional or multi-dimensional, depending on what the researcher determines makes more sense for the data analyzed. There are various statistical programs available for the analysis of large quantities of data that use algorithms that match different spatial configurations of legislators to the voting data in an attempt to obtain the best "goodness of fit" between the spatial map and the data.

I analyze the roll calls using W-NOMINATE (Poole and Rosenthal 1997: 23, 233), a statistical scaling program that estimates legislators' ideal points and "cutting lines" for each vote in a common space based on the binary choices, yes or no, recorded for each member on multiple roll call votes. "The closeness of two legislators on the map shows how similar their voting records are and distribution of legislators shows what the dimensions are" (Poole 2005: 1).

The roll call analysis has several potential benefits. First, it reduces the multi-dimensionality of the political space, in which each legislative vote constitutes a dimension, to a limited number of dimensions, usually no more than two or three. Second, it allows the identification of legislators' ideal points on a map defined by the respective dimensions. Third, it permits identification of the pro-reform and anti-reform coalitions on each vote. Finally, it allows the prediction of how a legislator will vote on a given issue based on his or her ideal point on the map.

There are at least two potential limitations of using a roll call analysis to estimate party spatial positions. First, NOMINATE constrains legislators whose ideal points are extreme to lie on a circle with a radius of one, and therefore it underestimates the extremes. Second, individual ideal points (or, in the aggregate, the clusters of points that constitute party positions) determined by roll call analysis are more specific to a given legislative term than those obtained using alternative methods because the model overestimates the closeness of parties forming the governing coalition, which tend to vote together more often than the opposition parties do, and it underestimates the closeness between the parties in the opposition. The two limitations of the method do not, however, affect the validity of the results because I am only interested in obtaining a spatial map of the relative positions of the parties; the conclusions of this study do not rely in any way on the absolute position of a legislator or party.

The sources of the roll calls for this study are represented by the Web pages of the Polish, Hungarian, Romanian, and Slovak parliaments:

Poland: www.sejm.gov.pl
Hungary: www.mkogy.hu
Romania: www.cdep.ro
Slovakia: www.nrsr.sk

Appendix C

The Expert Survey of Party Positions

In order to validate the results obtained by the roll call analysis, I compare them with party positions given by expert evaluations. The data come from an expert survey conducted in 2003–2004 (Benoit and Laver 2006). Country experts were asked to rank party positions on various policy issues using a scale of 1 to 20, as well as the salience of each issue for each party, also on a scale of 1 to 20. The total number of expert responses was 42 for Hungary, 32 for Poland, 18 for Romania, and 17 for Slovakia. Policy issues surveyed were as follows:

1. Economic (Spending vs. Taxes)
   Promotes raising taxes to increase public services (1)
   Promotes cutting public services to cut taxes (20)
2. Social
   Favors liberal policies on matters such as abortion, homosexuality, and euthanasia (1)
   Opposes liberal policies on matters such as abortion, homosexuality, and euthanasia (20)
3. Economic (Privatization)
   Promotes maximum state ownership of business and industry (1)
   Opposes all state ownership of business and industry (20)
4. EU Joining
   Opposes joining the European Union (1)
   Favors joining the European Union (20)
5. Environment
   Supports protection of the environment, even at the cost of economic growth (1)
   Supports economic growth, even at the cost of damage to the environment (20)
6. Former Communists
   Former communist party officials should have the same rights and opportunities as other citizens to participate in public life (1)

Former communist party officials should be kept out of public life as far as is possible (20)

7. Foreign Ownership of Land
Supports unrestricted rights of foreigners to purchase and own [our country's] land (1)
Opposes any rights of foreigners to purchase and own [our country's] land (20)

8. Media Freedom
The mass media should be completely free to publish any material they see fit (1)
The content of mass media should be regulated by the state in the public interest (20)

9. Nationalism
Strongly promotes a cosmopolitan rather than [our country's] national consciousness, history, and culture (1)
Strongly promotes [our country's] national rather than a cosmopolitan consciousness, history, and culture (20)

10. Religion
Supports Christian principles in politics (1)
Supports secular principles in politics (20)

11. Urban versus Rural Interests
Promotes interests of urban voters above others (1)
Promotes interests of rural voters above others (20)

12 Decentralization
Promotes decentralization of all administration and decision making (1)
Opposes any decentralization of administration and decision making (20)

13. Left-Right
Please locate each party on a general left-right dimension, taking all aspects of party policy into account. Left (1). Right (20)

99. Sympathetic/Close to Respondent
Taking all aspects of party policy into account, please score each party in terms of how close it is to your own personal views.
Same as respondent (1)
Farthest from respondent (20)

Table C.1   Political parties included in the survey[1]

Party abbreviation	Party name
HUNGARY	
Fidesz	Alliance of Young Democrats-Hungarian Civic Party
FKgP	Independent Smallholders Party
MDF	Hungarian Democratic Forum
MIÉP	Hungarian Justice and Life Party
MSzP	Hungarian Socialist Party
MUNKÁS	Workers' Party
SzDSz	Alliance of Free Democrats
POLAND	
AWS	Solidarity Electoral Action
PSL	Polish People's Party
ROP	Movement for the Reconstruction of Poland
SLD	Democratic Left Alliance
UW	Freedom Union
ROMANIA	
PD	Democratic Party
PNL	National Liberal Party
PNȚCD	National Peasant Christian Democratic Party
PRM	Great Romania Party
PSD	Social Democratic Party
PUR	Humanist Party of Romania
UDMR	Democratic Alliance of Hungarians in Romania
SLOVAKIA	
ANO	Alliance of a New Citizen
HZDS	Movement for a Democratic Slovakia
KDH	Christian Democratic Movement
KSS	Communist Party of Slovakia
SDL	Party of the Democratic Left
SDKU	Slovak Democratic and Christian Union
SMK	Party of the Hungarian Coalition
SNS	Slovak National Party
Smer	Direction-Social Democracy

NOTE

1. In addition to the large parliamentary parties, the survey included a series of small extra parliamentary parties that are left out because they did not participate in voting on pension reform, in order to simplify the spatial maps of party positions.

Appendix D

The Public Opinion Surveys of Party Constituencies

In addition to the roll call analysis and the expert survey, I use public opinion surveys to spatially position party constituencies. Data for Hungary and Slovakia come from the *Central and Eastern Eurobarometer 6: Economic and Political Trends, October–November 1995.* Data for Poland are from the *Central and Eastern Eurobarometer 8: Public Opinion and the European Union, October–November 1997.* Data for Romania are from the *Central and Eastern Eurobarometer 8: Public Opinion and the European Union, October–November 1997* and from the *Public Opinion Barometer October 2003*, realized by the Soros Foundation Romania.[1] For each country the surveys were conducted at that time when one or several bills of the pension reform package were debated in the parliaments of the respective countries.

The Central and Eastern Eurobarometer

Using factor analysis, I confirmed the existence of a two-dimensional space. One dimension reveals the attitudes toward a free-market economy as reflected by the answer to the question about whether the respondent feels that the creation of a market economy is right or wrong for the respondent's country. The responses are recoded as 1 = wrong, 2 = don't know, and 3 = right.

The second dimension corresponds to the nationalist/cosmopolitan divide and is represented by the answers to three questions about the respondent's attitude toward the European Union (EU) and NATO. Two of the questions asked how the respondent would vote in a referendum on the country's membership in the EU and NATO, respectively. I recoded the answers as 1 = vote against, 2 = undecided/would not vote, and 3 = vote for. The third question asked about the respondent's impressions on the EU, and I recoded the answers as 1 = negative, 2 = neutral, and 3 = positive. I attempted to create an index that measures the nationalist/cosmopolitan attitudes by summing up these three items. The score of the inter-item reliability check (Cronbach's alpha) varies across countries, from 0.68 for Slovakia to 0.65 for Poland and Romania to 0.62 for Hungary.[2] Because the values for alpha are lower than the generally accepted threshold of 0.7, I decided to use individual questions rather than the index.

I identified party constituencies using the answer to the question: "If there were a general election tomorrow, which party or block would you vote for, or might you be inclined to vote for?" On each dimension, I placed the constituency of each party at the mean of responses for the respective party and the reference lines at the mean of all responses (after excluding the respondents that do not have the right to vote) and mapped party constituencies in the four quadrants.

THE SOROS PUBLIC OPINION BAROMETER

Using factor analysis, I confirmed the existence of a two-dimensional space. One dimension reveals the attitudes toward a free-market economy as reflected by the answer to the question about whether the respondent feels that the companies should be state owned or private property: "In your view, is it better that the companies are:" The answers have been recoded as 1 = a majority are state owned; 2 = half are state owned, half privately owned/don't know/no answer; and 3 = a majority are privately owned.

The second dimension corresponds to the traditionalist/libertarian divide and is represented by the answer to a question about the respondent's attitude toward homosexuals: "To what extent do you agree with the statement that homosexuals should be accepted as any other person?" The answers are coded as 1 = totally disagree; 2 = somewhat disagree; 3 = don't know/no answer; 4 = somewhat agree; and 5 = totally agree.

I identified party constituencies using the answer to the question: "If there were a parliamentary election next Sunday, which of the following parties would you vote for?" On each dimension, I placed the constituency of each party at the mean of responses for the respective party and the reference lines at the mean of all responses (after excluding the respondents that do not have the right to vote) and mapped party constituencies in the four quadrants.

NOTES

1. Available at http://www.soros.ro/ro/program_articol.php?articol=107.
2. A lower value of alpha for some countries may be due to numerous missing values and, possibly, to coding errors.

Notes

1 Introduction: Dilemmas of Pension Reform in Central and Eastern Europe

1. The number of pensioners divided by the number of contributors (usually expressed as a percentage).
2. The corresponding ratio in the United States is one pensioner to four workers.

2 Assessing the Impact of Domestic Political Institutions

1. Freedom House scores of 2 and below = consolidated democracy: Czech Republic, Estonia, Hungary, Latvia, Lithuania, Poland, Slovak Republic, and Slovenia; 3 = semiconsolidated democracy: Albania, Bulgaria, Croatia, Macedonia, and Romania; 4 = hybrid regime: Georgia and Ukraine; 5 = semiconsolidated authoritarian regime: Armenia and Moldova; 6–7 = consolidated authoritarian regime: Azerbaijan, Belarus, Kazakhstan, Kyrgyzstan, Russian Federation, Tajikistan, Turkmenistan and Uzbekistan (Freedom House 2009).

3 Parties, Coalitions, and Policies: A Theoretical Framework

1. This amounted to up to 30 or 40 percent in some Latin American countries (Mitchell 1999).
2. Single-peaked preferences mean that the closer a policy proposal is to party's ideal point, the greater the support for it by that party. Symmetry implies that equal departures from the ideal in opposite directions yield equal declines in satisfaction (Hinich and Munger 1997).
3. For a discussion of why the median voter is likely to hold a position distant from both the status quo and the radical retrenchment see Schludi (2003).
4. The same reasoning applies if the outcome is in M's win set.

4   POLITICAL PARTIES AND PENSION REFORM IN COMPARATIVE PERSPECTIVE

1. The system dependency ratio is calculated as the number of pensioners divided by the number of contributors.
2. Poland, Sejm, http://orka.sejm.gov.pl/proc2.nsf/ustawy/2297_u.htm, accessed on 25 March 2010.
3. Poland, Sejm, http://orka.sejm.gov.pl/proc2.nsf/ustawy/2307_u.htm, accessed on 25 March 2010.
4. Poland, Sejm, http://orka.sejm.gov.pl/proc4.nsf/ustawy/1942_u.htm, accessed on 25 March 2010.
5. Poland, Sejm, http://orka.sejm.gov.pl/proc3.nsf/ustawy/339_u.htm, accessed on 25 March 2010.
6. The old-age dependency ratio is calculated as the ratio of individuals over 60 divided by the number of individuals aged 20–59.
7. Poland, Sejm, http://www.sejm.gov.pl/archiwum/prace/kadencja2/glos2/11002033.htm and http://www.sejm.gov.pl/archiwum/prace/kadencja2/glos2/11002036.htm, accessed on 25 March 2010.
8. Poland, Sejm, http://orka2.sejm.gov.pl/Debata3.nsf, sitting 36, day 2, 26 November 1998, *Sprawozdanie Komisji Nadzwyczajnej o rządowym projekcie ustawy o emeryturach i rentach z Funduszu Ubezpieczeń Społecznych,* accessed 20 December 2009.
9. For a visualization of parties' positions on various policy issues, see Figures 5.1 and 5.2 in chapter 5.
10. Ibid. 5.
11. Ibid. 2.
12. Ibid. 3.
13. Poland, Sejm, http://orka.sejm.gov.pl/proc4.nsf/ustawy/855_u.htm, accessed 26 July 2010.
14. Ibid. 4.
15. Poland, Sejm, http://orka.sejm.gov.pl/SQL.nsf/glosowania?OpenAgent&4&108&11, accessed 7 January 2010.
16. Ibid.
17. Poland, Sejm, http://orka.sejm.gov.pl/SQL.nsf/glosowania?OpenAgent&6&28&95, accessed 9 January 2010.
18. The wage-based indexation is more generous because it takes into account not only inflation, but also the increase in wages due to economic growth. The most radical reform uses a price-based indexation.
19. For a visualization of parties' positions on various policy issues, see Figures 5.3 and 5.4 in chapter 5.
20. Hungary, National Assembly, http://www.complex.hu/kzlcim/tv997.htm, accessed 29 July 2010.
21. Ibid.
22. Hungary, National Assembly, http://www.complex.hu/kzlcim/tv993.htm, accessed 29 July 2010.

23. Hungary, National Assembly, http://www.complex.hu/kzlcim/ tv996.htm, accessed 29 July 2010.

24. Romania, Chamber of Deputies, http://www.cdep.ro/pls/dic/legis_ acte_parlam?cam=0&tip=1&an=2000, accessed 6 March 2010.

25. Romania, Chamber of Deputies, http://www.cdep.ro/pls/legis/ legis_pck.htp_act?ida=24081&frame=0, accessed 6 March 2010.

26. Romania, Chamber of Deputies, http://www.cdep.ro/pls/legis/ legis_pck.htp_act?ida=53022&frame=0, accessed 6 March 2010.

27. Romania, Chamber of Deputies, http://www.cdep.ro/pls/legis/ legis_pck.htp_act?ida=64898&frame=0, accessed 6 March 2010.

28. President Băsescu was accused of violating the Constitution, although the Constitutional Court did not find evidence of unconstitutional conduct. The reunited chambers of the Parliament suspended him from function on 19 April 2007 (Chamber of Deputies, http:// www.cdep.ro/pls/steno/steno.stenograma?ids=6286&idm=6&idl= 1, accessed on 14 March 2010). He was reinstated after the 19 May 2007 referendum in which 74.48% of voters decided to keep the president in office (Biroul Electoral Central 2007).

29. Romania, Chamber of Deputies, Extraordinary Session of 13 August 2008, http://www.cdep.ro/pls/steno/steno.stenograma?ids=6512 &idm=10&idl=1, accessed 9 March 2010.

30. Ibid 26.

31. For a visualization of parties' positions on various policy issues, see Figures 5.5–5.7 in chapter 5.

32. Ibid 28.

33. Romania, Chamber of Deputies session of 9/28/2009, available at http:// www.cdep.ro/pls/steno/steno.stenograma?ids=5731&idm=3,22

34. Ibid 29.

35. Romania, Chamber of Deputies, http://www.cdep.ro/pls/steno/ eVot.Nominal?idv=1241 , accessed 30 March 2010.

36. Romania, Chamber of Deputies, http://www.cdep.ro/pls/steno/ eVot.Nominal?idv=2648, accessed 30 March 2010.

37. Romania, Chamber of Deputies, http://www.cdep.ro/pls/proiecte/ upl_pck.proiect?cam=2&idp=11088, accessed 30 July 2010.

38. According to previous legislation, retirement age was raised gradually to 60 for women and 65 for men until 2015.

39. Slovakia, National Council, http://www.nrsr.sk/Default.aspx?sid= schodze/hlasovanie/hlasklub&ID=13061, accessed 30 July 2010.

40. Slovakia, National Council, http://www.nrsr.sk/Default.aspx?sid= schodze/hlasovanie/hlasklub&ID=14217, accessed 30 July 2010.

41. Slovakia, National Council, http://www.nrsr.sk/Default.aspx?sid= schodze/hlasovanie/hlasklub&ID=16293, accessed 30 July 2010.

42. For a visualization of parties' positions on various policy issues, see Figures 5.8 and 5.9 in chapter 5.

43. The bill was vetoed by President Rudolf Schuster on 22 October 2003, but the parliament overrode the president's veto on 30 October 2003.

44. Ibid 44.
45. This bill was also vetoed by President Rudolf Schuster in January 2004, but the parliament overrode the president's veto on 20 January 2004.
46. Ibid 45.
47. Ibid 46.
48. Market shares are calculated according to the total net asset value of funds of the given pension fund management company.
49. Ibid.
50. For a visualization of Smer positions on various policy issues, see Figures 5.8 and 5.9 in chapter 5.

5 MAPPING PARTIES' SPATIAL POSITIONS WITH ROLL CALL ANALYSES AND EXPERT SURVEYS IN POLAND, HUNGARY, ROMANIA, AND SLOVAKIA

1. The Sejm passed the bill on public pension system reform on 26 November 1998. Afterwards, the bill went to the Senate, which proposed several amendments. The Sejm voted on these amendments on 17 December 1998, but the bill as a whole was not submitted for vote again. The official date of the bill is 17 December, because this date marks the closing of the votes on the bill.
2. Poland, Sejm, http://orka.sejm.gov.pl/proc3.nsf/opisy/339.htm, accessed December 2009.
3. The scales for "nationalism" and "social" have been reversed compared to the original dataset in order to correspond to the other two scales.
4. The scales for "nationalism" and "social" have been reversed compared to the original dataset in order to correspond to the other two scales.
5. The scales for "nationalism" and "social" have been reversed compared to the original dataset in order to correspond to the other two scales.
6. Available at http://www.soros.ro/ro/program_articol.php?articol=107.
7. PSD Web site, http://www.psd.ro/perioade.php, accessed on 18 August 2009.
8. Ibid.
9. Ibid.
10. Info News, http://www.infonews.ro/article201.html, accessed on 13 August 2009.
11. Realitatea.net, http://www.realitatea.net/miron-mitrea-a-anuntat-oficial-ca-se-va-retrage-din-parlament_331316.html, accessed on 13 August 2009.

12. Mediafax.ro, http://www.mediafax.ro/justitie/dna-cere-camerei-deputatilor-aviz-pentru-urmarirea-penala-a-lui-miron-mitrea. html?4727;2572274, accessed on 13 August 2009.
13. Ziare.com, http://www.ziare.com/Iliescu_nu_este_singurul_veteran_care_isi_pregateste_retragerea-363394.html, accessed on 13 August 2009.
14. The scales for "nationalism" and "social" have been reversed compared to the original dataset in order to correspond to the other two scales.

6 Ideology, Interest Group Politics, and Pension Reform

1. Poland, Sejm, http://orka2.sejm.gov.pl/Debata3.nsf, sitting 36, day 2, 26 November 1998, *Sprawozdanie Komisji Nadzwyczajnej o rządowym projekcie ustawy o emeryturach i rentach z Funduszu Ubezpieczeń Społecznych*, accessed December 2009.
2. Poland, Sejm, http://orka.sejm.gov.pl/proc3.nsf/opisy/339.htm, accessed December 2009.

REFERENCES

Aleksandrowicz, Paula. 2007. "Pension Reform in Poland since Transition—From Path Departure to Path Dependence." *European Journal of Social Security* 9 (4): 323–344.

Andrews, Emily S. and Mansoora Rashid. 1996. "The Financing of Pension Systems in Central and Eastern Europe. An Overview of Major Trends and their Determinants, 1990–1993." World Bank Technical Paper 339. Social Challenges of Transition Series. Washington, DC: The World Bank.

Armeanu, Oana. 2010. "The Battle over Privileges and Pension Reform: Evidence from Legislative Roll Call Analysis in Poland." *Europe-Asia Studies* 62 (4): 571–595, http://www.informaworld.com.

Agh, Attila. 1995. "Partial Consolidation of the East-Central European parties: the case of the Hungarian Socialist Party." *Party Politics* 1 (4): 491–514.

Augusztinovics, Maria and Janos Köllő. 2009. "Decreased Employment and Pensions: The Case of Hungary." In Robert Holzmann, Landos Mackellar, and Jana Repanšek (eds.), *Pension Reform in Southeastern Europe: Linking to Labor and Financial Market Reform*. Washington, DC: The World Bank.

Bailey, Michael. 2001. "Ideal Point Estimation with a Small Number of Votes: A Random-Effects Approach." *Political Analysis* 9 (3): 192–210.

BBC News. 2007. Romania's MPs suspend president. 19 April. http://news.bbc.co.uk/2/hi/europe/6572003.stm (accessed 10 March 2010).

Beattie, Roger and Warren McGillivray. 1995. "A Risky Strategy: Reflections on the World Bank Report 'Averting the Old Age Crisis.'" *International Social Security Review* 48 (3–4): 5–22.

Bednárik, Rastislav. 2004. "Pension Reform Finally a Reality," European Industrial Relations Observatory On-line. http://www.eurofound.europa.eu/eiro/2004/04/feature/sk0404102f.htm (accessed 18 March 2010).

Benoit, Kenneth and Michael Laver. 2006. *Party Policy in Modern Democracies*. London: Routledge.

Biroul Electoral Central. 2004. Alegeri pentru Camera Deputaţilor, Senat şi Preşedintele României-anul 2004. http://www.bec2004.ro/ (accessed 30 July 2010).

Biroul Electoral Central. 2007. Comunicat privind rezultatele parţiale ale referendumului naţional din data de 19 mai 2007 pentru demiterea

preşedintelui României. http://www.becreferendum2007.ro/document3/
rez%20finale.pdf (accessed 30 July 2010).

Biroul Electoral Central. 2008. Alegeri pentru Camera Deputaţilor şi Senat
30 Noiembrie 2008. http://www.becparlamentare2008.ro/ (accessed 30
July 2010).

Biroul Electoral Central. 2009. Biroul Electoral Central pentru alegerea
Preşedintelui României din anul 2009 şi pentru referendumul naţional
din 22 noiembrie 2009. http://www.bec2009p.ro/rezultate.html
(accessed 8 March 2010).

Bohl, Martin T., Judith Lischewschi and Svitlana Voronkova. 2008. *Does
Regulation Hurt Pension Funds' Performance? Evidence from Strongly
Regulated Pension Fund Industries.* Discussion Paper PI-0813. London:
City University, The Pensions Institute.

Bonoli, Giuliano. 2000. *The Politics of Pension Reform. Institutions and Policy
Change in Western Europe.* Cambridge, UK: Cambridge University Press.

Brooks, Sarah. 2001. "The Diffusion of Pension Privatization over Time and
Space." Paper prepared for the Annual Meeting of the American Political
Science Association, 29 August–2 September, San Francisco, CA.

———. 2002. "Social Protection and Economic Integration. The Politics
of Pension Reform in an Era of Capital Mobility." *Comparative Political
Studies* 35 (5): 491–523.

———. 2004. "What Was the Role of International Financial Institutions
in the Diffusion of Social Security Reform in Latin America?" In Kurt
Weyland (ed.). *Learning from Foreign Models in Latin American Policy
Reform.* Washington, DC: Woodrow Wilson Center Press and John
Hopkins University Press.

———. 2005. "Interdependent and Domestic Foundations of Policy Change:
The Diffusion of Pension Privatization around the World." *International
Studies Quarterly* 49 (2): 273–294.

Bugajski, Janusz. 2002. *Political Parties of Eastern Europe. A Guide to Politics
in the Postcommunist Era.* New York: M. E. Sharpe.

Casa Naţională de Pensii şi Alte Drepturi de Asigurări Sociale. n.d. http://
www.cnpas.org/ (accessed 10 March 2010)

Chiriţoiu, Bogdan. 2001. "Păşind cu Greutate—Reforma Pensiilor în România."
Early Warning Report. Bucharest: Societatea Academică din România. http://
www.policy.hu/Chiriţoiu/reformapensiilor.pdf (accessed 29 March 2010).

Chłoń, Agnieszka, Marek Góra, and Michał Rutkowski. 1999. *Shaping
Pension Reform in Poland: Security through Diversity.* Washington, DC:
The World Bank.

Chłoń-Dominczak, A. 2004. "Pension Reform in Poland." In *Reforming
Public Pensions. Sharing the Experiences of Transition and OECD
Countries.* 27–28 May 2002, Warsaw. Paris: OECD.

Chłoń-Dominczak, Agnieszka. 2007. "Pension System and Employment
Incentives—Polish Experience." http://www.cef-see.org/pension_re-
form/ChlonDominczak.pdf (accessed 7 January 2010).

Ciobanu, Monica. 2007. "Romania's Travails with Democracy and Accession
to the European Union." *Europe-Asia Studies* 59 (8): 1429–1450.

Clayton, Richard and Jonas Pontusson. 1998. "Welfare-State Retrenchment Revisited: Entitlement Cuts, Public Sector Restructuring, and Inegalitarian Trends in Advanced Capitalist Societies." *World Politics* 51 (1): 67–98.

Condon, Christopher and Stefan Wagstyl. 2007. Romanian parliament suspends president. *Financial Times.* 19 April. http://www.ft.com/cms/s/0/d3be5f1a-ee6e-11db-b5e9-000b5df10621.html?nclick_check=1 (accessed 9 March 2010).

Cook, Linda J. 2007. *Postcommunist Welfare States: Reform Politics in Russia and Eastern Europe.* Ithaca, NY: Cornell University Press.

Cook, Linda J., Mitchell Orenstein, and Marilyn Rueschemeyer (eds.). 1999. *Left Parties and Social Policy in Postcommunist Europe.* Boulder, CO: Westview Press.

Cornea, Andrei. 2007. Mi-e teama de teamă lor. *Revista 22.* 20 April. http://www.revista22.ro/mi-e-teama-de-teama-lor-3646.html (accessed 9 March 2010).

Crepaz, Markus M. L. 1998. "Inclusion versus Exclusion. Political Institutions and Welfare Expenditures." Comparative Politics (October): 61–80.

De Castello Branco, Marta. 1998. "Pension Reform in the Baltics, Russia, and Other Countries of the Former Soviet Union (BRO)." IMF Working Paper 11 (February). Washington, DC: IMF.

De Menil, Georges and Eytan Sheshinski. 2001. "Romania's Pension System: From Crisis to Reform." Paper prepared for the Institute of World Economics Conference "Coping with the Pension Crisis—Where Does Europe Stand?" 21–22 March, Berlin.

Diaconu, Oana. 2008. "Pension Reform in Romania: How Far Should It Go?" In Robert W. McGee (ed.), *Taxation and Public Finance in Transition and Developing Economies,* 519–531. New York: Springer Science + Business Media.

Downs, William M. and Raluca V. Miller. 2006. "The 2004 Presidential and Parliamentary Elections in Romania." *Electoral Studies* 25: 393–415.

Early Warning Report. 2002. Administrarea Riscantă a Fondurilor de Asigurări Sociale. *Early Warning Report: Romania,* No. 4/2002. Bucharest: Societatea Academică din Romănia.

Economist. 1995. Getting Nastier. 4 February, Section: Europe, Romania, 334 (7900).

Elster, Jon, Claus Offe and Ulrich K. Preuss. 1998. *Institutional Design in Postcommunist Societies. Rebuilding the Ship at Sea.* New York: Cambridge University Press.

Esping-Andersen, Gøsta. 1985. *Politics against Markets.* Princeton, NJ: Princeton University Press.

———. 1990. *The Three Worlds of Welfare Capitalism.* Princeton, NJ: Princeton University Press.

European Commission. 1995. *Central and Eastern Eurobarometer 6: Economic and Political Trends, October–November 1995.* Distributed by Inter-university Consortium for Political and Social Research, Ann Arbor, MI (ICPSR 6835).

European Commission. 1997. Rapport Général 1997. Section 6. Élargissement. http://europa.eu/generalreport/fr/1997/frx60697.htm (accessed 25 March 2010).

———. Various years. *Central and Eastern Eurobarometer. Public Opinion and the European Union.* Distributed by Inter-university Consortium for Political and Social Research, Ann Arbor, MI (ICPSR 6835).

Feşnic, Florin and Oana Armeanu. 2008. "Does Education Make Voters More Leftist or More Rightist?" Paper presented at the Annual Meeting of the Midwest Political Science Association, 3–6 April, Chicago, IL.

———. 2009. "Strategic Effects of Electoral Rules: Testing the Impact of the 2008 Electoral Reform in Romania." Paper presented at the Annual Meeting of the Midwest Political Science Association, 1–5 April, Chicago, IL.

Fish, Steven M. 1999. "The End of Mečiarism." *East European Constitutional Review* 8 (1/2): 47–55.

Freedom House. 2009. Nations in Transit. http://www.freedomhouse.org/template.cfm?page=17 (accessed 21 July 2010).

Fultz, Elaine (ed.) 2002. *Pension Reform in Central and Eastern Europe.* Geneva, Switzerland: International Labour Organization.

Fultz, Elaine and Markus Ruck. 2001a. "Pension Reform in Central and Eastern Europe: Emerging Issues and Patterns." *International Labor Review* 140 (1): 19–43.

———. 2001b. *Pension Reform in Central and Eastern Europe: An Update on the Restructuring of National Pension Schemes in Selected Countries.* Geneva, Switzerland: International Labour Organization.

Garrett, Geoffrey. 1995. "Capital Mobility, Trade and the Domestic Politics of Economic Policy." *International Organization* 49 (4).

———. 1998. *Partisan Politics in the Global Economy.* Cambridge: Cambridge University Press.

Goliaš, Peter. 2005. "Pension Reform in Slovakia." International Organisation of Pension Supervisors, http://www.oecd.org/document/40/0,3343,en_35030657_38606785_39227944_1_1_1_1,00.html (accessed 18 March 2010).

Golinowska, Stanislawa. 1999. "Political Actors and Reform Paradigms in Old-Age Security in Poland." In Katharina Müller, Andreas Ryll, and Hans-Jurgen Wagener (eds.). *Transformation of Social Security: Pensions in Central-Eastern Europe.* New York: Physica-Verlag, 173–199.

Gongwer, John B. 2000. *Renaissance Program Strategic Plan.* http://www.jiu-valley.com/engl/tourism/history_pol_econ.pdf (accessed 30 July 2010).

Góra, Marek. 2001. "Going Beyond Transition: Pension Reform in Poland." In Blazyca, G. and R. Rapacki (eds), *Poland into the New Millennium.* Northampton, MA: Edward Elgar.

Gross, Peter and Vladimir Tismăneanu. 2005. "The End of Postcommunism in Romania." *Journal of Democracy* 16 (2): 146–162.

Grzymała-Busse, Anna. 2002. *Redeeming the Communist Past. The Regeneration of Communist Parties in East Central Europe.* New York: Cambridge University Press.

Guardiancich, I. 2004. "Welfare State Retrenchment in Central and Eastern Europe: The Case of Pension Reforms in Poland and Slovenia." *Managing Global Transitions* 2(1): 41–64.

Haggard, Stephan and Robert R. Kaufman (eds.). 1992. *The Politics of Economic Adjustment.* Princeton, NJ: Princeton University Press.

Haggard, Stephan and Steven Webb (eds.). 1996. *Voting for Reform: Democracy, Political Liberalization, and Structural Adjustment—An Overview.* San Francisco, CA: Institute for Contemporary Studies and the World Bank.

Hicks, Alexander and Duane H. Swank. 1992. "Politics, Institutions, and Welfare Spending in Industrialized Democracies, 1960–82." *American Political Science Review* 86 (3): 658–674.

Hinich, Melvin and Michael Munger. 1997. *Analytical Politics.* New York: Cambridge University Press.

Hinz, Richard P., Asta Zviniene, and Anna-Marie Vilamovska. 2005. *The New Pensions in Kazakhstan: Challenges in Making the Transition.* Social Protection Discussion Paper No. 0537. Washington DC: The World Bank.

Holzmann, Robert. 1993. "Reforming Old-age Pensions Systems in Central and Eastern European Countries in Transition." *Journal of Economics* 7 (Supplement 1): 191–218.

Holzmann, Robert and Joseph E. Stiglitz (eds.) 2001. *New Ideas about Old Age Security.* Washington, DC: The World Bank.

Holzmann, Robert, Mitchell Orenstein, and Michal Rutkowski. 2003. "Accelerating the European Pension Reform Agenda: Need, Progress, and Conceptual Underpinnings." In Robert Holzmann, Mitchell Orenstein, and Michal Rutkowski (eds.). *Pension Reform in Europe: Process and Progress.* Washington, DC: The World Bank, 1–47.

Holzmann, Robert and Robert Palacios. 2001. "Individual Accounts as Social Insurance: A World Bank Perspective." World Bank Social Protection Discussion Paper 0114. Washington, DC: The World Bank.

Holzmann, Robert and Ufuk Guven. 2009. *Adequacy of Retirement Income after Pension Reforms in Central, Eastern, and Southern Europe.* Washington, DC: The World Bank.

Huber, Evelyne, Charles Ragin, and John D. Stephens. 1993. "Social Democracy, Christian Democracy, Constitutional Structure, and the Welfare State." *American Journal of Sociology* 99 (3): 711–749.

Huber, Evelyne and John D. Stephens. 2000. "The Political Economy of Pension Reform." UNRISD Occasional Paper 7. Geneva: UNRISD.

———. 2001. *Development and Crisis of the Welfare State. Parties and Policies in Global Markets.* Chicago: The University of Chicago Press.

Hungarian Financial Supervisory Authority. 2009. Annual Report 2008. http://www.pszaf.hu/data/cms2084265/pszaf_annual_2008_kor3.pdf (accessed 25 March 2010).

Hungarian Financial Supervisory Authority. 2010. Times series of sectors supervised by HFSA-Pension funds. http://www.pszaf.hu/en/left_menu/pszafen_publication/timeseries (accessed 28 July 2010)

Immergut, Ellen. 1998. "The Theoretical Core of the New Institutionalism." *Politics & Society* 26 (1): 5–34.

Impavido, Gregorio and Roberto Rocha. 2006. "Competition and Performance in the Hungarian Second Pillar." World Bank Policy Research Working Paper 3876, April. Washington, D C: The World Bank.

International Labour Organization (ILO). 1997. *19th International Inquiry into the Cost of Social Security.* Geneva: ILO.

—— (ILO). 2007. *On the Preliminary Assessment of the Pension Reform Process in Slovakia.* Social Security Department, Social Protection Sector, Geneva. Subregional Office for Central and Eastern Europe, Budapest. Geneva/Budapest: ILO.

International Monetary Fund (IMF). 1998. "Romania: Statistical Appendix." IMF Staff Country Report No. 98/123 (November). Washington, DC: International Monetary Fund.

—— (IMF). 2004. "Romania: Selected Issues and Statistical Appendix." IMF Country Report No. 04/220 (July). Washington, DC: International Monetary Fund.

International Organisation of Pension Supervisors. 2008a. Hungary Country Profile. http://www.iopsweb.org/document/33/0,3343,en_35030657_38606785_38684193_1_1_1_1,00.html (accessed 18 March 2010).

——. 2008b. Poland Country Profile. http://www.iopsweb.org/document/57/0,3343,en_35030657_38606785_39218489_1_1_1_1,00.html (accessed 18 March 2010).

——. 2008c. Romania Country Profile. http://www.iopsweb.org/document/39/0,3343,en_35030657_38606785_38708647_1_1_1_1,00.html (accessed 18 March 2010).

——. 2008d. Slovak Republic Country Profile. http://www.iopsweb.org/document/40/0,3343,en_35030657_38606785_39227944_1_1_1_1,00.html (accessed 18 March 2010).

International Social Security Association. n.d.a. Hungary. Reforms. http://www.issa.int/aiss/Observatory/Country-Profiles/Regions/Europe/Hungary/(link)/Reforms%201 (accessed 29 March 2010).

International Social Security Association. n.d.b. Poland. Reforms. http://www.issa.int/Observatory/Country-Profiles/Regions/Europe/Poland (accessed 26 July 2010).

International Social Security Association. 2008. Social Security Programs Throughout the World: Europe, 2008. https://www.socialsecurity.gov/policy/docs/progdesc/ssptw/2008-2009/europe/ (accessed 21 March 2010).

Ishiyama, John T. 1995. "Communist Parties in Transition. Structures, Leaders, and Processes of Democratization in Eastern Europe." *Comparative Politics* (January): 147–166.

———. 1997. "The Sickle or the Rose? Previous Regime Type and the Evolution of the Ex-Communist Parties in Postcommunist Politics." *Comparative Political Studies* 30 (3): 299–330.

———. 2006. "Europeanization and the Communist Successor Parties." *Politics & Policy* 34 (1): 3–29.

James, Estelle and Sarah Brooks. 2001. "The Political Economy of Structural Pension Reform." In Robert Holzmann and Joseph Stiglitz (eds.), *New Ideas about Old Age Security*. Washington, DC: The World Bank.

Kaminski, Marek M., Grzegorz Lissowski and Piotr Swistak. 1998. "The 'Revival of Communism' or the Effect of Institutions?: The 1993 Polish Parliamentary Elections." *Public Choice* 97 (3): 429–449.

Kapstein, Etan B. and Michael Mandelbaum (eds.). 1997. *Sustaining the Transition: The Social Safety Net in Postcommunist Europe*. New York: Council of Foreign Relations.

Kitschelt, Herbert. 1992. "The Formation of Party Systems in East Central Europe." *Politics and Society* 20 (1): 7–50.

———. 1995. "Formation of Party Cleavages in Postcommunist Democracies: Theoretical Propositions." *Party Politics* 1: 447–472.

———. 2001. "Partisan Competition and Welfare State Retrenchment. When Do Politicians Choose Unpopular Polices?" In Paul Pierson (ed.), *The New Politics of the Welfare State*. New York: Oxford University Press.

Kitschelt, Herbert, Zdenka Mansfeldova, Radoslaw Markowski, and Gabor Toka (eds.). 1999. *Postcommunist Party Systems. Competition, Representation, and Inter-Party Cooperation*. New York: Cambridge University Press.

Korpi, W. 1983. *The Democratic Class Struggle*. London: Routledge and Kegan Paul.

Lambru, Mihaela and Bogdan Chirițoiu. 2002. Impact Study No. 10– Romanian Social Insurance and the Integration to European Union. http://www.policy.hu/Chirițoiu/final_report.pdf (accessed 30 March 2010).

Lijphart, Arend. 1984. *Democracies*. New Haven, CT: Yale University Press.

Lindeman, David, Michal Rutkowski, and Oleksiy Sluchynskyy. 2000 (August). *The Evolution of Pension Systems in Eastern Europe and Central Asia: Opportunities, Constraints, Dilemmas and Emerging Practices*. Washington, DC: The World Bank.

Lipsmeyer, Christine S. 2000. "Reading between the Welfare Lines: Politics and Policy Structure in Postcommunist Europe." *Europe-Asia Studies* 52 (7): 1191–1211.

Mahr, Alison and John Nagle. 1995. "Resurrection of the Successor Parties and Democratization in East-Central Europe." *Communist and Post-Communist Studies* 28, 4: 393–409.

Markowski, Radoslaw. 2002. "The Polish SLD in 1990s. From Opposition to Incumbents and Back." In András Bozóki and John T. Ishiyama (eds.). *The Communist Successor Parties of Central and Eastern Europe*. New York: M. E. Sharpe.

Mediafax. 2010. Şeitan: Prin recalcularea pensiilor speciale se vor face economii lunare de 300 de milioane de lei. http://www.mediafax.ro/social/seitan-prin-recalcularea-pensiilor-speciale-se-vor-face-economii-lunare-de-300-de-milioane-de-lei-6472259/ (accessed 30 July 2010).

Mihuţ, Liliana. 1994. "The Emergence of Political Pluralism in Romania." *Communist and Postcommunist Studies* 27 (4): 411–422.

Ministerul Muncii, Familiei şi Protecţiei Sociale. 2008. Lege nr. 204 din 22 mai 2006 privind pensiile facultative. http://www.mmuncii.ro/pub/imagemanager/images/file/Legislatie/LEGI/L204–2006_act.pdf (accessed 30 March 2010).

———. 2009. Quarterly Statistical Bulletin on Labour and Social Protection 4(68)/2009. http://www.mmuncii.ro/ro/653-view.html (accessed 29 March 2010).

Ministerul Muncii, Familiei şi Protecţiei Sociale. 2010. Quarterly Statistical Bulletin on Labour and Social Protection 1/2010. http://www.mmuncii.ro/ro/680-view.html (accessed 30 July 2010).

Ministry of Labour and Social Policy. n.d. Social Insurance. Pension Insurance. http://www.mpips.gov.pl/index.php?gid=876 (accessed 23 March 2010).

Mitchell, Olivia S. 1999. *Evaluating Administrative Costs in Mexico's AFORES Pension System*. Working Paper 1999–01. Philadelphia, PA: The Pension Research Council/Boettner Center.

Moise, Lidia. 2009. Statul nu mai poate finanţa pensile de lux. *Revista 22*. 2 June. http://www.revista22.ro/statul-nu-mai-poate-finan355a-pensiile-de-lux-6143.html (accessed 25 March 2010).

Müller, Katharina. 1999. *The Political Economy of Pension Reform in Central-Eastern Europe*. Northampton, MA: Edward Elgar.

———. 2002. "Between State and Market: Czech and Slovene Pension Reform in Comparison." In Elaine Fultz (ed.), *Pension Reform in Central and Eastern Europe Volume 2: Restructuring of Public Pension Schemes: Case Studies of the Czech Republic and Slovenia*. Budapest: International Labour Organization.

Mungiu-Pippidi, Alina. 2004. "Romania." *Nations in Transit*. Washington, DC: Freedom House.

———. 2008. "Romania." *Nations in Transit*. Washington, DC: Freedom House.

Národná banka Slovenska. 2009. Analysis of the Slovak Financial Sector for the Year 2008. http://www.nbs.sk/_img/Documents/DFT/PUBLIK/ANALYZA/2008–2a.pdf (accessed 25 March 2010).

———. n.d. Supplementary Pension Asset Management Companies. http://www.nbs.sk/en/financial-market-supervision/pension-saving-supervision/supplementary-pension-asset-management-companies (accessed 19 March 2010).

Nelson, Joan M. 1992. "Poverty, Equity, and the Politics of Adjustment." In Stephan Haggard and Robert R. Kaufman (eds.), *The Politics of Economic Adjustment*. Princeton, NJ: Princeton University Press.

———. 1993. "The Politics of Economic Transformation: Is Third World Experience Relevant in Eastern Europe?" *World Politics* 45 (April): 433–463.

Noghiu, Bernard. 2009. Pensionarii de lux ne costă peste 20 de milioane de euro annual. *Revista 22.* 19 March. http://www.revista22.ro/pension-arii-de-lux-ne-cost259-peste-20-de-milioane-de-euro-anual-5761.html (accessed 25 March 2010).

Orenstein, Mitchell. 1998. "A Genealogy of Communist Successor Parties in East-Central Europe and the Determinants of their Success." *East European Politics and Societies* 12 (3): 472–499.

———. 2000. "How Politics and Institutions Affect Pension Reform in Three Postcommunist Countries." World Bank Policy Research Working Paper 2310. Washington, DC: The World Bank.

———. 2003. "Mapping the Diffusion of Pension Innovation." In Robert Holzmann, Mitchell Orenstein, and Michal Rutkowski (eds.). *Pension Reform in Europe: Process and Progress.* Washington, DC: The World Bank, 171–193.

———. 2008. *Privatizing Pensions: The Transnational Campaign for Social Security Reform.* Princeton, NJ: Princeton University Press.

Palacios, Robert and Montserrat Pallarès-Miralles. 2000. "International Patterns of Pension Provision." World Bank Social Protection Discussion Paper 0009. Washington, DC: The World Bank.

Palata, Lubos. 2009. Slovakia: Battle of the Sexes and Far More. *Transitions Online.* 6 April. https://login.lib-proxy.usi.edu/login?url=http://search.ebscohost.com/login.aspx?direct=true&db=aph&AN=38125244&loginpage=login.asp&site=ehost-live&scope=site (accessed 29 March 2010).

PD-L. n.d. http://www.pdl.org.ro/index.php?page=PDL&textPag=12 (accessed 14 March 2010).

Pénzeš, Peter. 2007. "Private Pension System in Slovakia." Presentation at the CEIOPS OPC meeting, 7 September, Frankfurt am Main, Germany.

Pierson, Christopher. 1998 (2nd edition). *Beyond the Welfare State. The New Political Economy of Welfare.* University Park, PA: Pennsylvania State University Press.

Pierson, Paul. 1994. *Dismantling the Welfare State? Reagan, Thatcher, and the Politics of Retrenchment.* Cambridge, NY: Cambridge University Press.

———. 1998. "Irresistible Forces, Immovable Objects: Post-industrial Welfare States Confront Permanent Austerity." *Journal of European Public Policy* 5 (4): 539–560.

———. 2000. "Three Worlds of Welfare State Research." *Comparative Political Studies* 33 (6/7).

——— (ed.). 2001. *The New Politics of the Welfare State.* New York: Oxford University Press.

Pierson, Paul and R. Kent Weaver. 1993. "Imposing Losses in Pension Policy." In R. Kent Weaver and Bert A. Rockman (eds.), *Do Institutions Matter? Government Capabilities in the United States and Abroad.* Washington, DC: The Brookings Institution.

PNL. n.d. Programul prezidential. http://crinantonescu.ro/intra-in-dezbat-ere.html (accessed 14 March 2010).

Polish Financial Supervision Authority. 2010. Pension system. Financial and statistical data. Quarterly data. http://www.knf.gov.pl/en/about_the_market/Pension_system/index.html (accessed 26 July 2010).

Polska Agencja Prasowa. 2008. Legal Bulletin, Week 46, 13/11/08 - 19/11/08. http://www.girodivite.it/IMG/pdf/BPP46A.pdf (accessed 9 January 2010).

Poole, Keith T. 2005. *Spatial Models of Legislative Voting*. New York: Cambridge University Press.

Poole, Keith T. and Howard Rosenthal. 1997. *Congress: A Political-Economic History of Roll Call Voting*. New York: Oxford University Press.

Pop-Elecheş, Grigore. 1999. "Separated at Birth or Separated by Birth? The Communist Successor Parties in Romania and Hungary." *East European Politics and Societies* 13 (1): 117–147.

———. 2008. "A Party for All Seasons: Electoral Adaptation of Romanian Communist Successor Parties." *Communist and Postcommunist Studies* 41: 465–479.

Popescu, Marina. 2003. "The Parliamentary and Presidential Elections in Romania, November 2000." *Electoral Studies* 22: 325–395.

Popescu, Simona. 2009. Coaliţiile de dreapta, reţeta insuccesului. *Revista 22*. 6 October. http://www.revista22.ro/coali355iile-de-dreapta-re355e-ta-insuccesului-6704.html (accessed 14 March 2010).

Pora, Andreea. 2009. Noua arma antibăsesciană: prefraudarea ONG-istă. *Revista 22*. 29 October. http://www.revista22.ro/noua-arma-antibases-ciana-prefraudarea-ong-ista-6895.html (accessed 8 March 2010).

Pridham, Geoffrey (ed.). 1986. *Coalitional Behaviour in Theory and Practice: An Inductive Model for Western Europe*. New York: Cambridge University Press.

———. 2008. "Status Quo Bias or Institutionalisation for Reversibility?: The EU's Political Conditionality, Post-Accession Tendencies and Democratic Consolidation in Slovakia." *Europe-Asia Studies* 60 (3): 423–454.

Project on Political Transformation and the Electoral Process in Postcommunist Europe. 2002. http://www2.essex.ac.uk/elect/database/indexCountry.asp?country=ROMANIA&opt=elc. University of Essex (accessed 7 March 2010).

Revista 22. 2009. Băsescu: 2007 şi 2008 au fost un eşec pentru reforma din cauza relaţiei cu Tăriceanu. 20 September. http://www.revista22.ro/-basescu-2007-si-2008-au-fost-un-esec-pentru-reforma-din-cauza-relatie-6602.html (accessed 14 March 2010).

Rodrik, Dani. 1996. "Understanding Economic Policy Reform." *Journal of Economic Literature* XXXIV (March).

———. 1998. "Why Do More Open Economies Have Larger Governments?" *Journal of Political Economy* 106 (October).

Scarbrough, Elinor. 2000. "West European Welfare States: The Old Politics of Retrenchment." *European Journal of Political Research* 38 (6): 225–259.

Schludi, Martin. 2003. "Politics of Pension Reform—The French Case in a Comparative Perspective." *French Politics* 1 (2): 199–224.

Shepsle, K. 1979. "Institutional Arrangements and Equilibrium in Multidimensional Voting Models." *American Journal of Political Science* 23 (1): 27–59.

Shepsle, K. and B. Weingast. 1981. "Structure Induced Equilibrium and Legislative Choice." *Public Choice* 37 (3): 503–519.

Slovak Spectator. 2004. Pension plan is most popular reform. 13 December. http://spectator.sme.sk/articles/view/18128// (accessed 19 March 2010).

———. 2009a. More pension changes loom. 9 March. http://spectator.sme.sk/articles/view/34575/3/more_pension_changes_loom.html (accessed 23 March 2010).

———. 2009b. A round-up of the year in business. http://spectator.sme.sk/articles/view/37482/24/a_round_up_of_the_year_in_business.html (accessed 23 March 2010).

———. 2010. Coming into force: new and amended laws for 2010. http://spectator.sme.sk/articles/view/37582/24/coming_into_force_new_and_amended_laws_for2010.html (accessed 23 March 2010).

Snyder, Jack. 1993. "Nationalism and the Crisis of the Post-Soviet State." In Michael E. Brown (ed.), *Ethnic Conflict and International Security.* Princeton, NJ: Princeton University Press.

Sociálna Poisťovňa. n.d. Social Insurance Agency in Slovakia. http://www.socpoist.sk/?lang=en (accessed 20 March 2010).

Stan, Lavinia. 2005a. "From Riches to Rags: The Romanian National Christian Democrat Peasant Party." *East European Quarterly* 39 (2): 179–227.

———. 2005b. "The Opposition Takes Charge: The Romanian General Elections of 2004." *Problems of Post-Communism* 52 (3): 3–15.

Statistical Office of the Slovak Republic. 2006. Elections to the Parliament of the Slovak Republic in the year 2006. http://app.statistics.sk/nrsr_2006/angl/index.jsp (accessed 30 July 2010).

Stephens, John D. 1979. *The Transition from Capitalism to Socialism.* London: Macmillan.

Svoreňová, Mária. 2006. "Pension Reform and Trade Unions in the Slovak Republic." In *Social Security for All: Trade Union Policies,* special issue of *Labour Education 2006/4* (145): 99–107.

Tismăneanu, Vladimir. 2003. *Stalinism for All Seasons: A Political History of Romanian Communism.* Berkeley: University of California Press.

Thelen, Kathleen. 1999. "Historical Institutionalism in Comparative Politics." *Annual Review of Political Science* 2: 369–404.

Transparency International. 2009. *Corruption Perceptions Index.* http://www.transparency.org/policy_research/surveys_indices/cpi/200 (accessed 30 July 2010).

Tudoroiu, Theodor, Peter Horváth and Marek Hrušovský. 2009. "Ultra-Nationalism and Geopolitical Exceptionalism in Mečiar's Slovakia." *Problems of Post-Communism* 56 (4): 3–14.

Vachudova, Milada Anna. 2008. "Tempered by the EU? Political Parties and Party Systems Before and After Accession." *Journal of European Public Policy* 15 (6): 861–879.

Voinea, Liviu. 2003. "FDI in Romania Matures." *Early Warning Report-Romania 01/2003* (January): 11–13. Central and Eastern European Online Library.

Weingast, Barry R. 1996. "Political Institutions: Rational Choice Perspectives." In Robert E. Goodin and Hans-Dieter Klingeman (eds.). *A New Handbook of Political Science.* New York: Oxford University Press.

Wenzel, Michal. 1998. "Solidarity and Akcja Wyborcza 'Solidarnosc. An Attempt at Reviving the Legend." *Communist and Post-Communist Studies* 31 (2): 139–156.

Wiatr, Jerzy J. 1997. "Poland's Three Parliaments in the Era of Transition, 1989–1995." *International Political Science Review* 18 (4): 443–450.

Williamson, John (ed.). 1994. *The Political Economy of Policy Reform.* Washington, DC: Institute for International Studies.

Wilson, James Q. (ed.). 1980. *The Politics of Regulation.* New York: Basic Books.

Woleková, Helena. 1997. "Governmental Social Policy and the Social Situation of Slovakia's Inhabitants in 1995." In Martin Bútora and Péter Hunčik (eds.), *Global Report on Slovakia. Comprehensive Analyses from 1995 and Trends from 1996.* Bratislava: Sándor Márai Foundation.

World Bank. 1994. *Averting the Old Age Crisis: Policies to Protect the Old and Promote Growth.* New York: Oxford University Press.

World Bank. 1997. *Poland – Country Economic Memorandum. Reform and Growth on the Road to the EU. Report No. 16858-POL.* Washington, DC: The World Bank.

———. 2004. *Slovak Republic: Pension Policy Reform Note.* Washington, DC: The World Bank.

———. Various years. *World Development Report.* Washington, DC: The World Bank.

———. n.d. www.worldbank.org/pensions (accessed 7 July 2005).

World Economic Outlook. 1999. Washington, DC: International Monetary Fund. http://www.imf.org/external/pubs/ft/weo/1999/01/data/ (accessed 29 March 2010).

Young, Patricia T. 2009. "Political Parties and Democratic Governance in Romania." Paper presented at the American Political Science Association Meeting, 2–6 September, Toronto, ON.

FURTHER READINGS

Amparo Cruz-Saco, Maria and Carmelo Mesa-Lago (eds.). 1998. *Do Options Exist? The Reform of Pension and Health Care Systems in Latin America.* PA: University of Pittsburgh Press.

Armeanu, Oana. 2004. "Experimenting with Pension Reform in Central and Eastern Europe. Parties, Coalitions, and Policies." Paper presented at the Annual Meeting of the Midwest Political Science Association, 15–18 April, Chicago, IL.

———. 2006. "Party Systems, Coalitions, and Pension Reform. Legislative Roll Call Analyses and Expert Surveys in Poland, Slovakia, and Hungary." Paper presented at the Annual Meeting of the Midwest Political Science Association, 20–23 April, Chicago, IL.

Armeanu, Oana and Alin Ceobanu. 2004. "Do Ideology and Party Preference Matter? Cross-Regional Variation in Public Attitudes toward the Welfare State in Romania." Paper presented at the American Political Science Association, 2–5 September, Chicago, IL.

Arza, Camila and Martin Kohli. 2007. *Pension Reform in Europe: Politics, Policies and Outcomes.* London, UK: Routledge.

Barr, Nicholas. 1992. *Income Transfers and the Social Safety Net in Russia. Studies of Economies in Transformation.* Washington, DC: The World Bank.

——— (ed.) 1994. *Labor Markets and Social Policy in Central and Eastern Europe. The Transition and Beyond.* New York: Oxford University Press.

———. 1998 (3rd edition). *The Economics of the Welfare State.* New York: Oxford University Press.

———. 2000. "Reforming Pensions: Myths, Truths, and Policy Choices." IMF Working Paper 139. Washington, DC: IMF.

Barr, Nicholas and David Whynes (eds.). 1993. *Current Issues in the Economics of Welfare.* New York: St. Martin's Press.

Bennett, Andrew and Alexander George. 1997. "An Alliance of Statistical and Case Study Methods: Research on the Interdemocratic Peace." *APSA-CP. Newsletter of the APSA Organized Section in Comparative Politics* 9 (1): 6–9.

Bielasiak, Jack. 1997. "Substance and Process in the Development of Party Systems in East Central Europe." *Communist and Postcommunist Studies* 30 (1): 23–44.

Blondel, Jean and Ferdinand Müller-Rommel. 2001. *Cabinets in Eastern Europe.* New York: Palgrave.

Bodnarová, Bernardína. 1999. "Social Policy." In Grigorij Mesežnikov, Michal Ivantyšyn, and Tom Nicholson (eds.), *A Global Report on the State of Society.* Bratislava: Institute for Public Affairs.

Bonoli, Giuliano. 2003. "Two Worlds of Pension Reform in Western Europe." *Comparative Politics* (July): 399–416.

Bozóki, András and John T. Ishiyama (eds.). 2002. *The Communist Successor Parties of Central and Eastern Europe.* New York: M. E. Sharpe.

Brady, Henry E. and David Collier (eds.). 2001. *Rethinking Social Inquiry: Diverse Tools, Shared Standards.* Lanham, MD: Rowan & Littlefield Publishers and Institute of Governmental Studies/UC Berkeley.

Brooks, Sarah and Estelle James. 1999. "The Political Economy of Pension Reform." Paper presented at World Bank Conference "New Ideas About Old-Age Security," Washington, DC (September).

Buchanan, James. 1988. *The Political Economy of the Welfare State.* Stockholm, Sweden: The Industrial Institute for Economic and Social Research.

Caldwell, Michael. 1994. *The Influence of Democratic Structure: Presidents, Parliaments, and Welfare.* A study submitted to the Department of Political Science of Stanford University. Stanford, CA. (December).

Cashu, Ilean. 2000. "The Politics and Policy Trade-Offs of Reforming the Public Pension System in Postcommunist Moldova." *Europe-Asia Studies* 52 (4): 741–757.

———. 2001. "Negotiating Public Pension Reform in Russia, Romania, and Latvia: The Role of Compromise Mechanisms." Budapest: Open Society Institute, International Policy Fellowship Program.

———. 2001. "The Politics of Pension Retrenchment in Transitional Regimes: A Political Institutional Analysis of Russia, Romania, and Latvia." Budapest: Open Society Institute, International Policy Fellowship Program.

Coppedge, Michael. 1999. "Thickening Thin Concepts and Theories: Combining Large N and Small N in Comparative Politics." *Comparative Politics* 31 (4): 465–476.

Cotta, Maurizio. 1994. "Building Party Systems after Dictatorship. East European Cases in a Comparative Perspective." In Geoffrey Pridham and Tatu Vanhanen (eds.), *Democratization in Eastern Europe: Domestic and International Perspectives.* New York: Routledge.

Deacon, Bob and Julia Szalai. 1990. *Social Policy in the New Eastern Europe. What Future for Socialist Welfare?* Brookfield, VT: Gower Publishing Co.

Deacon, Bob, Mita Castle-Kanerova, Nick Manning, Frances Millard, Eva Orosz, Julia Szalai, and Anna Vidinova. 1992. *The New Eastern Europe. Social Policy Past, Present, and Future.* Newbury Park, CA: Sage Publications.

Disney, Richard. 1999. "Notional Accounts as a Pension Reform Strategy: An Evaluation." World Bank Social Protection Discussion Paper 9928. Washington, DC: The World Bank.

Esping-Andersen, Gøsta (ed.). 1996. *Welfare States in Transition. National Adaptations in Global Economies.* Thousand Oaks, CA: Sage Publications in association with the United Nations Research Institute for Social Development.

———. 1999. *Social Foundations of Postindustrial Economies.* New York: Oxford University Press.

Feldstein, Martin. 1996. "The Missing Piece in Policy Analysis: Social Security Reform." *The American Economic Review* 86 (2): 1–14.

Feşnic, Florin. 2003. "Modernization, Transition, and Vote in Romania." Paper presented at the Annual Conference of the Midwest Political Science Association, April 2003, Chicago, IL.

Focus, Center for Social and Market Analysis. 2003. "The New Slovak Government—The 100 First Days in Office." Public opinion poll (February). Bratislava, Slovak Republic.

Fox, Louise. 1994. "Old-Age Security in Transitional Economies." Policy Research Working Paper 1257 (February). Washington, DC: The World Bank.

Fox, Louise and Edward Palmer. 1999. "Latvian Pension Reform." Social Protection Discussion Paper Series 9922. Washington, DC: The World Bank.

Fultz, Elaine. 2003. "Recent Trends in Pension Reform and Implementation in the EU Accession Countries." Paper presented at the Informal Meeting of Ministers at the International Labour Conference, 10 June, Geneva.

Gallagher, Tom. 2005. *Modern Romania: The End of Communism, the Failure of Democratic Reform, and the Theft of a Nation.* New York: New York University Press.

Giersch, Herbert (ed.). 1997. *Reforming the Welfare State.* Berlin, Germany: Springer-Verlag.

Goodin, Robert E., Bruce Headey, Ruud Muffels, and Henk-Jan Dirven. 1999. *The Real Worlds of Welfare Capitalism.* Cambridge, UK: Cambridge University Press.

Gould, Arthur. 1993. *Capitalist Welfare Systems. A Comparison of Japan, Britain & Sweden.* New York: Longman.

Grzymała-Busse, Anna. 1998. "Reform Efforts in the Czech and Slovak Communist Parties and Their Successors, 1988–1993." *East European Politics and Societies* 12 (3): 442–471.

———. 2001. "Coalition Formation and the Regime Divide in New Democracies. East Central Europe." *Comparative Politics* (October): 85–104.

———. 2001. "Political Parties and State Politicization in East Central Europe." Paper presented at the APSA annual conference, 20 August–2 September, San Francisco, CA.

———. 2007. *Rebuilding Leviathan. Party Competition and State Exploitation in Postcommunist Democracies.* New York: Cambridge University Press.

Haas, Ernst B. 1986. "What Is Nationalism and Why Should We Study It?" *International Organization* 40 (3): 707–744.

Hasenfeld, Yeheskel, Jane A. Rafferty, and Mayer N. Zald. 1987. "The Welfare State, Citizenship, and Bureaucratic Encounters." *Annual Review of Sociology* 13: 387–415.

Hasselman, Chris. 2002. "The Distributional Consequences of Czech Privatization and Its Impact on Social Welfare Reform." Paper presented at the annual meeting of the Midwest Political Science Association (April), Chicago, IL.

———. "The Politics of Interest Representation: The Case of Pension Reform in Hungary." Paper presented at the annual meeting of the American Political Science Association (August), Boston, MA.

Haughton, Tim and Marek Rybář. 2008. "A Change of Direction: The 2006 Parliamentary Elections and Party Politics in Slovakia." *Journal of Communist Studies and Transition Politics* 24 (2): 232–255.

Hellman, Joel S. 1998. "Winners Take All. The Politics of Partial Reform in Postcommunist Transitions." *World Politics* 50 (January): 203–234.

Holmes, Leslie. 1997. *Post-communism. An Introduction.* Durham, NC: Duke University Press.

Huber, John and Ronald Inglehart. 1995. "Expert Interpretations of Party Space and Party Locations in 42 Societies." *Party Politics* 1 (1): 73–111.

Huber, Evelyne and John D. Stephens. 1998. "Internationalization and the Social Democratic Model." *Comparative Political Studies* 31: 353–397.

———. 2000. "Partisan Governance, Women's Employment, and the Social Democratic Service State." *American Sociological Review* 65 (June): 323–342.

Inglot, Tomasz. 1995. "The Politics of Social Policy Reform in Postcommunist Poland: Government Responses to the Social Insurance Crisis During 1989–1993." *Communist and Postcommunist Studies* 28 (3): 361–373.

———. 2008. *Welfare States in East Central Europe, 1919–2004.* New York: Cambridge University Press.

Ishiyama, John T. and Sahar Shafqat. 2000. "Party Identity Change in Postcommunist Politics: The Cases of the Successor Parties in Hungary, Poland and Russia." *Communist and Postcommunist Studies* 33: 439–455.

Iversen, Torben and Anne Wren. 1998. "Equality, Employment, and Budgetary Restraint. The Trilemma of the Service Economy." *World Politics* 50 (July): 507–546.

Iversen, Torben and David Soskice. 2001. "An Asset Theory of Social Policy Preferences." *American Political Science Review* 95 (4).

Iversen, Torben and Thomas R. Cusack. 2000. "The Causes of Welfare State Expansion. Deindustrialization or Globalization?" *World Politics* 52 (April): 313–349.

Jacobs, Alan. 2004. "Backing into the Future: Reconceiving Policy Reform as Intertemporal Choice." Paper presented at the annual meeting of the American Political Science Association (September), Chicago, IL.

Janoski, Thomas and Alexander M. Hicks (eds.). 1994. *The Comparative Political Economy of the Welfare State.* New York: Cambridge University Press.

Kasek, Leszek, Thomas Laursen and Emilia Skrok. 2008. *Sustainability of Pension Systems in the New EU Member States and Croatia: Coping with Aging Challenges and Fiscal Pressures.* Washington, DC: The World Bank.

Katzenstein, Peter. 1985. *Small States in World Markets.* Ithaca, NY: Cornell University Press.

Keane, Michael P. and Eswar S. Prasad. 2000. "Inequality, Transfers and Growth: New Evidence from the Economic Transition in Poland." IMF Working Paper 117. Washington, DC: IMF.

Kolberg, Jon Eivind (ed.). 1992. *The Study of Welfare Regimes.* Armonk, NY: M. E. Sharpe.

Kopecky, Petr. 1995. "Developing Party Organizations in East-Central Europe. What Type of Party Is Likely to Emerge?" *Party Politics* 1 (4): 515–534.

Kornai, Janos. 1997. "Editorial: Reforming the Welfare State in Postsocialist Societies." *World Development* 25 (8): 1183–1186.

Kornai, Janos, Stephan Haggard, and Robert R. Kaufman. 2001. *Reforming the State. Fiscal and Welfare Reform in Post-Socialist Countries.* New York: Cambridge University Press.

Koslowski, Peter and Andreas Follesdal (eds.) 1997. *Restructuring the Welfare State. Theory and Reform of Social Policy.* Heidelberg, Germany: Springer-Verlag.

Kovacs, Janos Matyas. 2002. "Approaching the EU and Reaching the US? Rival Narratives on Transforming Welfare Regimes in East-Central Europe." *West European Politics* 25, Special Issue 2 (April): 175–204.

Laver, Michael and Kenneth A. Shepsle. 1996. *Making and Breaking Governments. Cabinets and Legislatures in Parliamentary Democracies.* Cambridge: Cambridge University Press.

Lazutka, Roman. 1998. "Comments on 'The Current State of Lithuanian Pension System and Discussions on Its Reform'." European Union's Phare ACE Programme Research Report P98-1023-R.

Lewis, Paul G. 2000. Political Parties in Postcommunist Europe. New York: Routledge.

——— (ed.). 2001. *Party Development and Democratic Change in Postcommunist Europe. The First Decade.* Portland, OR: Frank Cass.

———. 2008. "Changes in the Party Politics of the New EU Member States in Central Europe: Patterns of Europeanization and Democratization." *Journal of Southern Europe and the Balkans* 10 (2): 151–165.

Londregan, John B. 2000. *Legislative Institutions and Ideology in Chile.* Cambridge: Cambridge University Press.

Mareş, Isabela. 1997. "Is Unemployment Insurable? Employers and the Introduction of Unemployment Insurance." *Journal of Public Policy* 17 (3): 299–327.

Marier, Patrik. 2008. *Pension Politics. Consensus and Social Conflict in Ageing Societies.* New York: Routledge.

Melicherčik, Igor and Cyril Ungvarský. 2006. "Pension Reform in Slovakia: Perspectives on the Fiscal Debt and Pension Level." International Organisation of Pension Supervisors, http://www.oecd.org/document/40/0,3343,en_35030657_38606785_39227944_1_1_1_1,00.html (accessed 18 March 2010).

Mitchell William C. and Randy T. Simmons. 1994. *Beyond Politics. Markets, Welfare, and the Failure of Bureaucracy.* Boulder, CO: Westview Press.

Moene, Karl Ove and Michael Wallerstein. 2001. "Inequality, Social Insurance, and Redistribution." *American Political Science Review* 95 (4).

Morgan, Kimberly. 2001. "Gender and the Welfare State." *Comparative Politics* (October): 105–124.

Mudde, Cas. 2001. "In the Name of the Peasantry, the Proletariat, and the People: Populisms in Eastern Europe." *East European Politics and Societies* 15 (1): 33–53.

Müller, Katharina. 2003. "Pension Reform in the East European Accession Countries." *European Journal of Social Security* 5 (1): 7–37.

Müller, K. 2004. "The Political Economy of Pension Reform in Central and Eastern Europe." In *Reforming Public Pensions. Sharing the Experiences of Transition and OECD Countries.* Warsaw, 27–28 May, 2002. Paris: OECD.

Müller, Katharina, Andreas Ryll, and Hans-Jurgen Wagener (eds.). 1999. *Transformation of Social Security: Pensions in Central-Eastern Europe.* New York: Physica-Verlag.

Národná Banka Slovenska. 2007. Report on the Results of the Slovak Financial Sector Analysis for the First Half of the Year 2007. http://www.nbs.sk/_img/Documents/DFT/PUBLIK/ANALYZA/2007–1a.pdf (accessed 21 March 2010).

———. 2008. Financial Stability Report 2007. http://www.nbs.sk/_img/Documents/ZAKLNBS%5CPUBLIK%5CSFS%5CSFS2007A.PDF (Accessed 21 March 2010).

O'Connor, Julia. 1993. "Gender, Class and Citizenship in the Comparative Analysis of Welfare State Regimes: Theoretical and Methodological Issues." *British Journal of Sociology* 44: 501–518.

———. 1996. "From Women in the Welfare State to Gendering Welfare State Regimes." *Current Sociology* 44: 1–124.

O'Connor, Julia, Ann Shola Orloff, and Sheila Shaver. 1999. *States, Markets, Families: Gender, Liberalism and Social Policy in Australia, Canada, Great Britain, and the Unites States.* Cambridge: Cambridge University Press.

OECD. 2001. "A Proposal for Developing a Taxonomy of Private Pension Systems." Paper presented at the 'Private Pensions Conference' hosted by the Ministry of Labour and Social Policy of Bulgaria, OECD, and United States Agency for International Development. Sofia, Bulgaria (April).

———. 2002. "The Political Economy of Pension Reform in Lithuania or Why Pension Reform in Lithuania has been Debated so Long?" Paper presented at the conference 'Practical Lessons in Pension Reform: Sharing the Experience of Transition and OEDC Countries' organized by the OECD, the Ministry of Labour and Social Policy of Poland, and the Ministry of Foreign Affairs of the Netherlands, Warsaw, Poland (May).

Ohtsu, Sadayoshi. 2002. "Pension System in Russia. The Political Economy of Putin's Pension Reform." Paper presented at the International Workshop 'Population, Labor Market, Pension and Quality of Life in Transitional Countries.' Kunitachi, Tokio (February).

Orenstein, Mitchell A. and Martine R. Haas. 2002. "Globalization and the Development of Welfare States in Postcommunist Europe." BCSIA Discussion Paper 2002–02. Cambridge, MA: Kennedy School of Government, Harvard University.

Orloff, Ann Shola. 1993. "Gender and the Social Rights of Citizenship: The Comparative Analysis of Gender Relations and Welfare States." *American Sociological Review* 58: 303–328.

———. 1996. "Gender in the Welfare State." *Annual Review of Sociology* 22: 51–78.

Pedersen, Susan. 1993. *Family, Dependence, and the Origins of the Welfare State*. Cambridge: Cambridge University Press.

Peters, B. Guy. 1998. *Comparative Politics: Theory and Methods*. New York: New York University Press.

Pettai, Vello and Marcus Kreuzer. 1999. "Party Politics in the Baltic States: Social Bases and Institutional Context." *East European Politics and Societies* 13 (1): 148–189.

Pierson, Paul. 1996. "The New Politics of the Welfare State." *World Politics* 48 (January): 143–179.

Poole, Keith T. W-NOMINATE program page. http://voteview.uh.edu/w-nominate.htm.

Prizel, Ilya. 2001. "Populism as a Political Force in Postcommunist Russia and Ukraine." *East European Politics and Societies* 15 (1): 54–63.

Project Syndicate. 2010. Social Insecurity—A Survey of Pensions in Eastern Europe and the NIS1. http://www.project-syndicate.org/survey/pensi1.

Przeworski, Adam and Henry Teune. 1970. *The Logic of Comparative Social Inquiry*. New York: Wiley.

Quadagno, Jill. 1987. "Theories of the Welfare State." *Annual Review of Sociology* 13: 109–128.

Ragin, Charles. 1987. *The Comparative Method: Moving Beyond Qualitative and Quantitative Strategies*. Berkeley: University of California Press.

Riboud, Michelle and Hoaquan Chu. 1997. "Pension Reform, Growth, and the Labor Market in Ukraine." Policy Research Working Paper 1731 (February). Washington, DC: The World Bank.

Ringold, Dena. 1999. "Social Policy in Postcommunist Europe: Legacies and Transition." In Linda J. Cook, Mitchell Orenstein, and Marilyn Rueschemeyer (eds.). *Left Parties and Social Policy in Postcommunist Europe*, 11–46. Boulder, CO: Westview Press.

Rocha, Roberto and Dimitri Vittas. 2001. "The Hungarian Pension Reform: A Preliminary Assessment of the First Years of Implementation." World Bank Policy Research Working Paper 2631. Washington, DC: The World Bank.

Roper, Steven. 2000. *Romania: The Unfinished Revolution.* London: Routledge.

Roper, Steven and Florin Feşnic. 2003. "Historical Legacies and Their Impact on Postcommunist Voting Behavior." *Europe-Asia Studies* 55 (1): 119–131.

Rose, Richard and Christian Haerpfer. 1998. "New Democracies Barometer. A 12-Nation Survey." *Studies in Public Policy* 306. Glasgow, Scotland: University of Strathclyde, Center for the Study of Public Policy.

Rose, Richard and Toni Makkai. 1995. "Consensus or Dissensus about Welfare in Postcommunist Societies?" *European Journal of Political Research* 28: 203–224.

Sartori, Giovanni. 1966. "European Political Parties: The Case of Polarized Pluralism." In Joseph Palombara and Myron Weiner (eds.), *Political Parties and Political Development*, 137–176. Princeton, NJ: Princeton University Press.

Schamis, Hector E. 1999. "Distributional Coalitions and the Politics of Economic Reform in Latin America." *World Politics* 51 (January): 236–268.

Schiff, Jerald, Niko Hobdari, Axel Schimmelpfennig, and Roman Zytek. 2000. "Pension Reform in the Baltics. Issues and Prospects." IMF Occasional Paper 200. Washington, DC: IMF.

Sederlof, Hjalte S. A. 2000. *Russia: Note on Social Protection.* Washington, DC: World Bank.

Seldon, Arthur. 1996. *Re-Privatising Welfare: After the Lost Century.* London: The Institute of Economic Affairs.

Standing, Guy. 1997. "The Folly of Social Safety Nets: Why Basic Income Is Needed in Eastern Europe." *Social Research* (Winter): 1339–1379.

Stevenson Sanjian, Andrea. 1996. "The Russian Welfare System and Political and Economic Transition." Paper presented at the 37th annual convention of the International Studies Association (16–20 April), San Diego, CA.

Svallfors, Stefan and Peter Taylor-Gooby (eds.). 1999. *The End of the Welfare State? Responses to State Retrenchment.* New York: Routledge.

Swenson, P. 1997. "Arranged Alliance: Business Interests in the New Deal." *Politics and Society* 25: 66–116.

Taggart, Paul and Aleks Szczerbiak. 2001. "Crossing Europe: Patterns of Contemporary Party-Based Euroscepticism in EU Member States and the Candidate States of Central and Eastern Europe." Paper presented at the annual meeting of the American Political Science Association, 29 August–2 September, San Francisco, CA.

Taylor-Gooby, Peter (ed.). *Making a European Welfare State: Convergences and Conflicts Over European Social Policy.* Malden, MA: Blackwell Publishing.

Tismăneanu, Vladimir. 2001. "Hypotheses on Populism: The Politics of Charismatic Protest." *East European Politics and Societies* 15 (1): 10–17.

Vachudova, Milada Anna. 2008. "Centre-Right Parties and Political Outcomes in East Central Europe." *Party Politics* 14 (4): 387–405.

Vachudova, Milada Anna and Liesbet Hooghe. 2009. "Postcommunist Politics in a Magnetic Field: How Transition and EU Accession Structure Party Competition on European Integration." *Comparative European Politics* 7 (2): 179–213.

Vachudova, Milada Anna and Tim Snyder. 1997. "Are Transitions Transitory? Two Types of Political Change in Eastern Europe since 1989." *East European Politics and Societies* 11 (1): 1–35.

Vujacic, Veljko. 2003. "From Class to Nation: Left, Right, and the Ideological and Institutional Roots of Postcommunist 'National Socialism'." *East European Politics and Societies* 17 (3): 359–392.

Wagener, Hans-Jurgen. 2002. "The Welfare State in Transition Economies and Accession to the EU." *West European Politics* 25, Special Issue 2 (April): 152–174.

Wallerstein, Immanuel. 1974. *The Modern World-System: Capitalist Agriculture and the Origins of the European World-Economy in the Sixteenth Century.* New York: Academic Press.

Weyland, Kurt. 2001. "Clarifying a Contested Concept. Populism in the Study of Latin American Politics." *Comparative Politics* (October): 1–22.

Wightman, Gordon (ed.). 1995. *Party Formation in East-Central Europe. Postcommunist Politics in Czechoslovakia, Hungary, Poland, and Bulgaria.* Aldershot: Edward Elgar.

———. 1999. "Party Divisions in Slovakia." Paper presented at the workshop on European Aspects of Postcommunist Party Development, 26–31 March, Mannheim, Germany.

Williamson, John B. and Fred C. Pampel. 1993. *Old-Age Security in Comparative Perspective.* New York: Oxford University Press.

Woleková, Helena. 1998. "Social Policy." In Martin Bútora and Thomas W. Skladony (eds.), *Slovakia 1996–1997. A Global Report on the State and Society.* Bratislava: Institute for Public Affairs.

World Bank. 1992. "Hungary. Reform of Social Policy and Expenditures." A World Bank Country Study. Washington, DC: World Bank.

———. 1992. "Romania: Human Resources and the Transition to a Market Economy." A World Bank Country Study. Washington, DC: World Bank.

———. 1993. *Historically Planned Economies. A Guide to the Data.* Washington, DC: World Bank.

———. 2000. *Making Transition Work for Everyone: Poverty and Inequality in Europe and Central Asia.* Washington, DC: World Bank.

INDEX

Note: Page numbers in **bold** denote illustrations.